WALDEN

OR, LIFE IN THE WOODS

BY
HENRY DAVID THOREAU

I do not propose to write an ode to dejection, but
to brag as lustily as chanticleer in the morning,
standing on his roost, if only to wake the neighbors up.

CASTLE BOOKS

Originally published in Boston, 1854.

This edition published by Castle Books,
a division of Book Sales, Inc.
114 Northfield Avenue
Edison, NJ 08837

ISBN-13: 978-0-7858-2222-6
ISBN-10: 0-7858-2222-4

Printed in the United States of America

WALDEN;

OR,

LIFE IN THE WOODS.

By HENRY D. THOREAU,

AUTHOR OF "A WEEK ON THE CONCORD AND MERRIMACK RIVERS."

I do not propose to write an ode to dejection, but to brag as lustily as chanticleer in the morning, standing on his roost, if only to wake my neighbors up. — Page 92.

BOSTON:

TICKNOR AND FIELDS.

M DCCC LIV.

The title page from the original edition of *Walden*.
Courtesy Concord Free Public Library.

Henry David Thoreau in 1856, at the age of 39. *Courtesy Concord Free Public Library.*

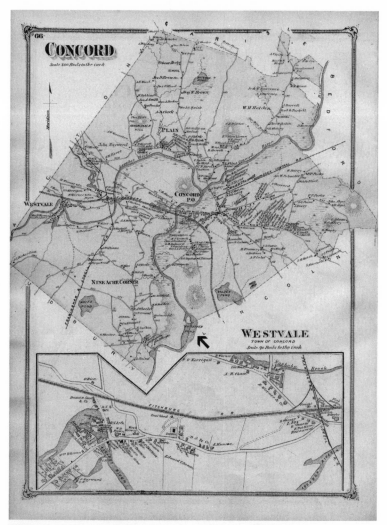

The town of Concored. The arrow is pointing to Walden Pond.
From *Beers Atlas of Middlesex County,* 1875. *Courtesy Frank Oppel.*

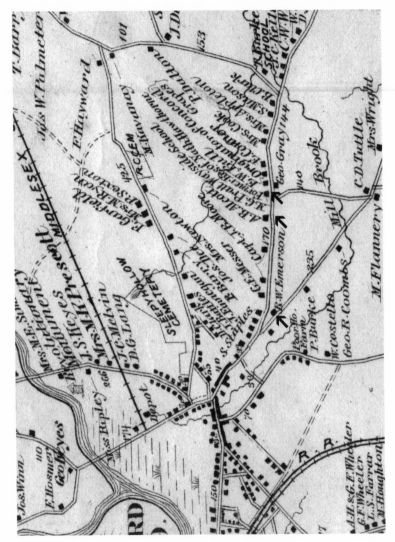

Concord was the center of New England's literary flowering.
Courtesy Concord Free Public Library.

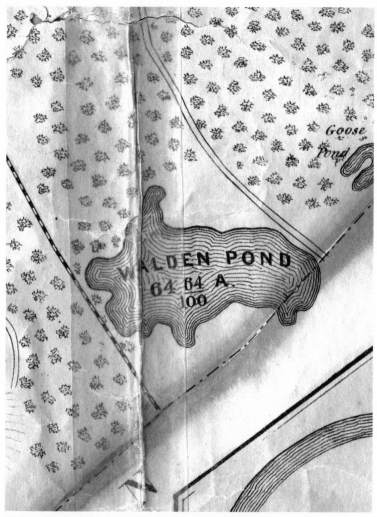

Walden Pond, close-up detail, of Walling's *Map of the Town of Concord, Middlesex County, Mass. Surveyed by the Authority of the Town.* Boston: H.F. Walling, 1852. *Courtesy Concord Free Public Library.*

Interior of the cabin at Walden Pond, and the desk at which Thoreau penned *Walden*. *Courtesy Concord Free Public Libarary.*

CONTENTS

		PAGE
INTRODUCTORY NOTE	. . . . . .	vii
I.	ECONOMY	7
II.	WHERE I LIVED, AND WHAT I LIVED FOR	128
III.	READING	156
IV.	SOUNDS	174
V.	SOLITUDE	202
VI.	VISITORS	218
VII.	THE BEAN-FIELD	241
VIII.	THE VILLAGE	261
IX.	THE PONDS	271
X.	BAKER FARM	314
XI.	HIGHER LAWS	327
XII.	BRUTE NEIGHBORS	347
XIII.	HOUSE-WARMING	369
XIV.	FORMER INHABITANTS, AND WINTER VIS-ITORS	396
XV.	WINTER ANIMALS	419
XVI.	THE POND IN WINTER	436
XVII.	SPRING	461
XVIII.	CONCLUSION	493

INTRODUCTORY NOTE

THOREAU lived in his Walden camp but
two years, 1845–1847, and, as his narrative
clearly shows, by no means exiled himself
from home and companions. His hermitage
was within easy walking distance of Concord; and, though his seclusion meant privacy at times, he was by no means debarred
from society. The life in the woods was a
characteristic expression of his stout independence of conditions, and served his purpose of living frugally and securing leisure
for observation, reading, and writing. But
since the act was in a way unique, it transferred something of its unique property to
the book which recorded it, and the book is
more closely identified with Thoreau's fame,
has done more to give him distinction, than
any other of his writings.

The book *Walden* was what William El-
lery Channing calls "the log-book of his
woodland cruise at Walden." Thoreau him-

self tells us that the bulk of the book was
written in his hermitage.   One bit of verse,

" Light-winged smoke, Icarian bird,"

he had printed in *The Dial ;* but nothing
else appears to have been garnered from
previous publications, and the book has thus
a unity of design which helps to preserve its
individual force.   *Walden* was not published, however, until 1854, when it was
brought out by Ticknor & Fields.

WALDEN.

———◆———

I.

ECONOMY.

WHEN I wrote the following pages, or rather the bulk of them, I lived alone, in the woods, a mile from any neighbor, in a house which I had built myself, on the shore of Walden Pond, in Concord, Massachusetts, and earned my living by the labor of my hands only. I lived there two years and two months. At present I am a sojourner in civilized life again.

I should not obtrude my affairs so much on the notice of my readers if very particular inquiries had not been made by my townsmen concerning my mode of life, which some would call impertinent, though they do not appear to me at all impertinent, but, considering the circumstances, very natural and pertinent. Some have asked what I got to eat; if I did not feel lonesome; if

I was not afraid; and the like. Others have
been curious to learn what portion of my income I devoted to charitable purposes; and
some, who have large families, how many
poor children I maintained. I will therefore ask those of my readers who feel no
particular interest in me to pardon me if I
undertake to answer some of these questions
in this book. In most books, the *I*, or first
person, is omitted; in this it will be retained; that, in respect to egotism, is the
main difference. We commonly do not remember that it is, after all, always the first
person that is speaking. I should not talk
so much about myself if there were anybody else whom I knew as well. Unfortunately, I am confined to this theme by the
narrowness of my experience. Moreover, I,
on my side, require of every writer, first or
last, a simple and sincere account of his own
life, and not merely what he has heard of
other men's lives; some such account as he
would send to his kindred from a distant
land; for if he has lived sincerely, it must
have been in a distant land to me. Perhaps these pages are more particularly addressed to poor students. As for the rest
of my readers, they will accept such portions

as apply to them. I trust that none will
stretch the seams in putting on the coat, for
it may do good service to him whom it fits.

I would fain say something, not so much
concerning the Chinese and Sandwich Is-
landers as you who read these pages, who
are said to live in New England; something about your condition, especially your
outward condition or circumstances in this
world, in this town, what it is, whether it is
necessary that it be as bad as it is, whether
it cannot be improved as well as not. I
have travelled a good deal in Concord; and
everywhere, in shops, and offices, and fields,
the inhabitants have appeared to me to be
doing penance in a thousand remarkable
ways. What I have heard of Bramins sitting exposed to four fires and looking in the
face of the sun; or hanging suspended, with
their heads downward, over flames; or looking at the heavens over their shoulders "until it becomes impossible for them to resume
their natural position, while from the twist
of the neck nothing but liquids can pass into
the stomach;" or dwelling, chained for life,
at the foot of a tree; or measuring with their
bodies, like caterpillars, the breadth of vast
empires; or standing on one leg on the tops

of pillars, — even these forms of conscious
penance are hardly more incredible and as-
tonishing than the scenes which I daily witness. The twelve labors of Hercules were
trifling in comparison with those which my
neighbors have undertaken ; for they were
only twelve, and had an end ; but I could
never see that these men slew or captured
any monster or finished any labor. They
have no friend Iolas to burn with a hot iron
the root of the hydra's head, but as soon as
one head is crushed, two spring up.

I see young men, my townsmen, whose
misfortune it is to have inherited farms,
houses, barns, cattle, and farming tools ; for
these are more easily acquired than got rid
of. Better if they had been born in the
open pasture and suckled by a wolf, that
they might have seen with clearer eyes what
field they were called to labor in. Who
made them serfs of the soil ? Why should
they eat their sixty acres, when man is con-
demned to eat only his peck of dirt ? Why
should they begin digging their graves as
soon as they are born ? They have got to
live a man's life, pushing all these things
before them, and get on as well as they can.
How many a poor immortal soul have I met

well nigh crushed and smothered under its load, creeping down the road of life, pushing before it a barn seventy-five feet by forty, its Augean stables never cleansed, and one hundred acres of land, tillage, mowing, pasture, and wood-lot! The portionless, who struggle with no such unnecessary inherited encumbrances, find it labor enough to subdue and cultivate a few cubic feet of flesh.

But men labor under a mistake. The better part of the man is soon ploughed into the soil for compost. By a seeming fate, commonly called necessity, they are employed, as it says in an old book, laying up treasures which moth and rust will corrupt and thieves break through and steal. It is a fool's life, as they will find when they get to the end of it, if not before. It is said that Deucalion and Pyrrha created men by throwing stones over their heads behind them : —

> Inde genus durum sumus, experiensque laborum,
> Et documenta damus quâ simus origine nati.

Or, as Raleigh rhymes it in his sonorous way, —

> "From thence our kind hard-hearted is, enduring pain and care,
> Approving that our bodies of a stony nature are."

So much for a blind obedience to a blunder-ing oracle, throwing the stones over their heads behind them, and not seeing where they fell.

Most men, even in this comparatively free country, through mere ignorance and mis-take, are so occupied with the factitious cares and superfluously coarse labors of life that its finer fruits cannot be plucked by them. Their fingers, from excessive toil, are too clumsy and tremble too much for that. Actually, the laboring man has not leisure for a true integrity day by day ; he cannot afford to sustain the manliest rela-tions to men ; his labor would be depreciated in the market. He has no time to be any-thing but a machine. How can he remem-ber well his ignorance — which his growth requires — who has so often to use his knowledge ? We should feed and clothe him gratuitously sometimes, and recruit him with our cordials, before we judge of him. The finest qualities of our nature, like the bloom on fruits, can be preserved only by the most delicate handling. Yet we do not treat ourselves nor one another thus ten-derly.

Some of you, we all know, are poor, find

it hard to live, are sometimes, as it were, gasping for breath. I have no doubt that some of you who read this book are unable to pay for all the dinners which you have actually eaten, or for the coats and shoes which are fast wearing or are already worn out, and have come to this page to spend borrowed or stolen time, robbing your creditors of an hour. It is very evident what mean and sneaking lives many of you live, for my sight has been whetted by experience; always on the limits, trying to get into business and trying to get out of debt, a very ancient slough, called by the Latins *æs alienum*, another's brass, for some of their coins were made of brass; still living, and dying, and buried by this other's brass; always promising to pay, promising to pay, to-morrow, and dying to-day, insolvent; seeking to curry favor, to get custom, by how many modes, only not state-prison offences; lying, flattering, voting, contracting yourselves into a nutshell of civility, or dilating into an atmosphere of thin and vaporous generosity, that you may persuade your neighbor to let you make his shoes, or his hat, or his coat, or his carriage, or import his groceries for him; making yourselves sick, that you may lay up something against a sick day, something to be tucked away in an old chest, or in a stocking behind the plastering, or, more safely, in the brick bank; no matter where, no matter how much or how little.

I sometimes wonder that we can be so frivolous, I may almost say, as to attend to the gross but somewhat foreign form of servitude called Negro Slavery, there are so many keen and subtle masters that enslave both North and South. It is hard to have a Southern overseer; it is worse to have a Northern one; but worst of all when you are the slave-driver of yourself. Talk of a divinity in man! Look at the teamster on the highway, wending to market by day or night; does any divinity stir within him? His highest duty to fodder and water his horses! What is his destiny to him compared with the shipping interests? Does not he drive for Squire Make-a-stir? How godlike, how immortal, is he? See how he cowers and sneaks, how vaguely all the day he fears, not being immortal nor divine, but the slave and prisoner of his own opinion of himself, a fame won by his own deeds. Public opinion is a weak tyrant compared with our own private opinion. What a man thinks of himself, that it is which determines, or rather indicates, his fate. Self-emancipation even in the West Indian provinces of the fancy and imagination, — what Wilberforce is there to bring that about? Think, also, of the ladies of the land weaving toilet cushions against the last day, not to betray too green an interest in their fates! As if you could kill time without injuring eternity.

The mass of men lead lives of quiet desperation. What is called resignation is confirmed desperation. From the desperate city you go into the desperate country, and have to console yourself with the bravery of minks and muskrats. A stereotyped but unconscious despair is concealed even under what are called the games and amusements of mankind. There is no play in them, for this comes after work. But it is a characteristic of wisdom not to do desperate things.

When we consider what, to use the words of the catechism, is the chief end of man, and what are the true necessaries and means of life, it appears as if men had deliberately chosen the common mode of living because they preferred it to any other. Yet they honestly think there is no choice left. But alert and healthy natures remember that the sun rose clear. It is never too late to give up our prejudices. No way of thinking or doing, however ancient, can be trusted without proof. What everybody echoes or in silence passes by as true to-day may turn out to be falsehood to-morrow, mere smoke of opinion, which some had trusted for a cloud that would sprinkle fertilizing rain on their fields. What old people say you cannot do you try and find that you can. Old deeds for old people, and new deeds for new. Old people did not know enough once, perchance, to fetch fresh fuel to keep the fire a-going; new people put a little dry wood under a pot, and are whirled round the globe with the speed of birds, in a way to kill old people, as the phrase is. Age is no better, hardly so well, qualified for an instructor as youth, for it has not profited so much as it has lost. One may almost doubt if the wisest man has learned anything of absolute value by living. Practically, the old have no very important advice to give the young, their own experience has been so partial, and their lives have been such miserable failures, for private reasons, as they must believe; and it may be that they have some faith left which belies that experience, and they are only less young than they were. I have lived some thirty years on this planet, and I have yet to hear the first syllable of valuable or even earnest advice from my seniors. They have told me nothing, and probably cannot tell me anything to the purpose. Here is life, an experiment to a great extent untried by me; but it does not avail me that they have tried it. If I have any experience which I think valuable, I am sure to reflect that this my Mentors said nothing about.

One farmer says to me, "You cannot live on vegetable food solely, for it furnishes nothing to make bones with;" and so he religiously devotes a part of his day to supplying his system with the raw material of bones; walking all the while he talks behind his oxen, which, with vegetable-made bones, jerk him and his lumbering plough along in spite of every obstacle. Some things are really necessaries of life in some circles, the most helpless and diseased, which in others are luxuries merely, and in others still are entirely unknown.

The whole ground of human life seems to some to have been gone over by their predecessors, both the heights and the valleys, and all things to have been cared for. According to Evelyn, " the wise Solomon prescribed ordinances for the very distances of trees ; and the Roman prætors have decided how often you may go into your neighbor's land to gather the acorns which fall on it without trespass, and what share belongs to that neighbor." Hippocrates has even left directions how we should cut our nails ; that is, even with the ends of the fingers, neither shorter nor longer. Undoubtedly the very tedium and ennui which presume to have exhausted the variety and the joys of life are as old as Adam. But man's capacities have never been measured ; nor are we to judge of what he can do by any precedents, so little has been tried. Whatever have been thy failures hitherto, " be not afflicted, my child, for who shall assign to thee what thou hast left undone ? "

We might try our lives by a thousand simple tests ; as, for instance, that the same sun which ripens my beans illumines at once a system of earths like ours. If I had remembered this it would have prevented some mistakes. This was not the light in which I hoed them. The stars are the apexes of what wonderful triangles! What distant and different beings in the various mansions of the universe are contemplating the same one at the same moment! Nature and human life are as various as our several constitutions. Who shall say what prospect life offers to another? Could a greater miracle take place than for us to look through each other's eyes for an instant? We should live in all the ages of the world in an hour; ay, in all the worlds of the ages. History, Poetry, Mythology! — I know of no reading of another's experience so startling and informing as this would be.

The greater part of what my neighbors call good I believe in my soul to be bad, and if I repent of anything, it is very likely to be my good behavior. What demon possessed me that I behaved so well? You may say the wisest thing you can, old man, — you who have lived seventy years, not without honor of a kind, — I hear an irresistible voice which invites me away from all that. One generation abandons the enterprises of another like stranded vessels.

I think that we may safely trust a good

deal more than we do. We may waive just so much care of ourselves as we honestly bestow elsewhere. Nature is as well adapted to our weakness as to our strength. The incessant anxiety and strain of some is a well-nigh incurable form of disease. We are made to exaggerate the importance of what work we do; and yet how much is not done by us! or, what if we had been taken sick? How vigilant we are! determined not to live by faith if we can avoid it; all the day long on the alert, at night we unwillingly say our prayers and commit ourselves to uncertainties. So thoroughly and sincerely are we compelled to live, reverencing our life, and denying the possibility of change. This is the only way, we say; but there are as many ways as there can be drawn radii from one centre. All change is a miracle to contemplate; but it is a miracle which is taking place every instant. Confucius said, " To know that we know what we know, and that we do not know what we do not know, that is true knowledge." When one man has reduced a fact of the imagination to be a fact to his understanding, I foresee that all men will at length establish their lives on that basis.

Let us consider for a moment what most of the trouble and anxiety which I have referred to is about, and how much it is necessary that we be troubled, or at least careful. It would be some advantage to live a primitive and frontier life, though in the midst of an outward civilization, if only to learn what are the gross necessaries of life and what methods have been taken to obtain them; or even to look over the old day-books of the merchants, to see what it was that men most commonly bought at the stores, what they stored, that is, what are the grossest groceries. For the improvements of ages have had but little influence on the essential laws of man's existence : as our skeletons, probably, are not to be distinguished from those of our ancestors.

By the words, *necessary of life*, I mean whatever, of all that man obtains by his own exertions, has been from the first, or from long use has become, so important to human life that few, if any, whether from savageness, or poverty, or philosophy, ever attempt to do without it. To many creatures there is in this sense but one necessary of life, Food. To the bison of the prairie it is a few inches of palatable grass, with water to drink; unless he seeks the Shelter of the forest or the mountain's shadow. None of the brute creation requires more than Food and Shelter. The necessaries of life for man in this climate may, accurately enough, be distributed under the several heads of Food, Shelter, Clothing, and Fuel; for not till we have secured these are we prepared to entertain the true problems of life with freedom and a prospect of success. Man has invented, not only houses, but clothes and cooked food; and possibly from the accidental discovery of the warmth of fire, and the consequent use of it, at first a luxury, arose the present necessity to sit by it. We observe cats and dogs acquiring the same second nature. By proper Shelter and Clothing we legitimately retain our own internal heat; but with an excess of these, or of Fuel, that is, with an external heat greater than our own internal, may not cookery properly be said to begin? Darwin, the naturalist, says of the inhabitants of Tierra del Fuego, that while his own party, who were well clothed and sitting close to a fire, were far from too warm, these naked savages, who were farther off, were observed, to his great surprise, " to be streaming with

perspiration at undergoing such a roasting."
So, we are told, the New Hollander goes
naked with impunity, while the European
shivers in his clothes. Is it impossible to
combine the hardiness of these savages with
the intellectualness of the civilized man ?
According to Liebig, man's body is a stove,
and food the fuel which keeps up the internal combustion in the lungs. In cold
weather we eat more, in warm less. The
animal heat is the result of a slow combustion, and disease and death take place when
this is too rapid ; or for want of fuel, or
from some defect in the draught, the fire
goes out. Of course the vital heat is not to
be confounded with fire ; but so much for
analogy. It appears, therefore, from the
above list, that the expression, *animal life*,
is nearly synonymous with the expression,
animal heat ; for while Food may be regarded as the Fuel which keeps up the fire
within us, — and Fuel serves only to prepare that Food or to increase the warmth
of our bodies by addition from without, —
Shelter and Clothing also serve only to retain the *heat* thus generated and absorbed.

The grand necessity, then, for our bodies,
is to keep warm, to keep the vital heat in

us. What pains we accordingly take, not only with our Food, and Clothing, and Shelter, but with our beds, which are our night-clothes, robbing the nests and breasts of birds to prepare this shelter within a shelter, as the mole has its bed of grass and leaves at the end of its burrow! The poor man is wont to complain that this is a cold world; and to cold, no less physical than social, we refer directly a great part of our ails. The summer, in some climates, makes possible to man a sort of Elysian life. Fuel, except to cook his Food, is then unnecessary; the sun is his fire, and many of the fruits are sufficiently cooked by its rays; while Food generally is more various, and more easily obtained, and Clothing and Shelter are wholly or half unnecessary. At the present day, and in this country, as I find by my own experience, a few implements, a knife, an axe, a spade, a wheelbarrow, etc., and for the studious, lamplight, stationery, and access to a few books, rank next to necessaries, and can all be obtained at a trifling cost. Yet some, not wise, go to the other side of the globe, to barbarous and unhealthy regions, and devote themselves to trade for ten or twenty years, in order that they may live, — that is, keep comfortably warm, — and die in New England at last. The luxuriously rich are not simply kept comfortably warm, but unnaturally hot ; as I implied before, they are cooked, of course *à la mode.*

Most of the luxuries, and many of the so-called comforts of life, are not only not indispensable, but positive hindrances to the elevation of mankind. With respect to luxuries and comforts, the wisest have ever lived a more simple and meagre life than the poor. The ancient philosophers, Chinese, Hindoo, Persian, and Greek, were a class than which none has been poorer in outward riches, none so rich in inward. We know not much about them. It is remarkable that *we* know so much of them as we do. The same is true of the more modern reformers and benefactors of their race. None can be an impartial or wise observer of human life but from the vantage ground of what *we* should call voluntary poverty. Of a life of luxury the fruit is luxury, whether in agriculture, or commerce, or literature, or art. There are nowadays professors of philosophy, but not philosophers. Yet it is admirable to profess because it was once

admirable to live. To be a philosopher is
not merely to have subtle thoughts, nor even
to found a school, but so to love wisdom
as to live according to its dictates, a life of
simplicity, independence, magnanimity, and
trust. It is to solve some of the problems
of life, not only theoretically, but practically. The success of great scholars and
thinkers is commonly a courtier-like success, not kingly, not manly. They make
shift to live merely by conformity, practically as their fathers did, and are in no
sense the progenitors of a nobler race of
men. But why do men degenerate ever?
What makes families run out? What is the
nature of the luxury which enervates and
destroys nations? Are we sure that there is
none of it in our own lives? The philosopher is in advance of his age even in the
outward form of his life. He is not fed,
sheltered, clothed, warmed, like his contemporaries. How can a man be a philosopher
and not maintain his vital heat by better
methods than other men?

When a man is warmed by the several
modes which I have described, what does he
want next? Surely not more warmth of the
same kind, as more and richer food, larger

and more splendid houses, finer and more
abundant clothing, more numerous incessant
and hotter fires, and the like. When he has
obtained those things which are necessary to
life, there is another alternative than to obtain the superfluities; and that is, to adventure on life now, his vacation from humbler
toil having commenced. The soil, it appears, is suited to the seed, for it has sent
its radicle downward, and it may now send
its shoot upward also with confidence. Why
has man rooted himself thus firmly in the
earth, but that he may rise in the same proportion into the heavens above? — for the
nobler plants are valued for the fruit they
bear at last in the air and light, far from the
ground, and are not treated like the humbler
esculents, which, though they may be bien-
nials, are cultivated only till they have per-
fected their root, and often cut down at top
for this purpose, so that most would not
know them in their flowering season.

I do not mean to prescribe rules to strong
and valiant natures, who will mind their own
affairs whether in heaven or hell, and perchance build more magnificently and spend
more lavishly than the richest, without ever
impoverishing themselves, not knowing how

they live, — if, indeed, there are any such, as has been dreamed ; nor to those who find their encouragement and inspiration in precisely the present condition of things, and cherish it with the fondness and enthusiasm of lovers, — and, to some extent, I reckon myself in this number; I do not speak to those who are well employed, in whatever circumstances, and they know whether they are well employed or not ; — but mainly to the mass of men who are discontented, and idly complaining of the hardness of their lot or of the times, when they might improve them. There are some who complain most energetically and inconsolably of any, because they are, as they say, doing their duty. I also have in my mind that seemingly wealthy, but most terribly impoverished class of all, who have accumulated dross, but know not how to use it, or get rid of it, and thus have forged their own golden or silver fetters.

If I should attempt to tell how I have desired to spend my life in years past, it would probably surprise those of my readers who are somewhat acquainted with its actual history ; it would certainly astonish those who know nothing about it. I will only hint at

some of the enterprises which I have cher-
ished.

In any weather, at any hour of the day or
night, I have been anxious to improve the
nick of time, and notch it on my stick too ;
to stand on the meeting of two eternities,
the past and future, which is precisely the
present moment ; to toe that line. You will
pardon some obscurities, for there are more
secrets in my trade than in most men's, and
yet not voluntarily kept, but inseparable
from its very nature. I would gladly tell
all that I know about it, and never paint
" No Admittance " on my gate.

I long ago lost a hound, a bay horse, and
a turtle-dove, and am still on their trail.
Many are the travellers I have spoken concerning them, describing their tracks and
what calls they answered to. I have met
one or two who had heard the hound, and
the tramp of the horse, and even seen the
dove disappear behind a cloud, and they
seemed as anxious to recover them as if
they had lost them themselves.

To anticipate, not the sunrise and the
dawn merely, but, if possible, Nature herself! How many mornings, summer and
winter, before yet any neighbor was stir-

ring about his business, have I been about mine! No doubt, many of my townsmen have met me returning from this enterprise, farmers starting for Boston in the twilight, or woodchoppers going to their work. It is true, I never assisted the sun materially in his rising, but, doubt not, it was of the last importance only to be present at it.

So many autumn, ay, and winter days, spent outside the town, trying to hear what was in the wind, to hear and carry it express! I well-nigh sunk all my capital in it, and lost my own breath into the bargain, running in the face of it. If it had concerned either of the political parties, depend upon it, it would have appeared in the Gazette with the earliest intelligence. At other times watching from the observatory of some cliff or tree, to telegraph any new arrival; or waiting at evening on the hilltops for the sky to fall, that I might catch something, though I never caught much, and that, manna-wise, would dissolve again in the sun.

For a long time I was reporter to a journal, of no very wide circulation, whose editor has never yet seen fit to print the bulk of my contributions, and, as is too common with writers, I got only my labor for my pains. However, in this case my pains were their own reward.

For many years I was self-appointed inspector of snow storms and rain storms, and did my duty faithfully; surveyor, if not of highways, then of forest paths and all across-lot routes, keeping them open, and ravines bridged and passable at all seasons, where the public heel had testified to their utility.

I have looked after the wild stock of the town, which give a faithful herdsman a good deal of trouble by leaping fences; and I have had an eye to the unfrequented nooks and corners of the farm; though I did not always know whether Jonas or Solomon worked in a particular field to-day; that was none of my business. I have watered the red huckleberry, the sand cherry and the nettle tree, the red pine and the black ash, the white grape and the yellow violet, which might have withered else in dry seasons.

In short, I went on thus for a long time (I may say it without boasting), faithfully minding my business, till it became more and more evident that my townsmen would not after all admit me into the list of town officers, nor make my place a sinecure with

a moderate allowance. My accounts, which
I can swear to have kept faithfully, I have,
indeed, never got audited, still less accepted,
still less paid and settled. However, I have
not set my heart on that.

Not long since, a strolling Indian went
to sell baskets at the house of a well-known
lawyer in my neighborhood. " Do you wish
to buy any baskets ? " he asked. " No, we
do not want any," was the reply. " What ! "
exclaimed the Indian as he went out the
gate, " do you mean to starve us ? " Having
seen his industrious white neighbors so well
off, — that the lawyer had only to weave arguments, and by some magic wealth and
standing followed, — he had said to himself :
I will go into business ; I will weave baskets ; it is a thing which I can do. Thinking that when he had made the baskets he
would have done his part, and then it would
be the white man's to buy them. He had
not discovered that it was necessary for him
to make it worth the other's while to buy
them, or at least make him think that it was
so, or to make something else which it would
be worth his while to buy. I too had woven
a kind of basket of a delicate texture, but I
had not made it worth any one's while to

buy them. Yet not the less, in my case, did I think it worth my while to weave them, and instead of studying how to make it worth men's while to buy my baskets, I studied rather how to avoid the necessity of selling them. The life which men praise and regard as successful is but one kind. Why should we exaggerate any one kind at the expense of the others?

Finding that my fellow-citizens were not likely to offer me any room in the court house, or any curacy or living anywhere else, but I must shift for myself, I turned my face more exclusively than ever to the woods, where I was better known. I determined to go into business at once, and not wait to acquire the usual capital, using such slender means as I had already got. My purpose in going to Walden Pond was not to live cheaply nor to live dearly there, but to transact some private business with the fewest obstacles; to be hindered from accomplishing which for want of a little common sense, a little enterprise and business talent, appeared not so sad as foolish.

I have always endeavored to acquire strict business habits; they are indispensable to every man. If your trade is with the Celes-

tial Empire, then some small counting house
on the coast, in some Salem harbor, will be
fixture enough.   You will export such articles as the country affords, purely native
products, much ice and pine timber and
a little granite, always in native bottoms.
These will be good ventures.   To oversee
all the details yourself in person; to be at
once pilot and captain, and owner and un-
derwriter; to buy and sell and keep the accounts; to read every letter received, and
write or read every letter sent; to superin-
tend the discharge of imports night and
day; to be upon many parts of the coast almost at the same time, — often the richest
freight will be discharged upon a Jersey
shore; — to be your own telegraph, un-
weariedly sweeping the horizon, speaking
all passing vessels bound coastwise; to keep
up a steady despatch of commodities, for
the supply of such a distant and exorbitant
market; to keep yourself informed of the
state of the markets, prospects of war and
peace everywhere, and anticipate the ten-
dencies of trade and civilization, — taking
advantage of the results of all exploring expeditions, using new passages and all improvements in navigation; — charts to be

studied, the position of reefs and new lights
and buoys to be ascertained, and ever, and
ever, the logarithmic tables to be corrected,
for by the error of some calculator the vessel often splits upon a rock that should have
reached a friendly pier, — there is the un-
told fate of La Perouse; — universal science
to be kept pace with, studying the lives of
all great discoverers and navigators, great
adventurers and merchants, from Hanno
and the Phœnicians down to our day; in
fine, account of stock to be taken from time
to time, to know how you stand. It is a
labor to task the faculties of a man, — such
problems of profit and loss, of interest, of
tare and tret, and gauging of all kinds in it,
as demand a universal knowledge.

I have thought that Walden Pond would
be a good place for business, not solely on
account of the railroad and the ice trade;
it offers advantages which it may not be
good policy to divulge; it is a good post and
a good foundation. No Neva marshes to be
filled; though you must everywhere build
on piles of your own driving. It is said that
a flood-tide, with a westerly wind, and ice in
the Neva, would sweep St. Petersburg from
the face of the earth.

As this business was to be entered into without the usual capital, it may not be easy to conjecture where those means, that will still be indispensable to every such undertaking, were to be obtained. As for Clothing, to come at once to the practical part of the question, perhaps we are led oftener by the love of novelty and a regard for the opinions of men, in procuring it, than by a true utility. Let him who has work to do recollect that the object of clothing is, first, to retain the vital heat, and secondly, in this state of society, to cover nakedness, and he may judge how much of any necessary or important work may be accomplished without adding to his wardrobe. Kings and queens who wear a suit but once, though made by some tailor or dressmaker to their majesties, cannot know the comfort of wearing a suit that fits. They are no better than wooden horses to hang the clean clothes on. Every day our garments become more assimilated to ourselves, receiving the impress of the wearer's character, until we hesitate to lay them aside, without such delay and medical appliances and some such solemnity even as our bodies. No man ever stood the lower in my estimation for having a patch in his clothes; yet I am sure that there is greater anxiety, commonly, to have fashionable, or at least clean and unpatched clothes, than to have a sound conscience. But even if the rent is not mended, perhaps the worst vice betrayed is improvidence. I sometimes try my acquaintances by such tests as this, — Who could wear a patch, or two extra seams only, over the knee? Most behave as if they believed that their prospects for life would be ruined if they should do it. It would be easier for them to hobble to town with a broken leg than with a broken pantaloon. Often if an accident happens to a gentleman's legs, they can be mended; but if a similar accident happens to the legs of his pantaloons, there is no help for it; for he considers, not what is truly respectable, but what is respected. We know but few men, a great many coats and breeches. Dress a scarecrow in your last shift, you standing shiftless by, who would not soonest salute the scarecrow? Passing a cornfield the other day, close by a hat and coat on a stake, I recognized the owner of the farm. He was only a little more weather-beaten than when I saw him last. I have heard of a dog that barked at every stranger who ap-

proached his master's premises with clothes
on, but was easily quieted by a naked thief.
It is an interesting question how far men
would retain their relative rank if they were
divested of their clothes. Could you, in
such a case, tell surely of any company of
civilized men which belonged to the most
respected class ? When Madam Pfeiffer, in
her adventurous travels round the world,
from east to west, had got so near home as
Asiatic Russia, she says that she felt the
necessity of wearing other than a travelling
dress, when she went to meet the authorities, for she " was now in a civilized country, where . . . people are judged of by
their clothes." Even in our democratic New
England towns the accidental possession of
wealth, and its manifestation in dress and
equipage alone, obtain for the possessor almost universal respect. But they who yield
such respect, numerous as they are, are so
far heathen, and need to have a missionary
sent to them. Beside, clothes introduced
sewing, a kind of work which you may call
endless ; a woman's dress, at least, is never
done.

A man who has at length found something to do will not need to get a new suit

to do it in ; for him the old will do, that has
lain dusty in the garret for an indeterminate
period. Old shoes will serve a hero longer
than they have served his valet, — if a hero
ever has a valet, — bare feet are older than
shoes, and he can make them do. Only they
who go to soirées and legislative halls must
have new coats, coats to change as often as
the man changes in them. But if my jacket
and trousers, my hat and shoes, are fit to
worship God in, they will do ; will they not ?
Who ever saw his old clothes, — his old
coat, actually worn out, resolved into its
primitive elements, so that it was not a deed
of charity to bestow it on some poor boy,
by him perchance to be bestowed on some
poorer still, or shall we say richer, who
could do with less ? I say, beware of all enterprises that require new clothes, and not
rather a new wearer of clothes. If there is
not a new man, how can the new clothes be
made to fit ? If you have any enterprise
before you, try it in your old clothes. All
men want, not something to *do with*, but
something to *do*, or rather something to *be*.
Perhaps we should never procure a new suit,
however ragged or dirty the old, until we
have so conducted, so enterprised or sailed

in some way, that we feel like new men in the old, and that to retain it would be like keeping new wine in old bottles. Our moulting season, like that of the fowls, must be a crisis in our lives. . The loon retires to solitary ponds to spend it. Thus also the snake casts its slough, and the caterpillar its wormy coat, by an internal industry and expansion ; for clothes are but our outmost cuticle and mortal coil. Otherwise we shall be found sailing under false colors, and be inevitably cashiered at last by our own opinion, as well as that of mankind.

We don garment after garment, as if we grew like exogenous plants by addition without. Our outside and often thin and fanciful clothes are our epidermis, or false skin, which partakes not of our life, and may be stripped off here and there without fatal injury ; our thicker garments, constantly worn, are our cellular integument, or cortex ; but our shirts are our liber, or true bark, which cannot be removed without girdling and so destroying the man. I believe that all races at some seasons wear something equivalent to the shirt. It is desirable that a man be clad so simply that he can lay his hands on himself in the dark, and that he live in all respects so compactly and preparedly, that, if an enemy take the town, he can, like the old philosopher, walk out the gate empty-handed without anxiety. While one thick garment is, for most purposes, as good as three thin ones, and cheap clothing can be obtained at prices really to suit customers; while a thick coat can be bought for five dollars, which will last as many years, thick pantaloons for two dollars, cowhide boots for a dollar and a half a pair, a summer hat for a quarter of a dollar, and a winter cap for sixty-two and a half cents, or a better be made at home at a nominal cost, where is he so poor that, clad in such a suit, *of his own earning*, there will not be found wise men to do him reverence?

When I ask for a garment of a particular form, my tailoress tells me gravely, "They do not make them so now," not emphasizing the "They" at all, as if she quoted an authority as impersonal as the Fates, and I find it difficult to get made what I want, simply because she cannot believe that I mean what I say, that I am so rash. When I hear this oracular sentence, I am for a moment absorbed in thought, emphasizing to myself each word separately that I may come at the meaning of it, that I may find out by what degree of consanguinity *They* are related to *me*, and what authority they may have in an affair which affects me so nearly; and, finally, I am inclined to answer her with equal mystery, and without any more emphasis of the "they," — "It is true, they did not make them so recently, but they do now." Of what use this measuring of me if she does not measure my character, but only the breadth of my shoulders, as it were a peg to hang the coat on? We worship not the Graces, nor the Parcæ, but Fashion. She spins and weaves and cuts with full authority. The head monkey at Paris puts on a traveller's cap, and all the monkeys in America do the same. I sometimes despair of getting anything quite simple and honest done in this world by the help of men. They would have to be passed through a powerful press first, to squeeze their old notions out of them, so that they would not soon get upon their legs again; and then there would be some one in the company with a maggot in his head, hatched from an egg deposited there nobody knows when, for not even fire kills these things, and you would have lost your labor. Nevertheless, we will not forget that some Egyptian wheat was handed down to us by a mummy.

On the whole, I think that it cannot be maintained that dressing has in this or any country risen to the dignity of an art. At present men make shift to wear what they can get. Like shipwrecked sailors, they put on what they can find on the beach, and at a little distance, whether of space or time, laugh at each other's masquerade. Every generation laughs at the old fashions, but follows religiously the new. We are amused at beholding the costume of Henry VIII., or Queen Elizabeth, as much as if it was that of the King and Queen of the Cannibal Islands. All costume off a man is pitiful or grotesque. It is only the serious eye peering from and the sincere life passed within it which restrain laughter and consecrate the costume of any people. Let Harlequin be taken with a fit of the colic and his trappings will have to serve that mood too. When the soldier is hit by a cannon ball rags are as becoming as purple.

The childish and savage taste of men and women for new patterns keeps how many

shaking and squinting through kaleido-
scopes that they may discover the particular figure which this generation requires to-
day. The manufacturers have learned that
this taste is merely whimsical. Of two patterns which differ only by a few threads
more or less of a particular color, the one
will be sold readily, the other lie on the
shelf, though it frequently happens that
after the lapse of a season the latter becomes the most fashionable. Comparatively,
tattooing is not the hideous custom which it
is called. It is not barbarous merely because the printing is skin-deep and unalter-
able.

I cannot believe that our factory system
is the best mode by which men may get
clothing. The condition of the operatives
is becoming every day more like that of the
English ; and it cannot be wondered at,
since, as far as I have heard or observed,
the principal object is, not that mankind
may be well and honestly clad, but, unquestionably, that the corporations may be en-
riched. In the long run men hit only what
they aim at. Therefore, though they should
fail immediately, they had better aim at
something high.

As for a Shelter, I will not deny that this
is now a necessary of life, though there are
instances of men having done without it for
long periods in colder countries than this.
Samuel Laing says that " the Laplander
in his skin dress, and in a skin bag which
he puts over his head and shoulders, will
sleep night after night on the snow . . . in
a degree of cold which would extinguish
the life of one exposed to it in any woollen
clothing." He had seen them asleep thus.
Yet he adds, " They are not hardier than
other people." But, probably, man did not
live long on the earth without discovering
the convenience which there is in a house,
the domestic comforts, which phrase may
have originally signified the satisfactions of
the house more than of the family ; though
these must be extremely partial and occasional in those climates where the house is
associated in our thoughts with winter or the
rainy season chiefly, and two thirds of the
year, except for a parasol, is unnecessary.
In our climate, in the summer, it was formerly almost solely a covering at night. In
the Indian gazettes a wigwam was the symbol of a day's march, and a row of them cut
or painted on the bark of a tree signified

that so many times they had camped.　Man was not made so large limbed and robust but that he must seek to narrow his world, and wall in a space such as fitted him.　He was at first bare and out of doors; but though this was pleasant enough in serene and warm weather, by daylight, the rainy season and the winter, to say nothing of the torrid sun, would perhaps have nipped his race in the bud if he had not made haste to clothe himself with the shelter of a house. Adam and Eve, according to the fable, wore the bower before other clothes.　Man wanted a home, a place of warmth, or comfort, first of physical warmth, then the warmth of the affections.

We may imagine a time when, in the infancy of the human race, some enterprising mortal crept into a hollow in a rock for shelter.　Every child begins the world again, to some extent, and loves to stay out doors, even in wet and cold.　It plays house, as well as horse, having an instinct for it.　Who does not remember the interest with which, when young, he looked at shelving rocks, or any approach to a cave?　It was the natural yearning of that portion of our most primitive ancestor which still survived in us.

From the cave we have advanced to roofs
of palm leaves, of bark and boughs, of linen
woven and stretched, of grass and straw, of
boards and shingles, of stones and tiles. At
last, we know not what it is to live in the
open air, and our lives are domestic in more
senses than we think. From the hearth
the field is a great distance. It would be
well, perhaps, if we were to spend more of
our days and nights without any obstruction
between us and the celestial bodies, if the
poet did not speak so much from under a
roof, or the saint dwell there so long. Birds
do not sing in caves, nor do doves cherish
their innocence in dovecots.

However, if one designs to construct a
dwelling house, it behooves him to exercise
a little Yankee shrewdness, lest after all
he find himself in a workhouse, a labyrinth
without a clue, a museum, an almshouse, a
prison, or a splendid mausoleum instead.
Consider first how slight a shelter is absolutely necessary. I have seen Penobscot Indians, in this town, living in tents of thin
cotton cloth, while the snow was nearly a
foot deep around them, and I thought that
they would be glad to have it deeper to keep
out the wind. Formerly, when how to get

my living honestly, with freedom left for my
proper pursuits, was a question which vexed
me even more than it does now, for unfortunately I am become somewhat callous, I
used to see a large box by the railroad, six
feet long by three wide, in which the laborers locked up their tools at night ; and it
suggested to me that every man who was
hard pushed might get such a one for a dollar, and, having bored a few auger holes in
it, to admit the air at least, get into it when
it rained and at night, and hook down the
lid, and so have freedom in his love, and in
his soul be free. This did not appear the
worst, nor by any means a despicable alternative. You could sit up as late as you
pleased, and, whenever you got up, go
abroad without any landlord or house-lord
dogging you for rent. Many a man is har-
assed to death to pay the rent of a larger
and more luxurious box who would not have
frozen to death in such a box as this. I am
far from jesting. Economy is a subject
which admits of being treated with levity,
but it cannot so be disposed of. A comfortable house for a rude and hardy race, that
lived mostly out of doors, was once made
here almost entirely of such materials as

Nature furnished ready to their hands.
Gookin, who was superintendent of the Indians subject to the Massachusetts Colony,
writing in 1674, says, "The best of their
houses are covered very neatly, tight and
warm, with barks of trees, slipped from their
bodies at those seasons when the sap is up,
and made into great flakes, with pressure of
weighty timber, when they are green. . . .
The meaner sort are covered with mats
which they make of a kind of bulrush, and
are also indifferently tight and warm, but
not so good as the former. . . . Some I
have seen, sixty or a hundred feet long and
thirty feet broad. . . . I have often lodged
in their wigwams, and found them as warm
as the best English houses." He adds that
they were commonly carpeted and lined
within with well-wrought embroidered mats,
and were furnished with various utensils.
The Indians had advanced so far as to regulate the effect of the wind by a mat suspended over the hole in the roof and moved
by a string. Such a lodge was in the first
instance constructed in a day or two at most,
and taken down and put up in a few hours ;
and every family owned one, or its apartment in one.

In the savage state every family owns a shelter as good as the best, and sufficient for its coarser and simpler wants ; but I think that I speak within bounds when I say that, though the birds of the air have their nests, and the foxes their holes, and the savages their wigwams, in modern civilized society not more than one half the families own a shelter. In the large towns and cities, where civilization especially prevails, the number of those who own a shelter is a very small fraction of the whole. The rest pay an annual tax for this outside garment of all, become indispensable summer and winter, which would buy a village of Indian wigwams, but now helps to keep them poor as long as they live. I do not mean to insist here on the disadvantage of hiring compared with owning, but it is evident that the savage owns his shelter because it costs so little, while the civilized man hires his commonly because he cannot afford to own it ; nor can he, in the long run, any better afford to hire. But, answers one, by merely paying this tax the poor civilized man secures an abode which is a palace compared with the savage's. An annual rent of from twenty-five to a hundred dollars (these are the country rates) entitles him to the benefit of the improvements of centuries, spacious apartments, clean paint and paper, Rumford fireplace, back plastering, Venetian blinds, copper pump, spring lock, a commodious cellar, and many other things. But how happens it that he who is said to enjoy these things is so commonly a *poor* civilized man, while the savage, who has them not, is rich as a savage? If it is asserted that civilization is a real advance in the condition of man, — and I think that it is, though only the wise improve their advantages, — it must be shown that it has produced better dwellings without making them more costly; and the cost of a thing is the amount of what I will call life which is required to be exchanged for it, immediately or in the long run. An average house in this neighborhood costs perhaps eight hundred dollars, and to lay up this sum will take from ten to fifteen years of the laborer's life, even if he is not encumbered with a family, — estimating the pecuniary value of every man's labor at one dollar a day, for if some receive more, others receive less; — so that he must have spent more than half his life commonly before *his* wigwam will be earned. If we suppose him to pay a rent instead, this is but a doubtful choice of evils. Would the savage have been wise to exchange his wigwam for a palace on these terms ?

It may be guessed that I reduce almost the whole advantage of holding this superfluous property as a fund in store against the future, so far as the individual is concerned, mainly to the defraying of funeral expenses. But perhaps a man is not required to bury himself. Nevertheless this points to an important distinction between the civilized man and the savage ; and, no doubt, they have designs on us for our benefit, in making the life of a civilized people an *institution*, in which the life of the individual is to a great extent absorbed, in order to preserve and perfect that of the race. But I wish to show at what a sacrifice this advantage is at present obtained, and to suggest that we may possibly so live as to secure all the advantage without suffering any of the disadvantage. What mean ye by saying that the poor ye have always with you, or that the fathers have eaten sour grapes, and the children's teeth are set on edge ?

" As I live, saith the Lord God, ye shall

not have occasion any more to use this prov-
erb in Israel."

" Behold all souls are mine ; as the soul
of the father, so also the soul of the son is
mine : the soul that sinneth it shall die."

When I consider my neighbors, the farmers of Concord, who are at least as well off
as the other classes, I find that for the most
part they have been toiling twenty, thirty,
or forty years, that they may become the
real owners of their farms, which commonly
they have inherited with encumbrances, or
else bought with hired money, — and we
may regard one third of that toil as the cost
of their houses, — but commonly they have
not paid for them yet. It is true, the encumbrances sometimes outweigh the value
of the farm, so that the farm itself becomes
one great encumbrance, and still a man is
found to inherit it, being well acquainted
with it, as he says. On applying to the as-
sessors, I am surprised to learn that they
cannot at once name a dozen in the town
who own their farms free and clear. If you
would know the history of these homesteads,
inquire at the bank where they are mort-
gaged. The man who has actually paid for
his farm with labor on it is so rare that

every neighbor can point to him. I doubt
if there are three such men in Concord.
What has been said of the merchants, that
a very large majority, even ninety-seven in
a hundred, are sure to fail, is equally true
of the farmers. With regard to the merchants, however, one of them says perti-
nently that a great part of their failures are
not genuine pecuniary failures, but merely
failures to fulfil their engagements, because
it is inconvenient; that is, it is the moral
character that breaks down. But this puts
an infinitely worse face on the matter, and
suggests, beside, that probably not even the
other three succeed in saving their souls,
but are perchance bankrupt in a worse sense
than they who fail honestly. Bankruptcy
and repudiation are the spring-boards from
which much of our civilization vaults and
turns its somersets, but the savage stands
on the unelastic plank of famine. Yet the
Middlesex Cattle Show goes off here with
éclat annually, as if all the joints of the agricultural machine were suent.

The farmer is endeavoring to solve the
problem of a livelihood by a formula more
complicated than the problem itself. To get
his shoestrings he speculates in herds of

cattle. With consummate skill he has set
his trap with a hair springe to catch comfort
and independence, and then, as he turned
away, got his own leg into it. This is the
reason he is poor; and for a similar reason
we are all poor in respect to a thousand savage comforts, though surrounded by luxuries. As Chapman sings, —

> " The false society of men —
>   — for earthly greatness
>   All heavenly comforts rarefies to air."

And when the farmer has got his house,
he may not be the richer but the poorer for
it, and it be the house that has got him. As
I understand it, that was a valid objection
urged by Momus against the house which
Minerva made, that she " had not made it
movable, by which means a bad neighborhood might be avoided; " and it may still
be urged, for our houses are such unwieldy
property that we are often imprisoned rather
than housed in them; and the bad neighborhood to be avoided is our own scurvy selves.
I know one or two families, at least, in this
town, who, for nearly a generation, have
been wishing to sell their houses in the outskirts and move into the village, but have
not been able to accomplish it, and only
death will set them free.

Granted that the *majority* are able at last either to own or hire the modern house with all its improvements. While civilization has been improving our houses, it has not equally improved the men who are to inhabit them. It has created palaces, but it was not so easy to create noblemen and kings. And *if the civilized man's pursuits are no worthier than the savage's, if he is employed the greater part of his life in obtaining gross necessaries and comforts merely, why should he have a better dwelling than the former?*

But how do the poor *minority* fare? Perhaps it will be found that just in proportion as some have been placed in outward circumstances above the savage, others have been degraded below him. The luxury of one class is counterbalanced by the indigence of another. On the one side is the palace, on the other are the almshouse and " silent poor." The myriads who built the pyramids to be the tombs of the Pharaohs were fed on garlic, and it may be were not decently buried themselves. The mason who finishes the cornice of the palace returns at night perchance to a hut not so good as a wigwam. It is a mistake to sup-

pose that, in a country where the usual evidences of civilization exist, the condition of a
very large body of the inhabitants may not
be as degraded as that of savages. I refer to
the degraded poor, not now to the degraded
rich. To know this I should not need to
look farther than to the shanties which
everywhere border our railroads, that last
improvement in civilization ; where I see in
my daily walks human beings living in sties,
and all winter with an open door, for the
sake of light, without any visible, often imaginable, wood pile, and the forms of both
old and young are permanently contracted
by the long habit of shrinking from cold
and misery, and the development of all their
limbs and faculties is checked. It certainly
is fair to look at that class by whose labor
the works which distinguish this generation
are accomplished. Such too, to a greater
or less extent, is the condition of the operatives of every denomination in England,
which is the great workhouse of the world.
Or I could refer you to Ireland, which is
marked as one of the white or enlightened
spots on the map. Contrast the physical
condition of the Irish with that of the North
American Indian, or the South Sea Islander,

or any other savage race before it was degraded by contact with the civilized man. Yet I have no doubt that that people's rulers are as wise as the average of civilized rulers. Their condition only proves what squalidness may consist with civilization. I hardly need refer now to the laborers in our Southern States who produce the staple exports of this country, and are themselves a staple production of the South. But to confine myself to those who are said to be in *moderate* circumstances.

Most men appear never to have considered what a house is, and are actually though needlessly poor all their lives because they think that they must have such a one as their neighbors have. As if one were to wear any sort of coat which the tailor might cut out for him, or, gradually leaving off palmleaf hat or cap of woodchuck skin, complain of hard times because he could not afford to buy him a crown! It is possible to invent a house still more convenient and luxurious than we have, which yet all would admit that man could not afford to pay for. Shall we always study to obtain more of these things, and not sometimes to be content with less? Shall the respectable citizen thus gravely teach, by precept and example, the necessity of the young man's providing a certain number of superfluous glow-shoes, and umbrellas, and empty guest chambers for empty guests, before he dies? Why should not our furniture be as simple as the Arab's or the Indian's? When I think of the benefactors of the race, whom we have apotheosized as messengers from heaven, bearers of divine gifts to man, I do not see in my mind any retinue at their heels, any car-load of fashionable furniture. Or what if I were to allow — would it not be a singular allowance? — that our furniture should be more complex than the Arab's, in proportion as we are morally and intellectually his superiors! At present our houses are cluttered and defiled with it, and a good housewife would sweep out the greater part into the dust hole, and not leave her morning's work undone. Morning work! By the blushes of Aurora and the music of Memnon, what should be man's *morning work* in this world? I had three pieces of limestone on my desk, but I was terrified to find that they required to be dusted daily, when the furniture of my mind was all undusted still, and I threw them out the window in disgust. How, then, could I have a furnished house? I would rather sit in the open air, for no dust gathers on the grass, unless where man has broken ground.

It is the luxurious and dissipated who set the fashions which the herd so diligently follow. The traveller who stops at the best houses, so called, soon discovers this, for the publicans presume him to be a Sardanapalus, and if he resigned himself to their tender mercies he would soon be completely emasculated. I think that in the railroad car we are inclined to spend more on luxury than on safety and convenience, and it threatens without attaining these to become no better than a modern drawing room, with its divans, and ottomans, and sunshades, and a hundred other oriental things, which we are taking west with us, invented for the ladies of the harem and the effeminate natives of the Celestial Empire, which Jonathan should be ashamed to know the names of. I would rather sit on a pumpkin and have it all to myself than be crowded on a velvet cushion. I would rather ride on earth in an ox cart, with a free circulation, than go to heaven in the fancy car of an excursion train and breathe a *malaria* all the way.

The very simplicity and nakedness of
man's life in the primitive ages imply this
advantage, at least, that they left him still
but a sojourner in nature. When he was
refreshed with food and sleep he contemplated his journey again. He dwelt, as it
were, in a tent in this world, and was either
threading the valleys, or crossing the plains,
or climbing the mountain tops. But lo!
men have become the tools of their tools.
The man who independently plucked the
fruits when he was hungry is become a
farmer ; and he who stood under a tree for
shelter, a housekeeper. We now no longer
camp as for a night, but have settled down
on earth and forgotten heaven. We have
adopted Christianity merely as an improved
method of *agri-*culture. We have built for
this world a family mansion, and for the
next a family tomb. The best works of art
are the expression of man's struggle to free
himself from this condition, but the effect of
our art is merely to make this low state comfortable and that higher state to be forgotten. There is actually no place in this village for a work of *fine* art, if any had come
down to us, to stand, for our lives, our
houses and streets, furnish no proper ped-

estal for it. There is not a nail to hang a
picture on, nor a shelf to receive the bust of
a hero or a saint. When I consider how
our houses are built and paid for, or not
paid for, and their internal economy man-
aged and sustained, I wonder that the floor
does not give way under the visitor while he
is admiring the gewgaws upon the mantel-
piece, and let him through into the cellar,
to some solid and honest though earthy
foundation. I cannot but perceive that this
so-called rich and refined life is a thing
jumped at, and I do not get on in the enjoyment of the *fine* arts which adorn it, my
attention being wholly occupied with the
jump; for I remember that the greatest
genuine leap, due to human muscles alone,
on record, is that of certain wandering
Arabs, who are said to have cleared twenty-
five feet on level ground. Without factitious support, man is sure to come to earth
again beyond that distance. The first question which I am tempted to put to the proprietor of such great impropriety is, Who
bolsters you? Are you one of the ninety-
seven who fail, or the three who succeed?
Answer me these questions, and then perhaps I may look at your bawbles and find

them ornamental. The cart before the horse is neither beautiful nor useful. Before we can adorn our houses with beautiful objects the walls must be stripped, and our lives must be stripped, and beautiful housekeeping and beautiful living be laid for a foundation : now, a taste for the beautiful is most cultivated out of doors, where there is no house and no housekeeper.

Old Johnson, in his " Wonder-Working Providence," speaking of the first settlers of this town, with whom he was contemporary, tells us that " they burrow themselves in the earth for their first shelter under some hillside, and, casting the soil aloft upon timber, they make a smoky fire against the earth, at the highest side." They did not "provide them houses," says he, " till the earth, by the Lord's blessing, brought forth bread to feed them," and the first year's crop was so light that " they were forced to cut their bread very thin for a long season." The secretary of the Province of New Netherland, writing in Dutch, in 1650, for the information of those who wished to take up land there, states more particularly that " those in New Netherland, and especially in New England, who have no means to build farm houses at first according to their wishes, dig a square pit in the ground, cellar fashion, six or seven feet deep, as long and as broad as they think proper, case the earth inside with wood all round the wall, and line the wood with the bark of trees or something else to prevent the caving in of the earth; floor this cellar with plank, and wainscot it over-head for a ceiling, raise a roof of spars clear up, and cover the spars with bark or green sods, so that they can live dry and warm in these houses with their entire families for two, three, and four years, it being under-stood that partitions are run through those cellars which are adapted to the size of the family. The wealthy and principal men in New England, in the beginning of the colo-nies, commenced their first dwelling houses in this fashion for two reasons: firstly, in order not to waste time in building, and not to want food the next season; secondly, in order not to discourage poor laboring people whom they brought over in numbers from Fatherland. In the course of three or four years, when the country became adapted to agriculture, they built themselves handsome houses, spending on them several thousands."

In this course which our ancestors took there was a show of prudence at least, as if their principle were to satisfy the more pressing wants first. But are the more pressing wants satisfied now? When I think of acquiring for myself one of our luxurious dwellings, I am deterred, for, so to speak, the country is not yet adapted to *human* culture, and we are still forced to cut our *spiritual* bread far thinner than our forefathers did their wheaten. Not that all architectural ornament is to be neglected even in the rudest periods; but let our houses first be lined with beauty, where they come in contact with our lives, like the tenement of the shell-fish, and not overlaid with it. But, alas! I have been inside one or two of them, and know what they are lined with.

Though we are not so degenerate but that we might possibly live in a cave or a wigwam or wear skins to-day, it certainly is better to accept the advantages, though so dearly bought, which the invention and industry of mankind offer. In such a neighborhood as this, boards and shingles, lime and bricks, are cheaper and more easily obtained than suitable caves, or whole logs, or bark in sufficient quantities, or even well-tempered clay or flat stones. I speak understandingly on this subject, for I have made myself acquainted with it both theoretically and practically. With a little more wit we might use these materials so as to become richer than the richest now are, and make our civilization a blessing. The civilized man is a more experienced and wiser savage. But to make haste to my own experiment.

Near the end of March, 1845, I borrowed an axe and went down to the woods by Walden Pond, nearest to where I intended to build my house, and began to cut down some tall arrowy white pines, still in their youth, for timber. It is difficult to begin without borrowing, but perhaps it is the most generous course thus to permit your fellow-men to have an interest in your enterprise. The owner of the axe, as he released his hold on it, said that it was the apple of his eye ; but I returned it sharper than I received it. It was a pleasant hillside where I worked, covered with pine woods, through which I looked out on the pond, and a small open field in the woods where pines and hickories were springing up. The ice in the pond was not yet dissolved, though there were some open spaces, and it was all dark colored and saturated with water. There were some slight flurries of snow during the days that I worked there ; but for the most part when I came out on to the railroad, on my way home, its yellow sand heap stretched away gleaming in the hazy atmosphere, and the rails shone in the spring sun, and I heard the lark and pewee and other birds already come to commence another year with us. They were pleasant spring days, in which the winter of man's discontent was thawing as well as the earth, and the life that had lain torpid began to stretch itself. One day, when my axe had come off and I had cut a green hickory for a wedge, driving it with a stone, and had placed the whole to soak in a pond hole in order to swell the wood, I saw a striped snake run into the water, and he lay on the bottom, apparently without inconvenience, as long as I stayed there, or more than a quarter of an hour ; perhaps because he had not yet fairly come out of the torpid state. It appeared to me that for a like reason men remain in their present low and primitive condition ; but if

they should feel the influence of the spring
of springs arousing them, they would of
necessity rise to a higher and more ethereal
life. I had previously seen the snakes in
frosty mornings in my path with portions of
their bodies still numb and inflexible, waiting for the sun to thaw them. On the 1st
of April it rained and melted the ice, and
in the early part of the day, which was very
foggy, I heard a stray goose groping about
over the pond and cackling as if lost, or like
the spirit of the fog.

So I went on for some days cutting and
hewing timber, and also studs and rafters,
all with my narrow axe, not having many
communicable or scholar-like thoughts, singing to myself, —

> Men say they know many things;
> But lo! they have taken wings, —
> The arts and sciences,
> And a thousand appliances;
> The wind that blows
> Is all that anybody knows.

I hewed the main timbers six inches square,
most of the studs on two sides only, and the
rafters and floor timbers on one side, leaving
the rest of the bark on, so that they were
just as straight and much stronger than

sawed ones. Each stick was carefully mortised or tenoned by its stump, for I had borrowed other tools by this time. My days in the woods were not very long ones ; yet I usually carried my dinner of bread and butter, and read the newspaper in which it was wrapped, at noon, sitting amid the green pine boughs which I had cut off, and to my bread was imparted some of their fragrance, for my hands were covered with a thick coat of pitch. Before I had done I was more the friend than the foe of the pine tree, though I had cut down some of them, having become better acquainted with it. Sometimes a rambler in the wood was attracted by the sound of my axe, and we chatted pleasantly over the chips which I had made.

By the middle of April, for I made no haste in my work, but rather made the most of it, my house was framed and ready for the raising. I had already bought the shanty of James Collins, an Irishman who worked on the Fitchburg Railroad, for boards. James Collins' shanty was considered an uncommonly fine one. When I called to see it he was not at home. I walked about the outside, at first unobserved from within, the window was so deep and high. It was of

small dimensions, with a peaked cottage
roof, and not much else to be seen, the dirt
being raised five feet all around as if it were
a compost heap. The roof was the soundest
part, though a good deal warped and made
brittle by the sun. Door-sill there was none,
but a perennial passage for the hens under
the door board. Mrs. C. came to the door
and asked me to view it from the inside.
The hens were driven in by my approach.
It was dark, and had a dirt floor for the
most part, dank, clammy, and aguish, only
here a board and there a board which would
not bear removal. She lighted a lamp to
show me the inside of the roof and the walls,
and also that the board floor extended under
the bed, warning me not to step into the
cellar, a sort of dust hole two feet deep. In
her own words, they were "good boards
overhead, good boards all around, and a
good window," — of two whole squares originally, only the cat had passed out that way
lately. There was a stove, a bed, and a
place to sit, an infant in the house where it
was born, a silk parasol, gilt-framed looking-
glass, and a patent new coffee-mill nailed to
an oak sapling, all told. The bargain was
soon concluded, for James had in the mean

while returned. I to pay four dollars and twenty-five cents to-night, he to vacate at five to-morrow morning, selling to nobody else meanwhile : I to take possession at six. It were well, he said, to be there early, and anticipate certain indistinct but wholly unjust claims on the score of ground rent and fuel. This he assured me was the only encumbrance. At six I passed him and his family on the road. One large bundle held their all, — bed, coffee-mill, looking-glass, hens, — all but the cat ; she took to the woods and became a wild cat, and, as I learned afterward, trod in a trap set for woodchucks, and so became a dead cat at last.

I took down this dwelling the same morning, drawing the nails, and removed it to the pond side by small cart-loads, spreading the boards on the grass there to bleach and warp back again in the sun. One early thrush gave me a note or two as I drove along the woodland path. I was informed treacherously by a young Patrick that neighbor Seeley, an Irishman, in the intervals of the carting, transferred the still tolerable, straight, and drivable nails, staples, and spikes to his pocket, and then stood when I came back to pass the time of day, and look freshly up, unconcerned, with spring thoughts, at the devastation ; there being a dearth of work, as he said. He was there to represent spectatordom, and help make this seemingly insignificant event one with the removal of the gods of Troy.

I dug my cellar in the side of a hill sloping to the south, where a woodchuck had formerly dug his burrow, down through sumach and blackberry roots, and the lowest stain of vegetation, six feet square by seven deep, to a fine sand where potatoes would not freeze in any winter. The sides were left shelving, and not stoned ; but the sun having never shone on them, the sand still keeps its place. It was but two hours' work. I took particular pleasure in this breaking of ground, for in almost all latitudes men dig into the earth for an equable temperature. Under the most splendid house in the city is still to be found the cellar where they store their roots as of old, and long after the superstructure has disappeared posterity remark its dent in the earth. The house is still but a sort of porch at the entrance of a burrow.

At length, in the beginning of May, with the help of some of my acquaintances, rather

to improve so good an occasion for neighbor-
liness than from any necessity, I set up the
frame of my house. No man was ever more
honored in the character of his raisers than
I. They are destined, I trust, to assist at
the raising of loftier structures one day. I
began to occupy my house on the 4th of
July, as soon as it was boarded and roofed,
for the boards were carefully feather-edged
and lapped, so that it was perfectly impervious to rain, but before boarding I laid the
foundation of a chimney at one end, bringing two cartloads of stones up the hill from
the pond in my arms. I built the chimney
after my hoeing in the fall, before a fire became necessary for warmth, doing my cooking in the mean while out of doors on the
ground, early in the morning : which mode
I still think is in some respects more convenient and agreeable than the usual one.
When it stormed before my bread was
baked, I fixed a few boards over the fire,
and sat under them to watch my loaf, and
passed some pleasant hours in that way. In
those days, when my hands were much employed, I read but little, but the least scraps
of paper which lay on the ground, my holder,
or tablecloth, afforded me as much entertain-

ment, in fact answered the same purpose as the Iliad.

It would be worth the while to build still more deliberately than I did, considering, for instance, what foundation a door, a window, a cellar, a garret, have in the nature of man, and perchance never raising any superstructure until we found a better reason for it than our temporal necessities even. There is some of the same fitness in a man's building his own house that there is in a bird's building its own nest. Who knows but if men constructed their dwellings with their own hands, and provided food for themselves and families simply and honestly enough, the poetic faculty would be universally developed, as birds universally sing when they are so engaged? But alas! we do like cowbirds and cuckoos, which lay their eggs in nests which other birds have built, and cheer no traveller with their chattering and unmusical notes. Shall we forever resign the pleasure of construction to the carpenter? What does architecture amount to in the experience of the mass of men? I never in all my walks came across a man engaged in so simple and natural an occupation as build-

ing his house. We belong to the community. It is not the tailor alone who is the
ninth part of a man ; it is as much the
preacher, and the merchant, and the farmer.
Where is this division of labor to end ? and
what object does it finally serve ? No doubt
another *may* also think for me; but it is not
therefore desirable that he should do so to
the exclusion of my thinking for myself.

True, there are architects so called in this
country, and I have heard of one at least
possessed with the idea of making architectural ornaments have a core of truth, a necessity, and hence a beauty, as if it were a
revelation to him. All very well perhaps
from his point of view, but only a little
better than the common dilettantism. A
sentimental reformer in architecture, he began at the cornice, not at the foundation.
It was only now to put a core of truth within
the ornaments, that every sugar plum in fact
might have an almond or caraway seed in
it, — though I hold that almonds are most
wholesome without the sugar, — and not
how the inhabitant, the indweller, might
build truly within and without, and let the
ornaments take care of themselves. What
reasonable man ever supposed that orna-

ments were something outward and in the skin merely, — that the tortoise got his spotted shell, or the shellfish its mother-o'-pearl tints, by such a contract as the inhabitants of Broadway their Trinity Church? But a man has no more to do with the style of architecture of his house than a tortoise with that of its shell: nor need the soldier be so idle as to try to paint the precise *color* of his virtue on his standard. The enemy will find it out. He may turn pale when the trial comes. This man seemed to me to lean over the cornice, and timidly whisper his half truth to the rude occupants who really knew it better than he. What of architectural beauty I now see, I know has gradually grown from within outward, out of the necessities and character of the in-dweller, who is the only builder, — out of some unconscious truthfulness, and noble-ness, without ever a thought for the appear-ance ; and whatever additional beauty of this kind is destined to be produced will be preceded by a like unconscious beauty of life. The most interesting dwellings in this country, as the painter knows, are the most unpretending, humble log huts and cottages of the poor commonly ; it is the life of the

inhabitants whose shells they are, and not
any peculiarity in their surfaces merely,
which makes them *picturesque ;* and equally
interesting will be the citizen's suburban
box, when his life shall be as simple and as
agreeable to the imagination, and there is
as little straining after effect in the style of
his dwelling.   A great proportion of architectural ornaments are literally hollow, and
a September gale would strip them off, like
borrowed plumes, without injury to the sub-
stantials.   They can do without *architecture*
who have no olives nor wines in the cellar.
What if an equal ado were made about the
ornaments of style in literature, and the
architects of our bibles spent as much time
about their cornices as the architects of our
churches do ?   So are made the *belles-lettres*
and the *beaux-arts* and their professors.
Much it concerns a man, forsooth, how a few
sticks are slanted over him or under him,
and what colors are daubed upon his box.
It would signify somewhat, if, in any earnest sense, *he* slanted them and daubed it ;
but the spirit having departed out of the
tenant, it is of a piece with constructing his
own coffin, — the architecture of the grave,
and " carpenter," is but another name for

" coffin-maker." One man says, in his despair or indifference to life, take up a handful of the earth at your feet, and paint your house that color. Is he thinking of his last and narrow house? Toss up a copper for it as well. What an abundance of leisure he must have! Why do you take up a handful of dirt? Better paint your house your own complexion; let it turn pale or blush for you. An enterprise to improve the style of cottage architecture! When you have got my ornaments ready I will wear them.

Before winter I built a chimney, and shingled the sides of my house, which were already impervious to rain, with imperfect and sappy shingles made of the first slice of the log, whose edges I was obliged to straighten with a plane.

I have thus a tight shingled and plastered house, ten feet wide by fifteen long, and eight-feet posts, with a garret and a closet, a large window on each side, two trap doors, one door at the end, and a brick fireplace opposite. The exact cost of my house, paying the usual price for such materials as I used, but not counting the work, all of which was done by myself, was as follows; and I give the details because very few are able to

tell exactly what their houses cost, and fewer
still, if any, the separate cost of the various
materials which compose them : —

Boards	$8 03½,	mostly shanty boards.
Refuse shingles for roof and sides	4 00	
Laths	1 25	
Two second-hand windows with glass . .	2 43	
One thousand old brick	4 00	
Two casks of lime . .	2 40	That was high.
Hair	0 31	More than I needed.
Mantle-tree iron . . .	0 15	
Nails	3 90	
Hinges and screws . .	0 14	
Latch	0 10	
Chalk	0 01	
Transportation . . .	1 40	} I carried a good part on my back.

In all $28 12½

These are all the materials excepting the
timber, stones, and sand, which I claimed by
squatter's right. I have also a small wood-
shed adjoining, made chiefly of the stuff
which was left after building the house.

I intend to build me a house which will
surpass any on the main street in Concord
in grandeur and luxury, as soon as it pleases
me as much and will cost me no more than
my present one.

I thus found that the student who wishes for a shelter can obtain one for a lifetime at an expense not greater than the rent which he now pays annually. If I seem to boast more than is becoming, my excuse is that I brag for humanity rather than for myself; and my shortcomings and inconsistencies do not affect the truth of my statement. Notwithstanding much cant and hypocrisy, — chaff which I find it difficult to separate from my wheat, but for which I am as sorry as any man, — I will breathe freely and stretch myself in this respect, it is such a relief to both the moral and physical system; and I am resolved that I will not through humility become the devil's attorney. I will endeavor to speak a good word for the truth. At Cambridge College the mere rent of a student's room, which is only a little larger than my own, is thirty dollars each year, though the corporation had the advantage of building thirty-two side by side and under one roof, and the occupant suffers the inconvenience of many and noisy neighbors, and perhaps a residence in the fourth story. I cannot but think that if we had more true wisdom in these respects, not only less education would be needed, because, forsooth, more would already have been acquired, but the pecuniary expense of getting an education would in a great measure vanish. Those conveniences which the student requires at Cambridge or elsewhere cost him or somebody else ten times as great a sacrifice of life as they would with proper management on both sides. Those things for which the most money is demanded are never the things which the student most wants. Tuition, for instance, is an important item in the term bill, while for the far more valuable education which he gets by associating with the most cultivated of his contemporaries no charge is made. The mode of founding a college is, commonly, to get up a subscription of dollars and cents, and then following blindly the principles of a division of labor to its extreme, a principle which should never be followed but with circumspection, — to call in a contractor who makes this a subject of speculation, and he employs Irishmen or other operatives actually to lay the foundations, while the students that are to be are said to be fitting themselves for it ; and for these oversights successive generations have to pay. I think that it would be *better than this*, for the students, or those who desire to be benefited by it, even to lay the foundation themselves. The student who secures his coveted leisure and retirement by systematically shirking any labor necessary to man obtains but an ignoble and unprofitable leisure, defrauding himself of the experience which alone can make leisure fruitful. "But," says one, "you do not mean that the students should go to work with their hands instead of their heads?" I do not mean that exactly, but I mean something which he might think a good deal like that; I mean that they should not *play* life, or *study* it merely, while the community supports them at this expensive game, but earnestly *live* it from beginning to end. How could youths better learn to live than by at once trying the experiment of living? Methinks this would exercise their minds as much as mathematics. If I wished a boy to know something about the arts and sciences, for instance, I would not pursue the common course, which is merely to send him into the neighborhood of some professor, where anything is professed and practised but the art of life; — to survey the world through a telescope or a microscope, and never with his natural

eye ; to study chemistry, and not learn how
his bread is made, or mechanics, and not
learn how it is earned ; to discover new sat-
ellites to Neptune, and not detect the motes
in his eyes, or to what vagabond he is a
satellite himself ; or to be devoured by the
monsters that swarm all around him, while
contemplating the monsters in a drop of
vinegar. Which would have advanced the
most at the end of a month, — the boy who
had made his own jackknife from the ore
which he had dug and smelted, reading as
much as would be necessary for this — or
the boy who had attended the lectures on
metallurgy at the Institute in the mean
while, and had received a Rogers' penknife
from his father ? Which would be most
likely to cut his fingers ? . . . To my astonishment I was informed on leaving college that I had studied navigation ! — why,
if I had taken one turn down the harbor I should have known more about it.
Even the *poor* student studies and is taught
only *political* economy, while that economy of living which is synonymous with
philosophy is not even sincerely professed
in our colleges. The consequence is, that
while he is reading Adam Smith, Ricardo,

and Say, he runs his father in debt irretrievably.

As with our colleges, so with a hundred " modern improvements ; " there is an illusion about them ; there is not always a positive advance. The devil goes on exacting compound interest to the last for his early share and numerous succeeding investments in them. Our inventions are wont to be pretty toys, which distract our attention from serious things. They are but improved means to an unimproved end, an end which it was already but too easy to arrive at ; as railroads lead to Boston or New York. We are in great haste to construct a magnetic telegraph from Maine to Texas ; but Maine and Texas, it may be, have nothing important to communicate. Either is in such a predicament as the man who was earnest to be introduced to a distinguished deaf woman, but when he was presented, and one end of her ear trumpet was put into his hand, had nothing to say. As if the main object were to talk fast and not to talk sensibly. We are eager to tunnel under the Atlantic and bring the old world some weeks nearer to the new ; but perchance the first news that will leak through into the broad, flapping American ear will be that the Princess Adelaide has the whooping cough. After all, the man whose horse trots a mile in a minute does not carry the most important messages; he is not an evangelist, nor does he come round eating locusts and wild honey. I doubt if Flying Childers ever carried a peck of corn to mill.

One says to me, " I wonder that you do not lay up money; you love to travel; you might take the cars and go to Fitchburg to-day and see the country." But I am wiser than that. I have learned that the swiftest traveller is he that goes afoot. I say to my friend, Suppose we try who will get there first. The distance is thirty miles; the fare ninety cents. That is almost a day's wages. I remember when wages were sixty cents a day for laborers on this very road. Well, I start now on foot, and get there before night; I have travelled at that rate by the week together. You will in the mean while have earned your fare, and arrive there some time to-morrow, or possibly this evening, if you are lucky enough to get a job in season. Instead of going to Fitchburg, you will be working here the greater part of the day. And so, if the railroad reached round

the world, I think that I should keep ahead
of you ; and as for seeing the country and
getting experience of that kind, I should
have to cut your acquaintance altogether.

Such is the universal law, which no man
can ever outwit, and with regard to the railroad even we may say it is as broad as it is
long.   To make a railroad round the world
available to all mankind is equivalent to
grading the whole surface of the planet.
Men have an indistinct notion that if they
keep up this activity of joint stocks and
spades long enough all will at length ride
somewhere, in next to no time, and for nothing ; but though a crowd rushes to the depot,
and the conductor shouts " All aboard ! "
when the smoke is blown away and the vapor
condensed, it will be perceived that a few are
riding, but the rest are run over, — and it
will be called, and will be, " A melancholy
accident."   No doubt they can ride at last
who shall have earned their fare, that is, if
they survive so long, but they will probably
have lost their elasticity and desire to travel
by that time.   This spending of the best
part of one's life earning money in order to
enjoy a questionable liberty during the least
valuable part of it, reminds me of the Eng-

lishman who went to India to make a fortune first, in order that he might return to
England and live the life of a poet. He
should have gone up garret at once.
" What ! " exclaim a million Irishmen starting up from all the shanties in the land, " is
not this railroad which we have built a good
thing ? " Yes, I answer, *comparatively*
good, that is, you might have done worse ;
but I wish, as you are brothers of mine, that
you could have spent your time better than
digging in this dirt.

Before I finished my house, wishing to
earn ten or twelve dollars by some honest
and agreeable method, in order to meet my
unusual expenses, I planted about two acres
and a half of light and sandy soil near it
chiefly with beans, but also a small part with
potatoes, corn, peas, and turnips. The
whole lot contains eleven acres, mostly growing up to pines and hickories, and was sold
the preceding season for eight dollars and
eight cents an acre. One farmer said that
it was " good for nothing but to raise cheep-
ing squirrels on." I put no manure whatever on this land, not being the owner, but
merely a squatter, and not expecting to cul-

tivate so much again, and I did not quite hoe it all once. I got out several cords of stumps in ploughing, which supplied me with fuel for a long time, and left small circles of virgin mould, easily distinguishable through the summer by the greater luxuriance of the beans there. The dead and for the most part unmerchantable wood behind my house, and the driftwood from the pond, have supplied the remainder of my fuel. I was obliged to hire a team and a man for the ploughing, though I held the plough myself. My farm outgoes for the first season were, for implements, seed, work, etc., $14 72½. The seed corn was given me. This never costs anything to speak of, unless you plant more than enough. I got twelve bushels of beans, and eighteen bushels of potatoes, beside some peas and sweet corn. The yellow corn and turnips were too late to come to anything. My whole income from the farm was

$$
\begin{array}{lr}
& \$23\ 44 \\
\text{Deducting the outgoes} \quad . \quad . \quad . & 14\ 72\tfrac{1}{2} \\
\hline
\text{There are left} \quad . \quad . \quad . \quad . \quad . \quad . & \$8\ 71\tfrac{1}{2},
\end{array}
$$

beside produce consumed and on hand at the time this estimate was made of the value of

$4.50, — the amount on hand much more than balancing a little grass which I did not raise. All things considered, that is, considering the importance of a man's soul and of to-day, notwithstanding the short time oc· cupied by my experiment, nay, partly even because of its transient character, I believe that that was doing better than any farmer in Concord did that year.

The next year I did better still, for I spaded up all the land which I required, about a third of an acre, and I learned from the experience of both years, not being in the least awed by many celebrated works on husbandry, Arthur Young among the rest, that if one would live simply and eat only the crop which he raised, and raise no more than he ate, and not exchange it for an insufficient quantity of more luxurious and expensive things, he would need to cultivate only a few rods of ground, and that it would be cheaper to spade up that than to use oxen to plough it, and to select a fresh spot from time to time than to manure the old, and he could do all his necessary farm work as it were with his left hand at odd hours in the summer; and thus he would not be tied to an ox, or horse, or cow, or pig, as at present.

I desire to speak impartially on this point, and as one not interested in the success or failure of the present economical and social arrangements. I was more independent than any farmer in Concord, for I was not anchored to a house or farm, but could follow the bent of my genius, which is a very crooked one, every moment. Beside being better off than they already, if my house had been burned or my crops had failed, I should have been nearly as well off as before.

I am wont to think that men are not so much the keepers of herds as herds are the keepers of men, the former are so much the freer. Men and oxen exchange work; but if we consider necessary work only, the oxen will be seen to have greatly the advantage, their farm is so much the larger. Man does some of his part of the exchange work in his six weeks of haying, and it is no boy's play. Certainly no nation that lived simply in all respects, that is, no nation of philosophers, would commit so great a blunder as to use the labor of animals. True, there never was and is not likely soon to be a nation of philosophers, nor am I certain it is desirable that there should be. However, *I* should

never have broken a horse or bull and taken
him to board for any work he might do for
me, for fear I should become a horse-man or
a herds-man merely; and if society seems to
be the gainer by so doing, are we certain that
what is one man's gain is not another's loss,
and that the stable-boy has equal cause with
his master to be satisfied? Granted that
some public works would not have been constructed without this aid, and let man share
the glory of such with the ox and horse;
does it follow that he could not have accomplished works yet more worthy of himself in
that case? When men begin to do, not
merely unnecessary or artistic, but luxurious
and idle work, with their assistance, it is inevitable that a few do all the exchange work
with the oxen, or, in other words, become
the slaves of the strongest. Man thus not
only works for the animal within him, but,
for a symbol of this, he works for the animal
without him. Though we have many substantial houses of brick or stone, the pros-
perity of the farmer is still measured by the
degree to which the barn overshadows the
house. This town is said to have the largest
houses for oxen, cows, and horses hereabouts,
and it is not behindhand in its public build-

ings ; but there are very few halls for free worship or free speech in this county. It should not be by their architecture, but why not even by their power of abstract thought, that nations should seek to commemorate themselves ? How much more admirable the Bhagvat-Geeta than all the ruins of the East! Towers and temples are the luxury of princes. A simple and independent mind does not toil at the bidding of any prince. Genius is not a retainer to any emperor, nor is its material silver, or gold, or marble, except to a trifling extent. To what end, pray, is so much stone hammered ? In Arcadia, when I was there, I did not see any hammering stone. Nations are possessed with an insane ambition to perpetuate the memory of themselves by the amount of hammered stone they leave. What if equal pains were taken to smooth and polish their manners ? One piece of good sense would be more memorable than a monument as high as the moon. I love better to see stones in place. The grandeur of Thebes was a vulgar grandeur. More sensible is a rod of stone wall that bounds an honest man's field than a hundred-gated Thebes that has wandered farther from the true end of life. The reli-

gion and civilization which are barbaric and
heathenish build splendid temples ; but what
you might call Christianity does not. Most
of the stone a nation hammers goes toward
its tomb only. It buries itself alive. As
for the Pyramids, there is nothing to wonder
at in them so much as the fact that so many
men could be found degraded enough to
spend their lives constructing a tomb for
some ambitious booby, whom it would have
been wiser and manlier to have drowned in
the Nile, and then given his body to the
dogs. I might possibly invent some excuse
for them and him, but I have no time for it.
As for the religion and love of art of the
builders, it is much the same all the world
over, whether the building be an Egyptian
temple or the United States Bank. It costs
more than it comes to. The mainspring is
vanity, assisted by the love of garlic and
bread and butter. Mr. Balcom, a promising
young architect, designs it on the back of his
Vitruvius, with hard pencil and ruler, and
the job is let out to Dobson & Sons, stone-
cutters. When the thirty centuries begin
to look down on it, mankind begin to look
up at it. As for your high towers and
monuments, there was a crazy fellow once

in this town who undertook to dig through
to China, and he got so far that, as he said,
he heard the Chinese pots and kettles rattle ;
but I think that I shall not go out of my
way to admire the hole which he made.
Many are concerned about the monuments
of the West and the East, — to know who
built them. For my part, I should like to
know who in those days did not build them,
— who were above such trifling. But to
proceed with my statistics.

By surveying, carpentry, and day - labor
of various other kinds in the village in
the mean while, for I have as many trades
as fingers, I had earned $13.34. The ex-
pense of food for eight months, namely,
from July 4th to March 1st, the time when
these estimates were made, though I lived
there more than two years, — not counting
potatoes, a little green corn, and some peas,
which I had raised, nor considering the
value of what was on hand at the last date,
was

Rice $1 73½
Molasses . . . 1 73   Cheapest form of the
                           saccharine.
Rye meal . . . 1 04¾
Indian meal . . 0 99¾   Cheaper than rye.
Pork 0 22

Flour	0 88	} Costs more than Indian meal, both money and trouble.
Sugar	0 80	
Lard	0 65	
Apples	0 25	
Dried apple . .	0 22	
Sweet potatoes .	0 10	
One pumpkin .	0 6	
One watermelon .	0 2	
Salt	0 3	

All experiments which failed.

Yes, I did eat $8.74, all told; but I should not thus unblushingly publish my guilt, if I did not know that most of my readers were equally guilty with myself, and that their deeds would look no better in print. The next year I sometimes caught a mess of fish for my dinner, and once I went so far as to slaughter a woodchuck which ravaged my bean-field, — effect his transmigration, as a Tartar would say, — and devour him, partly for experiment's sake; but though it afforded me a momentary enjoyment, notwithstanding a musky flavor, I saw that the longest use would not make that a good practice, however it might seem to have your woodchucks ready dressed by the village butcher.

Clothing and some incidental expenses within the same dates, though little can be inferred from this item, amounted to

$8 40¾
Oil and some household utensils . . 2 00

So that all the pecuniary outgoes, excepting for washing and mending, which for the most part were done out of the house, and their bills have not yet been received, — and these are all and more than all the ways by which money necessarily goes out in this part of the world, — were

House	$28 12½
Farm one year	14 72¼
Food eight months	8 74
Clothing, etc., eight months . .	8 40¾
Oil, etc., eight months	2 00
In all	$61 99¾

I address myself now to those of my readers who have a living to get. And to meet this I have for farm produce sold

	$23 44
Earned by day-labor	13 34
In all	$36 78,

which subtracted from the sum of the outgoes leaves a balance of $25.21¾ on the one side, — this being very nearly the means with which I started, and the measure of expenses to be incurred, — and on the other, beside the leisure and independence and health thus secured, a comfortable house for me as long as I choose to occupy it.

These statistics, however accidental and therefore uninstructive they may appear, as they have a certain completeness, have a certain value also. Nothing was given me of which I have not rendered some account. It appears from the above estimate, that my food alone cost me in money about twenty-seven cents a week. It was, for nearly two years after this, rye and Indian meal without yeast, potatoes, rice, a very little salt pork, molasses, and salt; and my drink, water. It was fit that I should live on rice, mainly, who loved so well the philosophy of India. To meet the objections of some inveterate cavillers, I may as well state, that if I dined out occasionally, as I always had done, and I trust shall have opportunities to do again, it was frequently to the detriment of my domestic arrangements. But the dining out, being, as I have stated, a constant element, does not in the least affect a comparative statement like this.

I learned from my two years' experience that it would cost incredibly little trouble to obtain one's necessary food, even in this latitude ; that a man may use as simple a

diet as the animals, and yet retain health
and strength. I have made a satisfactory
dinner, satisfactory on several accounts,
simply off a dish of purslane (*Portulaca
oleracea*) which I gathered in my cornfield,
boiled and salted. I give the Latin on account of the savoriness of the trivial name.
And pray what more can a reasonable man
desire, in peaceful times, in ordinary noons,
than a sufficient number of ears of green
sweet-corn boiled, with the addition of salt?
Even the little variety which I used was a
yielding to the demands of appetite, and not
of health. Yet men have come to such a
pass that they frequently starve, not for
want of necessaries, but for want of luxuries;
and I know a good woman who thinks that
her son lost his life because he took to drinking water only.

The reader will perceive that I am treat-
ing the subject rather from an economic
than a dietetic point of view, and he will
not venture to put my abstemiousness to the
test unless he has a well-stocked larder.

Bread I at first made of pure Indian meal
and salt, genuine hoe-cakes, which I baked
before my fire out of doors on a shingle or
the end of a stick of timber sawed off in

building my house ; but it was wont to get
smoked and to have a piny flavor. I tried
flour also ; but have at last found a mixture
of rye and Indian meal most convenient and
agreeable. In cold weather it was no little
amusement to bake several small loaves of
this in succession, tending and turning them
as carefully as an Egyptian his hatching
eggs. They were a real cereal fruit which I
ripened, and they had to my senses a fragrance like that of other noble fruits, which
I kept in as long as possible by wrapping
them in cloths. I made a study of the ancient and indispensable art of bread-making,
consulting such authorities as offered, going
back to the primitive days and first invention of the unleavened kind, when from the
wildness of nuts and meats men first reached
the mildness and refinement of this diet,
and travelling gradually down in my studies
through that accidental souring of the dough
which, it is supposed, taught the leavening
process, and through the various fermenta-
tions thereafter, till I came to " good, sweet,
wholesome bread," the staff of life. Leaven,
which some deem the soul of bread, the *spir-
itus* which fills its cellular tissue, which is
religiously preserved like the vestal fire, —

some precious bottle-full, I suppose, first brought over in the Mayflower, did the business for America, and its influence is still rising, swelling, spreading, in cerealian billows over the land, — this seed I regularly and faithfully procured from the village, till at length one morning I forgot the rules, and scalded my yeast; by which accident I discovered that even this was not indispensable, — for my discoveries were not by the synthetic but analytic process, — and I have gladly omitted it since, though most housewives earnestly assured me that safe and wholesome bread without yeast might not be, and elderly people prophesied a speedy decay of the vital forces. Yet I find it not to be an essential ingredient, and after going without it for a year am still in the land of the living; and I am glad to escape the trivialness of carrying a bottle-full in my pocket, which would sometimes pop and discharge its contents to my discomfiture. It is simpler and more respectable to omit it. Man is an animal who more than any other can adapt himself to all climates and circumstances. Neither did I put any sal-soda, or other acid or alkali, into my bread. It would seem that I made it according to

the recipe which Marcus Porcius Cato gave
about two centuries before Christ. "Pa-
nem depsticium sic facito. Manus mortari-
umque bene lavato. Farinam in mortarium
indito, aquæ paulatim addito, subigitoque
pulchre. Ubi bene subegeris, defingito, co-
quitoque sub testu." Which I take to mean,
"Make kneaded bread thus. Wash your
hands and trough well. Put the meal into
the trough, add water gradually, and knead
it thoroughly. When you have kneaded it
well, mould it, and bake it under a cover,"
that is, in a baking-kettle. Not a word
about leaven. But I did not always use this
staff of life. At one time, owing to the
emptiness of my purse, I saw none of it for
more than a month.

Every New Englander might easily raise
all his own breadstuffs in this land of rye
and Indian corn, and not depend on distant
and fluctuating markets for them. Yet so
far are we from simplicity and independence that, in Concord, fresh and sweet
meal is rarely sold in the shops, and hominy
and corn in a still coarser form are hardly
used by any. For the most part the farmer
gives to his cattle and hogs the grain of his
own producing, and buys flour, which is at

least no more wholesome, at a greater cost, at the store. I saw that I could easily raise my bushel or two of rye and Indian corn, for the former will grow on the poorest land, and the latter does not require the best, and grind them in a hand-mill, and so do without rice and pork ; and if I must have some concentrated sweet, I found by experiment that I could make a very good molasses either of pumpkins or beets, and I knew that I needed only to set out a few maples to obtain it more easily still, and while these were growing I could use various substitutes beside those which I have named. " For," as the Forefathers sang, —

" we can make liquor to sweeten our lips
Of pumpkins and parsnips and walnut-tree chips."

Finally, as for salt, that grossest of groceries, to obtain this might be a fit occasion for a visit to the seashore, or, if I did without it altogether, I should probably drink the less water. I do not learn that the Indians ever troubled themselves to go after it.

Thus I could avoid all trade and barter, so far as my food was concerned, and having a shelter already, it would only remain to get clothing and fuel. The pantaloons which I now wear were woven in a farmer's

family, — thank Heaven there is so much
virtue still in man; for I think the fall
from the farmer to the operative as great
and memorable as that from the man to the
farmer ; — and in a new country, fuel is an
encumbrance. As for a habitat, if I were
not permitted still to squat, I might purchase one acre at the same price for which
the land I cultivated was sold — namely,
eight dollars and eight cents. But as it
was, I considered that I enhanced the value
of the land by squatting on it.

There is a certain class of unbelievers who
sometimes ask me such questions as, if I
think that I can live on vegetable food
alone; and to strike at the root of the matter at once, — for the root is faith, — I am
accustomed to answer such, that I can live
on board nails. If they cannot understand
that, they cannot understand much that I
have to say. For my part, I am glad to
hear of experiments of this kind being tried;
as that a young man tried for a fortnight to
live on hard, raw corn on the ear, using his
teeth for all mortar. The squirrel tribe tried
the same and succeeded. The human race
is interested in these experiments, though
a few old women who are incapacitated for

them, or who own their thirds in mills, may be alarmed.

My furniture, part of which I made myself, and the rest cost me nothing of which I have not rendered an account, consisted of a bed, a table, a desk, three chairs, a looking-glass three inches in diameter, a pair of tongs and andirons, a kettle, a skillet, and a frying-pan, a dipper, a wash-bowl, two knives and forks, three plates, one cup, one spoon, a jug for oil, a jug for molasses, and a japanned lamp. None is so poor that he need sit on a pumpkin. That is shiftlessness. There is a plenty of such chairs as I like best in the village garrets to be had for taking them away. Furniture! Thank God, I can sit and I can stand without the aid of a furniture warehouse. What man but a philosopher would not be ashamed to see his furniture packed in a cart and going up country exposed to the light of heaven and the eyes of men, a beggarly account of empty boxes? That is Spaulding's furniture. I could never tell from inspecting such a load whether it belonged to a so-called rich man or a poor one; the owner always seemed poverty-stricken. Indeed, the

more you have of such things the poorer
you are. Each load looks as if it contained
the contents of a dozen shanties; and if one
shanty is poor, this is a dozen times as poor.
Pray, for what do we *move* ever but to get
rid of our furniture, our *exuviæ;* at last to
go from this world to another newly furnished, and leave this to be burned? It is
the same as if all these traps were buckled
to a man's belt, and he could not move over
the rough country where our lines are cast
without dragging them, — dragging his
trap. He was a lucky fox that left his tail
in the trap. The muskrat will gnaw his
third leg off to be free. No wonder man
has lost his elasticity. How often he is at
a dead set! "Sir, if I may be so bold,
what do you mean by a dead set?" If you
are a seer, whenever you meet a man you
will see all that he owns, ay, and much that
he pretends to disown, behind him, even to
his kitchen furniture and all the trumpery
which he saves and will not burn, and he
will appear to be harnessed to it and making what headway he can. I think that the
man is at a dead set who has got through a
knot hole or gateway where his sledge load
of furniture cannot follow him. I cannot

but feel compassion when I hear some trig, compact - looking man, seemingly free, all girded and ready, speak of his " furniture," as whether it is insured or not. " But what shall I do with my furniture ? " My gay butterfly is entangled in a spider's web then. Even those who seem for a long while not to have any, if you inquire more narrowly you will find have some stored in somebody's barn. I look upon England to-day as an old gentleman who is travelling with a great deal of baggage, trumpery which has accumulated from long housekeeping, which he has not the courage to burn ; great trunk, little trunk, bandbox and bundle. Throw away the first three at least. It would surpass the powers of a well man nowadays to take up his bed and walk, and I should certainly advise a sick one to lay down his bed and run. When I have met an immigrant tottering under a bundle which contained his all — looking like an enormous wen which had grown out of the nape of his neck — I have pitied him, not because that was his all, but because he had all *that* to carry. If I have got to drag my trap, I will take care that it be a light one and do not nip me in a vital part. But perchance

it would be wisest never to put one's paw
into it.

I would observe, by the way, that it costs
me nothing for curtains, for I have no gaz-
ers to shut out but the sun and moon, and I
am willing that they should look in. The
moon will not sour milk nor taint meat of
mine, nor will the sun injure my furniture
or fade my carpet; and if he is sometimes
too warm a friend, I find it still better
economy to retreat behind some curtain
which nature has provided, than to add a
single item to the details of housekeeping.
A lady once offered me a mat, but as I had
no room to spare within the house, nor time
to spare within or without to shake it, I declined it, preferring to wipe my feet on the
sod before my door. It is best to avoid the
beginnings of evil.

Not long since I was present at the auction of a deacon's effects, for his life had not
been ineffectual : —

" The evil that men do lives after them."

As usual, a great proportion was trumpery
which had begun to accumulate in his father's day. Among the rest was a dried
tapeworm. And now, after lying half a

century in his garret and other dust holes, these things were not burned; instead of a *bonfire*, or purifying destruction of them, there was an *auction*, or increasing of them. The neighbors eagerly collected to view them, bought them all, and carefully transported them to their garrets and dust holes, to lie there till their estates are settled, when they will start again. When a man dies he kicks the dust.

The customs of some savage nations might, perchance, be profitably imitated by us, for they at least go through the semblance of casting their slough annually; they have the idea of the thing, whether they have the reality or not. Would it not be well if we were to celebrate such a " busk," or " feast of first fruits," as Bartram describes to have been the custom of the Mucclasse Indians? " When a town celebrates the busk," says he, " having previously provided themselves with new clothes, new pots, pans, and other household utensils and furniture, they collect all their worn out clothes and other despicable things, sweep and cleanse their houses, squares, and the whole town, of their filth, which with all the remaining grain and other old provisions

they cast together into one common heap,
and consume it with fire. After having
taken medicine, and fasted for three days,
all the fire in the town is extinguished.
During this fast they abstain from the grat-
ification of every appetite and passion whatever. A general amnesty is proclaimed ; all
malefactors may return to their town."

" On the fourth morning, the high priest,
by rubbing dry wood together, produces new
fire in the public square, from whence every
habitation in the town is supplied with the
new and pure flame."

They then feast on the new corn and
fruits, and dance and sing for three days,
" and the four following days they receive
visits and rejoice with their friends from
neighboring towns who have in like manner
purified and prepared themselves."

The Mexicans also practised a similar
purification at the end of every fifty-two
years, in the belief that it was time for the
world to come to an end.

I have scarcely heard of a truer sacra-
ment, that is, as the dictionary defines it,
" outward and visible sign of an inward
and spiritual grace," than this, and I have
no doubt that they were originally inspired

directly from Heaven to do thus, though
they have no biblical record of the revelation.

For more than five years I maintained
myself thus solely by the labor of my hands,
and I found, that by working about six
weeks in a year, I could meet all the expenses of living. The whole of my winters,
as well as most of my summers, I had free
and clear for study. I have thoroughly tried
school-keeping, and found that my expenses
were in proportion, or rather out of proportion, to my income, for I was obliged to dress
and train, not to say think and believe, accordingly, and I lost my time into the bargain. As I did not teach for the good of
my fellow-men, but simply for a livelihood,
this was a failure. I have tried trade ; but
I found that it would take ten years to get
under way in that, and that then I should
probably be on my way to the devil. I was
actually afraid that I might by that time be
doing what is called a good business. When
formerly I was looking about to see what I
could do for a living, some sad experience
in conforming to the wishes of friends being fresh in my mind to tax my ingenuity,

I thought often and seriously of picking huckleberries; that surely I could do, and its small profits might suffice, — for my greatest skill has been to want but little, — so little capital it required, so little distraction from my wonted moods, I foolishly thought. While my acquaintances went unhesitatingly into trade or the professions, I contemplated this occupation as most like theirs; ranging the hills all summer to pick the berries which came in my way, and thereafter carelessly dispose of them; so, to keep the flocks of Admetus. I also dreamed that I might gather the wild herbs, or carry evergreens to such villagers as loved to be reminded of the woods, even to the city, by hay-cart loads. But I have since learned that trade curses everything it handles; and though you trade in messages from heaven, the whole curse of trade attaches to the business.

As I preferred some things to others, and especially valued my freedom, as I could fare hard and yet succeed well, I did not wish to spend my time in earning rich carpets or other fine furniture, or delicate cookery, or a house in the Grecian or the Gothic style just yet. If there are any to whom it

is no interruption to acquire these things,
and who know how to use them when acquired, I relinquish to them the pursuit.
Some are " industrious," and appear to love
labor for its own sake, or perhaps because it
keeps them out of worse mischief ; to such I
have at present nothing to say.   Those who
would not know what to do with more leisure than they now enjoy, I might advise to
work twice as hard as they do, — work till
they pay for themselves, and get their free
papers.   For myself I found that the occupation of a day-laborer was the most independent of any, especially as it required only
thirty or forty days in a year to support one.
The laborer's day ends with the going down
of the sun, and he is then free to devote
himself to his chosen pursuit, independent of
his labor ; but his employer, who speculates
from month to month, has no respite from
one end of the year to the other.

In short, I am convinced, both by faith
and experience, that to maintain one's self
on this earth is not a hardship but a pastime, if we will live simply and wisely ; as
the pursuits of the simpler nations are still
the sports of the more artificial.   It is not
necessary that a man should earn his living

by the sweat of his brow, unless he sweats easier than I do.

One young man of my acquaintance, who has inherited some acres, told me that he thought he should live as I did, *if he had the means.* I would not have any one adopt *my* mode of living on any account; for, beside that before he has fairly learned it I may have found out another for myself, I desire that there may be as many different persons in the world as possible; but I would have each one be very careful to find out and pursue *his own* way, and not his father's or his mother's or his neighbor's instead. The youth may build or plant or sail, only let him not be hindered from doing that which he tells me he would like to do. It is by a mathematical point only that we are wise, as the sailor or the fugitive slave keeps the polestar in his eye; but that is sufficient guidance for all our life. We may not arrive at our port within a calculable period, but we would preserve the true course.

Undoubtedly, in this case, what is true for one is truer still for a thousand, as a large house is not proportionally more expensive than a small one, since one roof may

cover, one cellar underlie, and one wall separate several apartments.   But for my part,
I preferred the solitary dwelling.   Moreover, it will commonly be cheaper to build
the whole yourself than to convince another
of the advantage of the common wall ; and
when you have done this, the common parti-
tion, to be much cheaper, must be a thin one,
and that other may prove a bad neighbor,
and also not keep his side in repair.   The
only coöperation which is commonly possible
is exceedingly partial and superficial ; and
what little true coöperation there is, is as if
it were not, being a harmony inaudible to
men.   If a man has faith, he will coöperate
with equal faith everywhere ; if he has not
faith, he will continue to live like the rest of
the world, whatever company he is joined to.
To coöperate in the highest as well as the
lowest sense, means *to get our living together.*
I heard it proposed lately that two young
men should travel together over the world,
the one without money, earning his means as
he went, before the mast and behind the
plough, the other carrying a bill of exchange
in his pocket.   It was easy to see that they
could not long be companions or coöperate,
since one would not *operate* at all.   They

would part at the first interesting crisis in their adventures. Above all, as I have implied, the man who goes alone can start to-day ; but he who travels with another must wait till that other is ready, and it may be a long time before they get off.

But all this is very selfish, I have heard some of my townsmen say. I confess that I have hitherto indulged very little in philanthropic enterprises. I have made some sacrifices to a sense of duty, and among others have sacrificed this pleasure also. There are those who have used all their arts to persuade me to undertake the support of some poor family in the town ; and if I had nothing to do — for the devil finds employment for the idle — I might try my hand at some such pastime as that. However, when I have thought to indulge myself in this respect, and lay their Heaven under an obligation by maintaining certain poor persons in all respects as comfortably as I maintain myself, and have even ventured so far as to make them the offer, they have one and all unhesitatingly preferred to remain poor. While my townsmen and women are devoted in so many ways to the good of their fellows,

I trust that one at least may be spared to other and less humane pursuits. You must have a genius for charity as well as for anything else. As for Doing-good, that is one of the professions which are full. Moreover, I have tried it fairly, and, strange as it may seem, am satisfied that it does not agree with my constitution. Probably I should not consciously and deliberately forsake my particular calling to do the good which society demands of me, to save the universe from annihilation; and I believe that a like but infinitely greater steadfastness elsewhere is all that now preserves it. But I would not stand between any man and his genius; and to him who does this work, which I decline, with his whole heart and soul and life, I would say, Persevere, even if the world call it doing evil, as it is most likely they will.

I am far from supposing that my case is a peculiar one; no doubt many of my readers would make a similar defence. At doing something, — I will not engage that my neighbors shall pronounce it good, — I do not hesitate to say that I should be a capital fellow to hire; but what that is, it is for my employer to find out. What *good* I do, in the common sense of that word, must be aside from my main path, and for the most part wholly unintended. Men say, practically, Begin where you are and such as you are, without aiming mainly to become of more worth, and with kindness aforethought go about doing good. If I were to preach at all in this strain, I should say rather, Set about being good. As if the sun should stop when he had kindled his fires up to the splendor of a moon or a star of the sixth magnitude, and go about like a Robin Good-fellow, peeping in at every cottage window, inspiring lunatics, and tainting meats, and making darkness visible, instead of steadily increasing his genial heat and beneficence till he is of such brightness that no mortal can look him in the face, and then, and in the mean while too, going about the world in his own orbit, doing it good, or rather, as a truer philosophy has discovered, the world going about him getting good. When Phaeton, wishing to prove his heavenly birth by his beneficence, had the sun's chariot but one day, and drove out of the beaten track, he burned several blocks of houses in the lower streets of heaven, and scorched the surface of the earth, and dried up every spring, and made the great desert of Sahara, till at length Jupiter hurled him headlong to the earth with a thunderbolt, and the sun, through grief at his death, did not shine for a year.

There is no odor so bad as that which arises from goodness tainted. It is human, it is divine, carrion. If I knew for a certainty that a man was coming to my house with the conscious design of doing me good, I should run for my life, as from that dry and parching wind of the African deserts called the simoom, which fills the mouth and nose and ears and eyes with dust till you are suffocated, for fear that I should get some of his good done to me, — some of its virus mingled with my blood. No, — in this case I would rather suffer evil the natural way. A man is not a good *man* to me because he will feed me if I should be starving, or warm me if I should be freezing, or pull me out of a ditch if I should ever fall into one. I can find you a Newfoundland dog that will do as much. Philanthropy is not love for one's fellow-man in the broadest sense. Howard was no doubt an exceedingly kind and worthy man in his way, and has his reward; but, comparatively speaking, what are a hundred Howards to *us*, if their philanthropy do not help *us* in our best estate, when we are most worthy to be helped? I never heard of a philanthropic meeting in which it was sincerely proposed to do any good to me, or the like of me.

The Jesuits were quite balked by those Indians who, being burned at the stake, suggested new modes of torture to their tormentors. Being superior to physical suffering, it sometimes chanced that they were superior to any consolation which the missionaries could offer ; and the law to do as you would be done by fell with less persuasiveness on the ears of those who, for their part, did not care how they were done by, who loved their enemies after a new fashion, and came very near freely forgiving them all they did.

Be sure that you give the poor the aid they most need, though it be your example which leaves them far behind. If you give money, spend yourself with it, and do not merely abandon it to them. We make curious mistakes sometimes. Often the poor man is not so cold and hungry as he is dirty and ragged and gross. It is partly his taste, and not merely his misfortune. If you give him money, he will perhaps buy more rags with it. I was wont to pity the clumsy Irish laborers who cut ice on the pond, in such mean and ragged clothes, while I shivered in my more tidy and somewhat more fashionable garments, till, one bitter cold day, one who had slipped into the water came to my house to warm him, and I saw him strip off three pairs of pants and two pairs of stockings ere he got down to the skin, though they were dirty and ragged enough, it is true, and that he could afford to refuse the *extra* garments which I offered him, he had so many *intra* ones. This ducking was the very thing he needed. Then I began to pity myself, and I saw that it would be a greater charity to bestow on me a flannel shirt than a whole slop-shop on him. There are a thousand hacking at the branches of evil to one who is striking at the root, and it may be that he who bestows the largest amount of time and money on the needy is doing the most by his mode of life to produce that misery which he strives in vain to relieve. It is the pious slave-breeder devoting the proceeds of every tenth slave to buy a Sunday's liberty for the rest. Some show their kindness to the poor by employing them in their kitchens. Would they not be kinder if they

employed themselves there? You boast of
spending a tenth part of your income in
charity; may be you should spend the nine
tenths so, and done with it. Society recov-
ers only a tenth part of the property then.
Is this owing to the generosity of him in
whose possession it is found, or to the remiss-
ness of the officers of justice?

Philanthropy is almost the only virtue
which is sufficiently appreciated by mankind.
Nay, it is greatly overrated; and it is our
selfishness which overrates it. A robust
poor man, one sunny day here in Concord,
praised a fellow-townsman to me, because, as
he said, he was kind to the poor; meaning
himself. The kind uncles and aunts of the
race are more esteemed than its true spiritual fathers and mothers. I once heard a rev-
erend lecturer on England, a man of learning and intelligence, after enumerating her
scientific, literary, and political worthies,
Shakespeare, Bacon, Cromwell, Milton, New-
ton, and others, speak next of her Christian
heroes, whom, as if his profession required it
of him, he elevated to a place far above all
the rest, as the greatest of the great. They
were Penn, Howard, and Mrs. Fry. Every
one must feel the falsehood and cant of this.

The last were not England's best men and women ; only, perhaps, her best philanthropists.

I would not subtract anything from the praise that is due to philanthropy, but merely demand justice for all who by their lives and works are a blessing to mankind. I do not value chiefly a man's uprightness and benevolence, which are, as it were, his stem and leaves. Those plants of whose greenness withered we make herb tea for the sick serve but a humble use, and are most employed by quacks. I want the flower and fruit of a man ; that some fragrance be wafted over from him to me, and some ripeness flavor our intercourse. His goodness must not be a partial and transitory act, but a constant superfluity, which costs him nothing and of which he is unconscious. This is a charity that hides a multitude of sins. The philanthropist too often surrounds mankind with the remembrance of his own cast-off griefs as an atmosphere, and calls it sympathy. We should impart our courage, and not our despair, our health and ease, and not our disease, and take care that this does not spread by contagion. From what southern plains comes up

the voice of wailing? Under what latitudes
reside the heathen to whom we would send
light? Who is that intemperate and brutal
man whom we would redeem? If anything
ail a man, so that he does not perform his
functions, if he have a pain in his bowels
even, — for that is the seat of sympathy, —
he forthwith sets about reforming — the
world. Being a microcosm himself, he discovers — and it is a true discovery, and he
is the man to make it — that the world has
been eating green apples; to his eyes, in fact,
the globe itself is a great green apple, which
there is danger awful to think of that the
children of men will nibble before it is
ripe; and straightway his drastic philanthropy seeks out the Esquimaux and the
Patagonian, and embraces the populous Indian and Chinese villages; and thus, by a
few years of philanthropic activity, the powers in the mean while using him for their
own ends, no doubt, he cures himself of his
dyspepsia, the globe acquires a faint blush
on one or both of its cheeks, as if it were
beginning to be ripe, and life loses its cru-
dity and is once more sweet and wholesome to live. I never dreamed of any enor-
mity greater than I have committed. I

never knew, and never shall know, a worse
man than myself.

I believe that what so saddens the reformer is not his sympathy with his fellows
in distress, but, though he be the holiest son
of God, is his private ail. Let this be
righted, let the spring come to him, the
morning rise over his couch, and he will forsake his generous companions without apol-
ogy. My excuse for not lecturing against
the use of tobacco is, that I never chewed it,
that is a penalty which reformed tobacco-
chewers have to pay; though there are
things enough I have chewed which I could
lecture against. If you should ever be betrayed into any of these philanthropies, do
not let your left hand know what your right
hand does, for it is not worth knowing.
Rescue the drowning and tie your shoestrings. Take your time, and set about
some free labor.

Our manners have been corrupted by
communication with the saints. Our hymn-
books resound with a melodious cursing of
God and enduring him forever. One would
say that even the prophets and redeemers
had rather consoled the fears than confirmed
the hopes of man. There is nowhere re-

corded a simple and irrepressible satisfaction with the gift of life, any memorable praise of God. All health and success does me good, however far off and withdrawn it may appear; all disease and failure helps to make me sad and does me evil, however much sympathy it may have with me or I with it. If, then, we would indeed restore mankind by truly Indian, botanic, magnetic, or natural means, let us first be as simple and well as Nature ourselves, dispel the clouds which hang over our own brows, and take up a little life into our pores. Do not stay to be an overseer of the poor, but endeavor to become one of the worthies of the world.

I read in the Gulistan, or Flower Garden, of Sheik Sadi of Shiraz, that " They asked a wise man, saying : Of the many celebrated trees which the Most High God has created lofty and umbrageous, they call none azad, or free, excepting the cypress, which bears no fruit; what mystery is there in this? He replied: Each has its appropriate produce, and appointed season, during the continuance of which it is fresh and blooming, and during their absence dry and withered ; to neither of which states is the cypress exposed, being always flourishing; and of this nature are the azads, or religious independents. — Fix not thy heart on that which is transitory; for the Dijlah, or Tigris, will continue to flow through Bagdad after the race of caliphs is extinct: if thy hand has plenty, be liberal as the date tree; but if it affords nothing to give away, be an azad, or free man, like the cypress."

COMPLEMENTAL VERSES.

THE PRETENSIONS OF POVERTY.

Thou dost presume too much, poor needy wretch,
To claim a station in the firmament
Because thy humble cottage, or thy tub,
Nurses some lazy or pedantic virtue
In the cheap sunshine or by shady springs,
With roots and pot-herbs ; where thy right hand,
Tearing those humane passions from the mind,
Upon whose stocks fair blooming virtues flourish,
Degradeth nature, and benumbeth sense,
And, Gorgon-like, turns active men to stone.
We not require the dull society
Of your necessitated temperance,
Or that unnatural stupidity
That knows nor joy nor sorrow; nor your forc'd
Falsely exalted passive fortitude
Above the active.   This low abject brood,
That fix their seats in mediocrity,
Become your servile minds ; but we advance
Such virtues only as admit excess,
Brave, bounteous acts, regal magnificence,
All-seeing prudence, magnanimity
That knows no bound, and that heroic virtue
For which antiquity hath left no name,
But patterns only, such as Hercules,
Achilles, Theseus.   Back to thy loath'd cell ;
And when thou seest the new enlightened sphere,
Study to know but what those worthies were."

T. CAREW.

II

WHERE I LIVED, AND WHAT I LIVED FOR.

AT a certain season of our life we are accustomed to consider every spot as the possible site of a house. I have thus surveyed the country on every side within a dozen miles of where I live. In imagination I have bought all the farms in succession, for all were to be bought, and I knew their price. I walked over each farmer's premises, tasted his wild apples, discoursed on husbandry with him, took his farm at his price, at any price, mortgaging it to him in my mind ; even put a higher price on it, — took everything but a deed of it, — took his word for his deed, for I dearly love to talk, — cultivated it, and him too to some extent, I trust, and withdrew when I had enjoyed it long enough, leaving him to carry it on. This experience entitled me to be regarded as a sort of real-estate broker by my friends. Wherever I sat, there I might live, and the landscape radiated from me accordingly.

What is a house but a *sedes*, a seat ?—
better if a country seat. I discovered many
a site for a house not likely to be soon improved, which some might have thought too
far from the village, but to my eyes the village was too far from it. Well, there I
might live, I said ; and there I did live, for
an hour, a summer and a winter life ; saw
how I could let the years run off, buffet the
winter through, and see the spring come in.
The future inhabitants of this region, wherever they may place their houses, may be
sure that they have been anticipated. An
afternoon sufficed to lay out the land into
orchard, woodlot, and pasture, and to decide
what fine oaks or pines should be left to
stand before the door, and whence each
blasted tree could be seen to the best advantage ; and then I let it lie, fallow perchance,
for a man is rich in proportion to the number of things which he can afford to let
alone.

My imagination carried me so far that
I even had the refusal of several farms, —
the refusal was all I wanted, — but I never
got my fingers burned by actual possession.
The nearest that I came to actual possession
was when I bought the Hollowell place, and

had begun to sort my seeds, and collected
materials with which to make a wheelbarrow
to carry it on or off with; but before the
owner gave me a deed of it, his wife —
every man has such a wife — changed her
mind and wished to keep it, and he offered
me ten dollars to release him. Now, to
speak the truth, I had but ten cents in the
world, and it surpassed my arithmetic to tell,
if I was that man who had ten cents, or who
had a farm, or ten dollars, or all together.
However, I let him keep the ten dollars and
the farm too, for I had carried it far enough;
or rather, to be generous, I sold him the
farm for just what I gave for it, and, as he
was not a rich man, made him a present of
ten dollars, and still had my ten cents, and
seeds, and materials for a wheelbarrow left.
I found thus that I had been a rich man
without any damage to my poverty. But
I retained the landscape, and I have since
annually carried off what it yielded without a wheelbarrow. With respect to landscapes, —

> " I am monarch of all I *survey*,
> My right there is none to dispute."

I have frequently seen a poet withdraw,
having enjoyed the most valuable part of a

farm, while the crusty farmer supposed that he had got a few wild apples only. Why, the owner does not know it for many years when a poet has put his farm in rhyme, the most admirable kind of invisible fence, has fairly impounded it, milked it, skimmed it, and got all the cream, and left the farmer only the skimmed milk.

The real attractions of the Hollowell farm, to me, were : its complete retirement, being about two miles from the village, half a mile from the nearest neighbor, and sep- arated from the highway by a broad field ; its bounding on the river, which the owner said protected it by its fogs from frosts in the spring, though that was nothing to me ; the gray color and ruinous state of the house and barn, and the dilapidated fences, which put such an interval between me and the last occupant ; the hollow and lichen - covered apple trees, gnawed by rabbits, showing what kind of neighbors I should have ; but above all, the recollection I had of it from my earliest voyages up the river, when the house was concealed behind a dense grove of red maples, through which I heard the house- dog bark. I was in haste to buy it, before the proprietor finished getting out some rocks, cutting down the hollow apple trees, and grubbing up some young birches which had sprung up in the pasture, or, in short, had made any more of his improvements. To enjoy these advantages I was ready to carry it on ; like Atlas, to take the world on my shoulders, — I never heard what compensation he received for that, — and do all those things which had no other motive or excuse but that I might pay for it and be unmolested in my possession of it ; for I knew all the while that it would yield the most abundant crop of the kind I wanted if I could only afford to let it alone. But it turned out as I have said.

All that I could say, then, with respect to farming on a large scale, (I have always cultivated a garden,) was, that I had had my seeds ready. Many think that seeds improve with age. I have no doubt that time discriminates between the good and the bad ; and when at last I shall plant, I shall be less likely to be disappointed. But I would say to my fellows, once for all, As long as possible live free and uncommitted. It makes but little difference whether you are committed to a farm or the county jail.

Old Cato, whose " De Re Rusticâ " is my

" Cultivator," says, and the only translation I have seen makes sheer nonsense of the passage, " When you think of getting a farm turn it thus in your mind, not to buy greedily ; nor spare your pains to look at it, and do not think it enough to go round it once. The oftener you go there the more it will please you, if it is good." I think I shall not buy greedily, but go round and round it as long as I live, and be buried in it first, that it may please me the more at last.

The present was my next experiment of this kind, which I purpose to describe more at length, for convenience, putting the experience of two years into one. As I have said, I do not propose to write an ode to dejection, but to brag as lustily as chanticleer in the morning, standing on his roost, if only to wake my neighbors up. When first I took up my abode in the woods, that is, began to spend my nights as well as days there, which, by accident, was on Independence day, or the fourth of July, 1845, my house was not finished for winter, but was merely a defence against the rain, without plastering or chimney, the walls being of rough weather-stained boards, with wide chinks, which made it cool at night. The upright white hewn studs and freshly planed door and window casings gave it a clean and airy look, especially in the morning, when its timbers were saturated with dew, so that I fancied that by noon some sweet gum would exude from them. To my imagination it retained throughout the day more or less of this auroral character, reminding me of a certain house on a mountain which I had visited a year before. This was an airy and unplastered cabin, fit to entertain a travelling god, and where a goddess might trail her garments. The winds which passed over my dwelling were such as sweep over the ridges of mountains, bearing the broken strains, or celestial parts only, of terrestrial music. The morning wind forever blows, the poem of creation is uninterrupted ; but few are the ears that hear it. Olympus is but the outside of the earth everywhere.

The only house I had been the owner of before, if I except a boat, was a tent, which I used occasionally when making excursions in the summer, and this is still rolled up in my garret ; but the boat, after passing from hand to hand, has gone down the stream of

time. With this more substantial shelter
about me, I had made some progress toward settling in the world. This frame, so
slightly clad, was a sort of crystallization
around me, and reacted on the builder. It
was suggestive somewhat as a picture in
outlines. I did not need to go out doors to
take the air, for the atmosphere within had
lost none of its freshness. It was not so
much within doors as behind a door where I
sat, even in the rainest weather. The Hari-
vansa says, " An abode without birds is like
a meat without seasoning." Such was not
my abode, for I found myself suddenly
neighbor to the birds ; not by having imprisoned one, but having caged myself near
them. I was not only nearer to some of
those which commonly frequent the garden
and the orchard, but to those wilder and
more thrilling songsters of the forest which
never, or rarely, serenade a villager, — the
wood-thrush, the veery, the scarlet tanager,
the field - sparrow, the whippoorwill, and
many others.

I was seated by the shore of a small
pond, about a mile and a half south of the
village of Concord and somewhat higher
than it, in the midst of an extensive wood

between that town and Lincoln, and about two miles south of that our only field known to fame, Concord Battle Ground : but I was so low in the woods that the opposite shore, half a mile off, like the rest, covered with wood, was my most distant horizon.   For the first week, whenever I looked out on the pond it impressed me like a tarn high up on the side of a mountain, its bottom far above the surface of other lakes, and, as the sun arose, I saw it throwing off its nightly clothing of mist, and here and there, by degrees, its soft ripples or its smooth reflecting surface was revealed, while the mists, like ghosts, were stealthily withdrawing in every direction into the woods, as at the breaking up of some nocturnal conventicle.   The very dew seemed to hang upon the trees later into the day than usual, as on the sides of mountains.

This small lake was of most value as a neighbor in the intervals of a gentle rain storm in August, when, both air and water being perfectly still, but the sky overcast, mid-afternoon had all the serenity of evening, and the wood-thrush sang around, and was heard from shore to shore.   A lake like this is never smoother than at such a time ;

and the clear portion of the air above it
being shallow and darkened by clouds, the
water, full of light and reflections, becomes
a lower heaven itself so much the more important. From a hill top near by, where
the wood had been recently cut off, there
was a pleasing vista southward across the
pond, through a wide indentation in the hills
which form the shore there, where their
opposite sides sloping toward each other
suggested a stream flowing out in that direction through a wooded valley, but stream
there was none. That way I looked between and over the near green hills to
some distant and higher ones in the horizon, tinged with blue. Indeed, by standing
on tiptoe I could catch a glimpse of some of
the peaks of the still bluer and more distant
mountain ranges in the north-west, those
true-blue coins from heaven's own mint, and
also of some portion of the village. But in
other directions, even from this point, I
could not see over or beyond the woods
which surrounded me. It is well to have
some water in your neighborhood, to give
buoyancy to and float the earth. One value
even of the smallest well is, that when you
look into it you see that earth is not conti-

nent but insular. This is as important as
that it keeps butter cool. When I looked
across the pond from this peak toward the
Sudbury meadows, which in time of flood I
distinguished elevated perhaps by a mirage
in their seething valley, like a coin in a
basin, all the earth beyond the pond appeared like a thin crust insulated and
floated even by this small sheet of intervening water, and I was reminded that this on
which I dwelt was but *dry land.*

Though the view from my door was still
more contracted, I did not feel crowded or
confined in the least. There was pasture
enough for my imagination. The low shrub-
oak plateau to which the opposite shore
arose, stretched away toward the prairies of
the West and the steppes of Tartary, afford-
ing ample room for all the roving families of
men. "There are none happy in the world
but beings who enjoy freely a vast horizon,"
— said Damodara, when his herds required
new and larger pastures.

Both place and time were changed, and I
dwelt nearer to those parts of the universe
and to those eras in history which had most
attracted me. Where I lived was as far off
as many a region viewed nightly by astron-

omers. We are wont to imagine rare and
delectable places in some remote and more
celestial corner of the system, behind the
constellation of Cassiopeia's Chair, far from
noise and disturbance. I discovered that
my house actually had its site in such a
withdrawn, but forever new and unprofaned,
part of the universe. If it were worth the
while to settle in those parts near to the
Pleiades or the Hyades, to Aldebaran or
Altair, then I was really there, or at an
equal remoteness from the life which I had
left behind, dwindled and twinkling with as
fine a ray to my nearest neighbor, and to be
seen only in moonless nights by him. Such
was that part of creation where I had
squatted ; —

> " There was a shepherd that did live,
>   And held his thoughts as high
>   As were the mounts whereon his flocks
>   Did hourly feed him by."

What should we think of the shepherd's life
if his flocks always wandered to higher pastures than his thoughts ?

Every morning was a cheerful invitation
to make my life of equal simplicity, and I
may say innocence, with Nature herself. I
have been as sincere a worshipper of Aurora

as the Greeks. I got up early and bathed in the pond; that was a religious exercise, and one of the best things which I did. They say that characters were engraven on the bathing tub of king Tching-thang to this effect: " Renew thyself completely each day; do it again, and again, and forever again." I can understand that. Morning brings back the heroic ages. I was as much affected by the faint hum of a mosquito making its invisible and unimaginable tour through my apartment at earliest dawn, when I was sitting with door and windows open, as I could be by any trumpet that ever sang of fame. It was Homer's requiem; itself an Iliad and Odyssey in the air, singing its own wrath and wanderings. There was something cosmical about it; a standing advertisement, till forbidden, of the everlasting vigor and fertility of the world. The morning, which is the most memorable season of the day, is the awakening hour. Then there is least somnolence in us; and for an hour, at least, some part of us awakes which slumbers all the rest of the day and night. Little is to be expected of that day, if it can be called a day, to which we are not awakened by our Genius, but by the mechan-

ical nudgings of some servitor, are not awakened by our own newly-acquired force and
aspirations from within, accompanied by the
undulations of celestial music, instead of
factory bells, and a fragrance filling the air
— to a higher life than we fell asleep from ;
and thus the darkness bear its fruit, and
prove itself to be good, no less than the light.
That man who does not believe that each day
contains an earlier, more sacred, and auroral
hour than he has yet profaned, has despaired
of life, and is pursuing a descending and
darkening way. After a partial cessation of
his sensuous life, the soul of man, or its
organs rather, are reinvigorated each day,
and his Genius tries again what noble life it
can make. All memorable events, I should
say, transpire in morning time and in a
morning atmosphere. The Vedas say, " All
intelligences awake with the morning."
Poetry and art, and the fairest and most
memorable of the actions of men, date from
such an hour. All poets and heroes, like
Memnon, are the children of Aurora, and
emit their music at sunrise. To him whose
elastic and vigorous thought keeps pace with
the sun, the day is a perpetual morning. It
matters not what the clocks say or the atti-

tudes and labors of men.   Morning is when
I am awake and there is a dawn in me.
Moral reform is the effort to throw off sleep.
Why is it that men give so poor an account
of their day if they have not been slumbering ?   They are not such poor calculators.
If they had not been overcome with drowsi-
ness they would have performed something.
The millions are awake enough for physical
labor ; but only one in a million is awake
enough for effective intellectual exertion,
only one in a hundred millions to a poetic
or divine life.   To be awake is to be alive.
I have never yet met a man who was quite
awake.   How could I have looked him in
the face ?

We must learn to reawaken and keep
ourselves awake, not by mechanical aids, but
by an infinite expectation of the dawn, which
does not forsake us in our soundest sleep.
I know of no more encouraging fact than the
unquestionable ability of man to elevate his
life by a conscious endeavor.   It is something to be able to paint a particular picture,
or to carve a statue, and so to make a few
objects beautiful ; but it is far more glorious
to carve and paint the very atmosphere and
medium through which we look, which mor-

ally we can do. To affect the quality of the day, that is the highest of arts. Every man is tasked to make his life, even in its details, worthy of the contemplation of his most elevated and critical hour. If we refused, or rather used up, such paltry information as we get, the oracles would distinctly inform us how this might be done.

I went to the woods because I wished to live deliberately, to front only the essential facts of life, and see if I could not learn what it had to teach, and not, when I came to die, discover that I had not lived. I did not wish to live what was not life, living is so dear; nor did I wish to practise resignation, unless it was quite necessary. I wanted to live deep and suck out all the marrow of life, to live so sturdily and Spartan-like as to put to rout all that was not life, to cut a broad swath and shave close, to drive life into a corner, and reduce it to its lowest terms, and, if it proved to be mean, why then to get the whole and genuine meanness of it, and publish its meanness to the world; or if it were sublime, to know it by experience, and be able to give a true account of it in my next excursion. For most men, it appears to me, are in a strange uncertainty about it, whether it is of the devil or of God, and have *somewhat hastily* concluded that it is the chief end of man here to " glorify God and enjoy him forever."

Still we live meanly, like ants; though the fable tells us that we were long ago changed into men ; like pygmies we fight with cranes ; it is error upon error, and clout upon clout, and our best virtue has for its occasion a superfluous and evitable wretchedness. Our life is frittered away by detail. An honest man has hardly need to count more than his ten fingers, or in extreme cases he may add his ten toes, and lump the rest. Simplicity, simplicity, simplicity ! I say, let your affairs be as two or three, and not a hundred or a thousand ; instead of a million count half a dozen, and keep your accounts on your thumb nail. In the midst of this chopping sea of civilized life, such are the clouds and storms and quicksands and thousand-and-one items to be allowed for, that a man has to live, if he would not founder and go to the bottom and not make his port at all, by dead reckoning, and he must be a great calculator indeed who succeeds. Simplify, simplify. Instead of three meals a day, if it be necessary eat

but one; instead of a hundred dishes, five;
and reduce other things in proportion. Our
life is like a German Confederacy, made up
of petty states, with its boundary forever
fluctuating, so that even a German cannot
tell you how it is bounded at any moment.
The nation itself, with all its so-called internal improvements, which, by the way are all
external and superficial, is just such an unwieldy and overgrown establishment, cluttered with furniture and tripped up by its
own traps, ruined by luxury and heedless
expense, by want of calculation and a worthy aim, as the million households in the
land; and the only cure for it as for them
is in a rigid economy, a stern and more than
Spartan simplicity of life and elevation of
purpose. It lives too fast. Men think that
it is essential that the *Nation* have commerce, and export ice, and talk through a
telegraph, and ride thirty miles an hour,
without a doubt, whether *they* do or not;
but whether we should live like baboons or
like men, is a little uncertain. If we do not
get out sleepers, and forge rails, and devote
days and nights to the work, but go to tin-
kering upon our *lives* to improve *them*, who
will build railroads? And if railroads are

not built, how shall we get to heaven in season? But if we stay at home and mind our business, who will want railroads? We do not ride on the railroad; it rides upon us. Did you ever think what those sleepers are that underlie the railroad? Each one is a man, an Irishman, or a Yankee man. The rails are laid on them, and they are covered with sand, and the cars run smoothly over them. They are sound sleepers, I assure you. And every few years a new lot is laid down and run over; so that, if some have the pleasure of riding on a rail, others have the misfortune to be ridden upon. And when they run over a man that is walking in his sleep, a supernumerary sleeper in the wrong position, and wake him up, they suddenly stop the cars, and make a hue and cry about it, as if this were an exception. I am glad to know that it takes a gang of men for every five miles to keep the sleepers down and level in their beds as it is, for this is a sign that they may sometime get up again.

Why should we live with such hurry and waste of life? We are determined to be starved before we are hungry. Men say that a stitch in time saves nine, and so they

take a thousand stitches to-day to save nine
to-morrow. As for *work*, we have n't any of
any consequence. We have the Saint Vitus' dance, and cannot possibly keep our
heads still. If I should only give a few
pulls at the parish bell-rope, as for a fire,
that is, without setting the bell, there is
hardly a man on his farm in the outskirts
of Concord, notwithstanding that press of
engagements which was his excuse so many
times this morning, nor a boy, nor a woman,
I might almost say, but would forsake all
and follow that sound, not mainly to save
property from the flames, but, if we will
confess the truth, much more to see it burn,
since burn it must, and we, be it known, did
not set it on fire, — or to see it put out, and
have a hand in it, if that is done as handsomely ; yes, even if it were the parish
church itself. Hardly a man takes a half
hour's nap after dinner, but when he wakes
he holds up his head and asks, " What 's the
news ? " as if the rest of mankind had stood
his sentinels. Some give directions to be
waked every half hour, doubtless for no
other purpose ; and then, to pay for it, they
tell what they have dreamed. After a
night's sleep the news is as indispensable

as the breakfast. "Pray tell me anything new that has happened to a man anywhere on this globe," — and he reads it over his coffee and rolls, that a man has had his eyes gouged out this morning on the Wachito River; never dreaming the while that he lives in the dark unfathomed mammoth cave of this world, and has but the rudiment of an eye himself.

For my part, I could easily do without the post-office. I think that there are very few important communications made through it. To speak critically, I never received more than one or two letters in my life — I wrote this some years ago — that were worth the postage. The penny-post is, commonly, an institution through which you seriously offer a man that penny for his thoughts which is so often safely offered in jest. And I am sure that I never read any memorable news in a newspaper. If we read of one man robbed, or murdered, or killed by accident, or one house burned, or one vessel wrecked, or one steamboat blown up, or one cow run over on the Western Railroad, or one mad dog killed, or one lot of grasshoppers in the winter, — we never need read of another. One is enough. If you are acquainted with

the principle, what do you care for a myriad
instances and applications? To a philosopher all *news*, as it is called, is gossip, and
they who edit and read it are old women
over their tea. Yet not a few are greedy
after this gossip. There was such a rush, as
I hear, the other day at one of the offices to
learn the foreign news by the last arrival,
that several large squares of plate glass be-
longing to the establishment were broken
by the pressure, — news which I seriously
think a ready wit might write a twelvemonth
or twelve years beforehand with sufficient accuracy. As for Spain, for instance, if you
know how to throw in Don Carlos and the
Infanta, and Don Pedro and Seville and
Granada, from time to time in the right
proportions, — they may have changed the
names a little since I saw the papers, — and
serve up a bull-fight when other entertainments fail, it will be true to the letter, and
give us as good an idea of the exact state or
ruin of things in Spain as the most succinct
and lucid reports under this head in the
newspapers: and as for England, almost the
last significant scrap of news from that quarter was the revolution of 1649; and if you
have learned the history of her crops for an

average year, you never need attend to that
thing again, unless your speculations are of
a merely pecuniary character. If one may
judge who rarely looks into the newspapers,
nothing new does ever happen in foreign
parts, a French revolution not excepted.

What news! how much more important
to know what that is which was never old!
" Kieou-he-yu (great dignitary of the state
of Wei) sent a man to Khoung-tseu to know
his news. Khoung-tseu caused the messenger to be seated near him, and questioned
him in these terms : What is your master
doing? The messenger answered with respect : My master desires to diminish the
number of his faults, but he cannot come
to the end of them. The messenger being
gone, the philosopher remarked : What a
worthy messenger! What a worthy messenger!" The preacher, instead of vexing the
ears of drowsy farmers on their day of rest
at the end of the week, — for Sunday is the
fit conclusion of an ill-spent week, and not
the fresh and brave beginning of a new one,
— with this one other draggle-tail of a ser-
mon, should shout with thundering voice, —
" Pause! Avast! Why so seeming fast, but
deadly slow?"

Shams and delusions are esteemed for soundest truths, while reality is fabulous. If men would steadily observe realities only, and not allow themselves to be deluded, life, to compare it with such things as we know, would be like a fairy tale and the Arabian Nights' Entertainments. If we respected only what is inevitable and has a right to be, music and poetry would resound along the streets. When we are unhurried and wise, we perceive that only great and worthy things have any permanent and absolute existence, — that petty fears and petty pleasures are but the shadow of the reality. This is always exhilarating and sublime. By closing the eyes and slumbering, and consenting to be deceived by shows, men establish and confirm their daily life of routine and habit everywhere, which still is built on purely illusory foundations. Children, who play life, discern its true law and relations more clearly than men, who fail to live it worthily, but who think that they are wiser by experience, that is, by failure. I have read in a Hindoo book, that "there was a king's son, who, being expelled in infancy from his native city, was brought up by a forester, and, growing up to maturity in that state, imagined himself to belong to the barbarous race with which he lived. One of his father's ministers having discovered him, revealed to him what he was, and the misconception of his character was removed, and he knew himself to be a prince. So soul," continues the Hindoo philosopher, "from the circumstances in which it is placed, mistakes its own character, until the truth is revealed to it by some holy teacher, and then it knows itself to be *Brahme.*" I perceive that we inhabitants of New England live this mean life that we do because our vision does not penetrate the surface of things. We think that that *is* which *appears* to be. If a man should walk through this town and see only the reality, where, think you, would the " Mill-dam " go to? If he should give us an account of the realities he beheld there, we should not recognize the place in his description. Look at a meeting-house, or a court-house, or a jail, or a shop, or a dwelling-house, and say what that thing really is before a true gaze, and they would all go to pieces in your account of them. Men esteem truth remote, in the outskirts of the system, behind the farthest star, before Adam and after the last man. In eternity there is indeed something true and sublime. But all these times and places and occasions are now and here. God himself culminates in the present moment, and will never be more divine in the lapse of all the ages. And we are enabled to apprehend at all what is sublime and noble only by the perpetual instilling and drenching of the reality that surrounds us. The universe constantly and obediently answers to our conceptions; whether we travel fast or slow, the track is laid for us. Let us spend our lives in conceiving then. The poet or the artist never yet had so fair and noble a design but some of his posterity at least could accomplish it.

Let us spend one day as deliberately as Nature, and not be thrown off the track by every nutshell and mosquito's wing that falls on the rails. Let us rise early and fast, or break fast, gently and without perturbation; let company come and let company go, let the bells ring and the children cry, — determined to make a day of it. Why should we knock under and go with the stream? Let us not be upset and overwhelmed in that terrible rapid and whirlpool called a dinner, situated in the meridian shallows. Weather this danger and you are safe, for the rest

of the way is down hill. With unrelaxed
nerves, with morning vigor, sail by it, looking another way, tied to the mast like
Ulysses. If the engine whistles, let it
whistle till it is hoarse for its pains. If the
bell rings, why should we run? We will
consider what kind of music they are like.
Let us settle ourselves, and work and wedge
our feet downward through the mud and
slush of opinion, and prejudice, and tradition, and delusion, and appearance, that allu-
vion which covers the globe, through Paris
and London, through New York and Boston and Concord, through church and state,
through poetry and philosophy and religion,
till we come to a hard bottom and rocks
in place, which we can call *reality*, and say,
This is, and no mistake ; and then begin,
having a *point d'appui*, below freshet and
frost and fire, a place where you might found
a wall or a state, or set a lamp-post safely,
or perhaps a gauge, not a Nilometer, but a
Realometer, that future ages might know
how deep a freshet of shams and appearances
had gathered from time to time. If you
stand right fronting and face to face to a
fact, you will see the sun glimmer on both
its surfaces, as if it were a cimeter, and feel

its sweet edge dividing you through the heart and marrow, and so you will happily conclude your mortal career. Be it life or death, we crave only reality. If we are really dying, let us hear the rattle in our throats and feel cold in the extremities; if we are alive, let us go about our business.

Time is but the stream I go a-fishing in. I drink at it; but while I drink I see the sandy bottom and detect how shallow it is. Its thin current slides away, but eternity remains. I would drink deeper; fish in the sky, whose bottom is pebbly with stars. I cannot count one. I know not the first letter of the alphabet. I have always been regretting that I was not as wise as the day I was born. The intellect is a cleaver; it discerns and rifts its way into the secret of things. I do not wish to be any more busy with my hands than is necessary. My head is hands and feet. I feel all my best faculties concentrated in it. My instinct tells me that my head is an organ for burrowing, as some creatures use their snout and fore-paws, and with it I would mine and burrow my way through these hills. I think that the richest vein is somewhere hereabouts; so by the divining rod and thin rising vapors I judge; and here I will begin to mine.

III.

WITH a little more deliberation in the choice of their pursuits, all men would perhaps become essentially students and observers, for certainly their nature and destiny are interesting to all alike. In accumulating property for ourselves or our posterity, in founding a family or a state, or acquiring fame even, we are mortal; but in dealing with truth we are immortal, and need fear no change nor accident. The oldest Egyptian or Hindoo philosopher raised a corner of the veil from the statue of the divinity; and still the trembling robe remains raised, and I gaze upon as fresh a glory as he did, since it was I in him that was then so bold, and it is he in me that now reviews the vision. No dust has settled on that robe; no time has elapsed since that divinity was revealed. That time which we really improve, or which is improvable, is neither past, present, nor future.

My residence was more favorable, not only to thought, but to serious reading, than a university; and though I was beyond the range of the ordinary circulating library, I had more than ever come within the influence of those books which circulate round the world, whose sentences were first written on bark, and are now merely copied from time to time on to linen paper. Says the poet Mîr Camar Uddîn Mast, " Being seated to run through the region of the spiritual world ; I have had this advantage in books. To be intoxicated by a single glass of wine ; I have experienced this pleasure when I have drunk the liquor of the esoteric doctrines." I kept Homer's Iliad on my table through the summer, though I looked at his page only now and then. Incessant labor with my hands, at first, for I had my house to finish and my beans to hoe at the same time, made more study impossible. Yet I sustained myself by the prospect of such reading in future. I read one or two shallow books of travel in the intervals of my work, till that employment made me ashamed of myself, and I asked where it was then that *I* lived.

The student may read Homer or Æschy-

lus in the Greek without danger of dissipation or luxuriousness, for it implies that he
in some measure emulate their heroes, and
consecrate morning hours to their pages.
The heroic books, even if printed in the
character of our mother tongue, will always
be in a language dead to degenerate times;
and we must laboriously seek the meaning
of each word and line, conjecturing a larger
sense than common use permits out of what
wisdom and valor and generosity we have.
The modern cheap and fertile press, with all
its translations, has done little to bring us
nearer to the heroic writers of antiquity.
They seem as solitary, and the letter in
which they are printed as rare and curious,
as ever. It is worth the expense of youthful days and costly hours, if you learn only
some words of an ancient language, which
are raised out of the trivialness of the street,
to be perpetual suggestions and provoca-
tions. It is not in vain that the farmer remembers and repeats the few Latin words
which he has heard. Men sometimes speak
as if the study of the classics would at
length make way for more modern and practical studies; but the adventurous student
will always study classics, in whatever lan-

guage they may be written and however ancient they may be. For what are the classics but the noblest recorded thoughts of man? They are the only oracles which are not decayed, and there are such answers to the most modern inquiry in them as Delphi and Dodona never gave. We might as well omit to study Nature because she is old. To read well, that is, to read true books in a true spirit, is a noble exercise, and one that will task the reader more than any exercise which the customs of the day esteem. It requires a training such as the athletes underwent, the steady intention almost of the whole life to this object. Books must be read as deliberately and reservedly as they were written. It is not enough even to be able to speak the language of that nation by which they are written, for there is a memorable interval between the spoken and the written language, the language heard and the language read. The one is commonly transitory, a sound, a tongue, a dialect merely, almost brutish, and we learn it unconsciously, like the brutes, of our mothers. The other is the maturity and experience of that; if that is our mother tongue, this is our father tongue, a reserved and select expression, too significant to be heard by the ear, which we must be born again in order to speak. The crowds of men who merely *spoke* the Greek and Latin tongues in the middle ages were not entitled by the accident of birth to *read* the works of genius written in those languages; for these were not written in that Greek or Latin which they knew, but in the select language of literature. They had not learned the nobler dialects of Greece and Rome, but the very materials on which they were written were waste paper to them, and they prized instead a cheap contemporary literature. But when the several nations of Europe had acquired distinct though rude written languages of their own, sufficient for the purposes of their rising literatures, then first learning revived, and scholars were enabled to discern from that remoteness the treasures of antiquity. What the Roman and Grecian multitude could not *hear*, after the lapse of ages a few scholars *read*, and a few scholars only are still reading it.

However much we may admire the orator's occasional bursts of eloquence, the noblest written words are commonly as far behind or above the fleeting spoken language as the firmament with its stars is behind the clouds. *There* are the stars, and they who can may read them. The astronomers for-ever comment on and observe them. They are not exhalations like our daily colloquies and vaporous breath. What is called elo-quence in the forum is commonly found to be rhetoric in the study. The orator yields to the inspiration of a transient occasion, and speaks to the mob before him, to those who can *hear* him; but the writer, whose more equable life is his occasion, and who would be distracted by the event and the crowd which inspire the orator, speaks to the intellect and heart of mankind, to all in any age who can *understand* him.

No wonder that Alexander carried the Iliad with him on his expeditions in a pre-cious casket. A written word is the choicest of relics. It is something at once more in-timate with us and more universal than any other work of art. It is the work of art nearest to life itself. It may be translated into every language, and not only be read but actually breathed from all human lips; — not be represented on canvas or in mar-ble only, but be carved out of the breath of life itself. The symbol of an ancient man's thought becomes a modern man's speech. Two thousand summers have imparted to the monuments of Grecian literature, as to her marbles, only a maturer golden and autumnal tint, for they have carried their own serene and celestial atmosphere into all lands to protect them against the corrosion of time. Books are the treasured wealth of the world and the fit inheritance of generations and nations. Books, the oldest and the best, stand naturally and rightfully on the shelves of every cottage. They have no cause of their own to plead, but while they enlighten and sustain the reader his common sense will not refuse them. Their authors are a natural and irresistible aristocracy in every society, and, more than kings or emperors, exert an influence on mankind. When the illiterate and perhaps scornful trader has earned by enterprise and industry his coveted leisure and independence, and is admitted to the circles of wealth and fashion, he turns inevitably at last to those still higher but yet inaccessible circles of intellect and genius, and is sensible only of the imperfection of his culture and the vanity and insufficiency of all his riches, and further proves his good sense by the pains which he

takes to secure for his children that intellectual culture whose want he so keenly feels;
and thus it is that he becomes the founder
of a family.

Those who have not learned to read the
ancient classics in the language in which
they were written must have a very imperfect knowledge of the history of the human
race; for it is remarkable that no transcript
of them has ever been made into any modern tongue, unless our civilization itself may
be regarded as such a transcript. Homer
has never yet been printed in English, nor
Æschylus, nor Virgil even, — works as refined, as solidly done, and as beautiful almost as the morning itself; for later writers,
say what we will of their genius, have rarely,
if ever, equalled the elaborate beauty and
finish and the lifelong and heroic literary
labors of the ancients. They only talk of
forgetting them who never knew them. It
will be soon enough to forget them when we
have the learning and the genius which will
enable us to attend to and appreciate them.
That age will be rich indeed when those relics which we call Classics, and the still older
and more than classic but even less known
Scriptures of the nations, shall have still

further accumulated, when the Vaticans shall be filled with Vedas and Zendavestas and Bibles, with Homers and Dantes and Shakespeares, and all the centuries to come shall have successively deposited their trophies in the forum of the world. By such a pile we may hope to scale heaven at last.

The works of the great poets have never yet been read by mankind, for only great poets can read them. They have only been read as the multitude read the stars, at most astrologically, not astronomically. Most men have learned to read to serve a paltry convenience, as they have learned to cipher in order to keep accounts and not be cheated in trade ; but of reading as a noble intellectual exercise they know little or nothing ; yet this only is reading, in a high sense, not that which lulls us as a luxury and suffers the nobler faculties to sleep the while, but what we have to stand on tip-toe to read and devote our most alert and wakeful hours to.

I think that having learned our letters we should read the best that is in literature, and not be forever repeating our a b abs, and words of one syllable, in the fourth or fifth classes, sitting on the lowest and foremost form all our lives. Most men are sat-

isfied if they read or hear read, and perchance have been convicted by the wisdom
of one good book, the Bible, and for the rest
of their lives vegetate and dissipate their
faculties in what is called easy reading.
There is a work in several volumes in our
Circulating Library entitled Little Reading,
which I thought referred to a town of that
name which I had not been to. There are
those who, like cormorants and ostriches,
can digest all sorts of this, even after the
fullest dinner of meats and vegetables, for
they suffer nothing to be wasted. If others
are the machines to provide this provender,
they are the machines to read it. They read
the nine thousandth tale about Zebulon and
Sephronia, and how they loved as none had
ever loved before, and neither did the course
of their true love run smooth, — at any rate,
how it did run and stumble, and get up
again and go on! how some poor unfortunate got up on to a steeple, who had better
never have gone up as far as the belfry; and
then, having needlessly got him up there,
the happy novelist rings the bell for all the
world to come together and hear, O dear!
how he did get down again! For my part,
I think that they had better metamorphose

all such aspiring heroes of universal novel-
dom into man weather-cocks, as they used to
put heroes among the constellations, and let
them swing round there till they are rusty,
and not come down at all to bother honest
men with their pranks. The next time the
novelist rings the bell I will not stir though
the meeting-house burn down. " The Skip
of the Tip-Toe-Hop, a Romance of the Middle Ages, by the celebrated author of ' Tit-
tle-Tol-Tan,' to appear in monthly parts ; a
great rush ; don't all come together." All
this they read with saucer eyes, and erect
and primitive curiosity, and with unwearied
gizzard, whose corrugations even yet need
no sharpening, just as some little four-year-
old bencher his two-cent gilt-covered edition
of Cinderella, — without any improvement,
that I can see, in the pronunciation, or
accent, or emphasis, or any more skill in ex-
tracting or inserting the moral. The result
is dulness of sight, a stagnation of the vital
circulations, and a general deliquium and
sloughing off of all the intellectual faculties.
This sort of gingerbread is baked daily and
more sedulously than pure wheat or rye-and-
Indian in almost every oven, and finds a
surer market.

The best books are not read even by those who are called good readers. What does our Concord culture amount to? There is in this town, with a very few exceptions, no taste for the best or for very good books even in English literature, whose words all can read and spell. Even the college-bred and so-called liberally educated men here and elsewhere have really little or no acquaintance with the English classics; and as for the recorded wisdom of mankind, the ancient classics and Bibles, which are accessible to all who will know of them, there are the feeblest efforts anywhere made to become acquainted with them. I know a woodchopper, of middle age, who takes a French paper, not for news as he says, for he is above that, but to "keep himself in practice," he being a Canadian by birth; and when I ask him what he considers the best thing he can do in this world, he says, beside this, to keep up and add to his English. This is about as much as the college-bred generally do or aspire to do, and they take an English paper for the purpose. One who has just come from reading perhaps one of the best English books will find how many with whom he can converse about it?

Or suppose he comes from reading a Greek or Latin classic in the original, whose praises are familiar even to the so - called illiterate ; he will find nobody at all to speak to, but must keep silence about it. Indeed, there is hardly the professor in our colleges, who, if he has mastered the difficulties of the language, has proportionally mastered the difficulties of the wit and poetry of a Greek poet, and has any sympathy to impart to the alert and heroic reader ; and as for the sacred Scriptures, or Bibles of mankind, who in this town can tell me even their titles ? Most men do not know that any nation but the Hebrews have had a scripture. A man, any man, will go considerably out of his way to pick up a silver dollar ; but here are golden words, which the wisest men of antiquity have uttered, and whose worth the wise of every succeeding age have assured us of ; — and yet we learn to read only as far as Easy Reading, the primers and class-books, and when we leave school, the " Little Reading," and story books, which are for boys and beginners ; and our reading, our conversation and thinking, are all on a very low level, worthy only of pygmies and manikins.

I aspire to be acquainted with wiser men

than this our Concord soil has produced,
whose names are hardly known here. Or
shall I hear the name of Plato and never
read his book? As if Plato were my townsman and I never saw him, — my next neighbor and I never heard him speak or attended
to the wisdom of his words. But how actually is it? His Dialogues, which contain
what was immortal in him, lie on the next
shelf, and yet I never read them. We are
under-bred and low-lived and illiterate; and
in this respect I confess I do not make any
very broad distinction between the illiterateness of my townsman who cannot read at all
and the illiterateness of him who has learned
to read only what is for children and feeble
intellects. We should be as good as the
worthies of antiquity, but partly by first
knowing how good they were. We are a
race of tit-men, and soar but little higher in
our intellectual flights than the columns of
the daily paper.

It is not all books that are as dull as their
readers. There are probably words addressed to our condition exactly, which, if
we could really hear and understand, would
be more salutary than the morning or the
spring to our lives, and possibly put a new

aspect on the face of things for us. How many a man has dated a new era in his life from the reading of a book. The book exists for us perchance which will explain our miracles and reveal new ones. The at present unutterable things we may find somewhere uttered. These same questions that disturb and puzzle and confound us have in their turn occurred to all the wise men; not one has been omitted; and each has answered them, according to his ability, by his words and his life. Moreover, with wisdom we shall learn liberality. The solitary hired man on a farm in the outskirts of Concord, who has had his second birth and peculiar religious experience, and is driven as he believes into silent gravity and exclusiveness by his faith, may think it is not true; but Zoroaster, thousands of years ago, travelled the same road and had the same experience; but he, being wise, knew it to be universal, and treated his neighbors accordingly, and is even said to have invented and established worship among men. Let him humbly commune with Zoroaster then, and through the liberalizing influence of all the worthies, with Jesus Christ himself, and let " our church " go by the board.

We boast that we belong to the nineteenth
century and are making the most rapid
strides of any nation. But consider how little this village does for its own culture. I do
not wish to flatter my townsmen, nor to be
flattered by them, for that will not advance
either of us. We need to be provoked, —
goaded like oxen, as we are, into a trot. We
have a comparatively decent system of common schools, schools for infants only ; but
excepting the half-starved Lyceum in the
winter, and latterly the puny beginning of a
library suggested by the state, no school for
ourselves. We spend more on almost any
article of bodily aliment or ailment than on
our mental aliment. It is time that we had
uncommon schools, that we did not leave off
our education when we begin to be men and
women. It is time that villages were universities, and their elder inhabitants the fellows of universities, with leisure — if they
are indeed so well off — to pursue liberal
studies the rest of their lives. Shall the
world be confined to one Paris or one Ox-
ford forever ? Cannot students be boarded
here and get a liberal education under the
skies of Concord ? Can we not hire some
Abelard to lecture to us ? Alas ! what with

foddering the cattle and tending the store, we are kept from school too long, and our education is sadly neglected. In this country, the village should in some respects take the place of the nobleman of Europe. It should be the patron of the fine arts. It is rich enough. It wants only the magnanimity and refinement. It can spend money enough on such things as farmers and traders value, but it is thought Utopian to propose spending money for things which more intelligent men know to be of far more worth. This town has spent seventeen thousand dollars on a town-house, thank fortune or politics, but probably it will not spend so much on living wit, the true meat to put into that shell, in a hundred years. The one hundred and twenty-five dollars annually subscribed for a Lyceum in the winter is better spent than any other equal sum raised in the town. If we live in the nineteenth century, why should we not enjoy the advantages which the nineteenth century offers? Why should our life be in any respect provincial? If we will read newspapers, why not skip the gossip of Boston and take the best newspaper in the world at once? — not be sucking the pap of " neutral family " papers, or browsing

" Olive-Branches " here in New England.
Let the reports of all the learned societies
come to us, and we will see if they know anything. Why should we leave it to Harper
& Brothers and Redding & Co. to select our
reading ? As the nobleman of cultivated
taste surrounds himself with whatever con-
duces to his culture, — genius — learning
— wit — books — paintings — statuary —
music — philosophical instruments, and the
like ; so let the village do, — not stop short
at a pedagogue, a parson, a sexton, a parish
library, and three selectmen, because our
pilgrim forefathers got through a cold winter
once on a bleak rock with these. To act
collectively is according to the spirit of our
institutions ; and I am confident that, as our
circumstances are more flourishing, our
means are greater than the nobleman's.
New England can hire all the wise men in
the world to come and teach her, and board
them round the while, and not be provincial
at all. That is the *uncommon* school we
want. Instead of noblemen, let us have
noble villages of men. If it is necessary,
omit one bridge over the river, go round a
little there, and throw one arch at least over
the darker gulf of ignorance which surrounds us.

IV.

SOUNDS.

BUT while we are confined to books, though the most select and classic, and read only particular written languages, which are themselves but dialects and provincial, we are in danger of forgetting the language which all things and events speak without metaphor, which alone is copious and standard. Much is published, but little printed. The rays which stream through the shutter will be no longer remembered when the shutter is wholly removed. No method nor discipline can supersede the necessity of being forever on the alert. What is a course of history or philosophy, or poetry, no matter how well selected, or the best society, or the most admirable routine of life, compared with the discipline of looking always at what is to be seen? Will you be a reader, a student merely, or a seer? Read your fate, see what is before you, and walk on into futurity.

I did not read books the first summer; I hoed beans. Nay, I often did better than this. There were times when I could not afford to sacrifice the bloom of the present moment to any work, whether of the head or hands. I love a broad margin to my life. Sometimes, in a summer morning, having taken my accustomed bath, I sat in my sunny doorway from sunrise till noon, rapt in a revery, amidst the pines and hickories and sumachs, in undisturbed solitude and stillness, while the birds sang around or flitted noiseless through the house, until by the sun falling in at my west window, or the noise of some traveller's wagon on the distant highway, I was reminded of the lapse of time. I grew in those seasons like corn in the night, and they were far better than any work of the hands would have been. They were not time subtracted from my life, but so much over and above my usual allowance. I realized what the Orientals mean by contemplation and the forsaking of works. For the most part, I minded not how the hours went. The day advanced as if to light some work of mine; it was morning, and lo, now it is evening, and nothing memorable is accomplished. Instead of singing like the birds, I silently smiled at my incessant good fortune. As the sparrow had its trill, sitting on the hickory before my door, so had I my chuckle or suppressed warble which he might hear out of my nest. My days were not days of the week, bearing the stamp of any heathen deity, nor were they minced into hours and fretted by the ticking of a clock ; for I lived like the Puri Indians, of whom it is said that " for yesterday, to-day, and to-morrow they have only one word, and they express the variety of meaning by pointing backward for yesterday, forward for to-morrow, and overhead for the passing day." This was sheer idleness to my fellow-townsmen, no doubt; but if the birds and flowers had tried me by their standard, I should not have been found wanting. A man must find his occasions in himself, it is true. The natural day is very calm, and will hardly reprove his indolence.

I had this advantage, at least, in my mode of life, over those who were obliged to look abroad for amusement, to society and the theatre, that my life itself was become my amusement and never ceased to be novel. It was a drama of many scenes and without

an end. If we were always indeed getting
our living, and regulating our lives according to the last and best mode we had
learned, we should never be troubled with
ennui. Follow your genius closely enough,
and it will not fail to show you a fresh prospect every hour. Housework was a pleasant pastime. When my floor was dirty, I
rose early, and, setting all my furniture out
of doors on the grass, bed and bedstead
making but one budget, dashed water on
the floor, and sprinkled white sand from the
pond on it, and then with a broom scrubbed
it clean and white ; and by the time the villagers had broken their fast the morning sun
had dried my house sufficiently to allow me
to move in again, and my meditations were
almost uninterrupted. It was pleasant to
see my whole household effects out on the
grass, making a little pile like a gypsy's
pack, and my three-legged table, from which
I did not remove the books and pen and
ink, standing amid the pines and hickories.
They seemed glad to get out themselves,
and as if unwilling to be brought in. I
was sometimes tempted to stretch an awning
over them and take my seat there. It was
worth the while to see the sun shine on these

things, and hear the free wind blow on them ; so much more interesting most familiar objects look out of doors than in the house. A bird sits on the next bough, life-everlasting grows under the table, and blackberry vines run round its legs ; pine cones, chestnut burs, and strawberry leaves are strewn about. It looked as if this was the way these forms came to be transferred to our furniture, to tables, chairs, and bedsteads, — because they once stood in their midst.

My house was on the side of a hill, immediately on the edge of the larger wood, in the midst of a young forest of pitch pines and hickories, and half a dozen rods from the pond, to which a narrow footpath led down the hill. In my front yard grew the strawberry, blackberry, and life - everlasting, johnswort and golden - rod, shrub - oaks and sand-cherry, blueberry and ground-nut. Near the end of May, the sand-cherry (*cerasus pumila*) adorned the sides of the path with its delicate flowers arranged in umbels cylindrically about its short stems, which last, in the fall, weighed down with good sized and handsome cherries, fell over in wreaths like rays on every side. I tasted

them out of compliment to Nature, though
they were scarcely palatable. The sumach
(*rhus glabra*) grew luxuriantly about the
house, pushing up through the embankment
which I had made, and growing five or six
feet the first season. Its broad pinnate
tropical leaf was pleasant though strange to
look on. The large buds, suddenly pushing
out late in the spring from dry sticks which
had seemed to be dead, developed themselves as by magic into graceful green and
tender boughs, an inch in diameter; and
sometimes, as I sat at my window, so heedlessly did they grow and tax their weak
joints, I heard a fresh and tender bough
suddenly fall like a fan to the ground, when
there was not a breath of air stirring, broken
off by its own weight. In August, the large
masses of berries, which, when in flower,
had attracted many wild bees, gradually
assumed their bright velvety crimson hue,
and by their weight again bent down and
broke the tender limbs.

As I sit at my window this summer afternoon, hawks are circling about my clearing;
the tantivy of wild pigeons, flying by twos
and threes athwart my view, or perching

restless on the white-pine boughs behind my
house, gives a voice to the air; a fishhawk
dimples the glassy surface of the pond and
brings up a fish; a mink steals out of the
marsh before my door and seizes a frog by
the shore; the sedge is bending under the
weight of the reed-birds flitting hither and
thither; and for the last half hour I have
heard the rattle of railroad cars, now dying
away and then reviving like the beat of a
partridge, conveying travellers from Boston
to the country.   For I did not live so out of
the world as that boy, who, as I hear, was
put out to a farmer in the east part of the
town, but ere long ran away and came home
again, quite down at the heel and homesick.
He had never seen such a dull and out-of-
the-way place; the folks were all gone off;
why, you could n't even hear the whistle!
I doubt if there is such a place in Massachusetts now : —

> " In truth, our village has become a butt
> For one of those fleet railroad shafts, and o'er
> Our peaceful plain its soothing sound is — Concord."

The Fitchburg Railroad touches the pond
about a hundred rods south of where I
dwell.   I usually go to the village along its
causeway, and am, as it were, related to so-

ciety by this link. The men on the freight
trains, who go over the whole length of the
road, bow to me as to an old acquaintance,
they pass me so often, and apparently they
take me for an employee; and so I am. I
too would fain be a track-repairer somewhere
in the orbit of the earth.

The whistle of the locomotive penetrates
my woods summer and winter, sounding like
the scream of a hawk sailing over some
farmer's yard, informing me that many restless city merchants are arriving within the
circle of the town, or adventurous country
traders from the other side. As they come
under one horizon, they shout their warning
to get off the track to the other, heard sometimes through the circles of two towns.
Here come your groceries, country; your
rations, countrymen! Nor is there any
man so independent on his farm that he can
say them nay. And here's your pay for
them! screams the countryman's whistle;
timber like long battering rams going
twenty miles an hour against the city's
walls, and chairs enough to seat all the
weary and heavy laden that dwell within
them. With such huge and lumbering
civility the country hands a chair to the

city. All the Indian huckleberry hills are stripped, all the cranberry meadows are raked into the city. Up comes the cotton, down goes the woven cloth; up comes the silk, down goes the woollen; up come the books, but down goes the wit that writes them.

When I meet the engine with its train of cars moving off with planetary motion, — or, rather, like a comet, for the beholder knows not if with that velocity and with that direction it will ever revisit this system, since its orbit does not look like a returning curve, — with its steam cloud like a banner streaming behind in golden and silver wreaths, like many a downy cloud which I have seen, high in the heavens, unfolding its masses to the light, — as if this travelling demigod, this cloud-compeller, would ere long take the sunset sky for the livery of his train; when I hear the iron horse make the hills echo with his snort like thunder, shaking the earth with his feet, and breathing fire and smoke from his nostrils, (what kind of winged horse or fiery dragon they will put into the new Mythology I don't know,) it seems as if the earth had got a race now worthy to inhabit it. If all were as it seems,

and men made the elements their servants
for noble ends! If the cloud that hangs
over the engine were the perspiration of
heroic deeds, or as beneficent as that which
floats over the farmer's fields, then the elements and Nature herself would cheerfully
accompany men on their errands and be
their escort.

I watch the passage of the morning cars
with the same feeling that I do the rising
of the sun, which is hardly more regular.
Their train of clouds stretching far behind
and rising higher and higher, going to
heaven while the cars are going to Boston,
conceals the sun for a minute and casts my
distant field into the shade, a celestial train
beside which the petty train of cars which
hugs the earth is but the barb of the spear.
The stabler of the iron horse was up early
this winter morning by the light of the stars
amid the mountains, to fodder and harness
his steed. Fire, too, was awakened thus early
to put the vital heat in him and get him off.
If the enterprise were as innocent as it is
early! If the snow lies deep, they strap on
his snow-shoes, and with the giant plough
plough a furrow from the mountains to the
seaboard, in which the cars, like a following

drill-barrow, sprinkle all the restless men and floating merchandise in the country for seed. All day the fire-steed flies over the country, stopping only that his master may rest, and I am awakened by his tramp and defiant snort at midnight, when in some remote glen in the woods he fronts the elements incased in ice and snow; and he will reach his stall only with the morning star, to start once more on his travels without rest or slumber. Or perchance, at evening, I hear him in his stable blowing off the superfluous energy of the day, that he may calm his nerves and cool his liver and brain for a few hours of iron slumber. If the enterprise were as heroic and commanding as it is protracted and unwearied!

Far through unfrequented woods on the confines of towns, where once only the hunter penetrated by day, in the darkest night dart these bright saloons without the knowledge of their inhabitants; this moment stopping at some brilliant station-house in town or city, where a social crowd is gathered, the next in the Dismal Swamp, scaring the owl and fox. The startings and arrivals of the cars are now the epochs in the village day. They go and come with such regularity and precision, and their whistle can be heard so far, that the farmers set their clocks by them, and thus one well conducted institution regulates a whole country. Have not men improved somewhat in punctuality since the railroad was invented? Do they not talk and think faster in the depot than they did in the stage - office? There is something electrifying in the atmosphere of the former place. I have been astonished at the miracles it has wrought; that some of my neighbors, who, I should have prophesied, once for all, would never get to Boston by so prompt a conveyance, are on hand when the bell rings. To do things "railroad fashion" is now the by-word; and it is worth the while to be warned so often and so sincerely by any power to get off its track. There is no stopping to read the riot act, no firing over the heads of the mob, in this case. We have constructed a fate, an *Atropos*, that never turns aside. (Let that be the name of your engine.) Men are advertised that at a certain hour and minute these bolts will be shot toward particular points of the compass; yet it interferes with no man's business, and the children go to school on the other track. We live the steadier for it. We are all educated thus to be sons of Tell. The air is full of invisible bolts. Every path but your own is the path of fate. Keep on your own track, then.

What recommends commerce to me is its enterprise and bravery. It does not clasp its hands and pray to Jupiter. I see these men every day go about their business with more or less courage and content, doing more even than they suspect, and perchance better employed than they could have consciously devised. I am less affected by their heroism who stood up for half an hour in the front line at Buena Vista, than by the steady and cheerful valor of the men who inhabit the snow-plough for their winter quarters; who have not merely the three-o'-clock in the morning courage, which Bonaparte thought was the rarest, but whose courage does not go to rest so early, who go to sleep only when the storm sleeps or the sinews of their iron steed are frozen. On this morning of the Great Snow, perchance, which is still raging and chilling men's blood, I hear the muffled tone of their engine bell from out the fog bank of their chilled breath, which announces that the cars *are coming*, without long delay, not-

withstanding the veto of a New England
north-east snow - storm, and I behold the
ploughmen covered with snow and rime,
their heads peering above the mould-board
which is turning down other than daisies and
the nests of field-mice, like bowlders of the
Sierra Nevada, that occupy an outside place
in the universe.

Commerce is unexpectedly confident and
serene, alert, adventurous, and unwearied.
It is very natural in its methods withal, far
more so than many fantastic enterprises and
sentimental experiments, and hence its singular success. I am refreshed and expanded
when the freight train rattles past me, and
I smell the stores which go dispensing their
odors all the way from Long Wharf to Lake
Champlain, reminding me of foreign parts,
of coral reefs, and Indian oceans, and tropical climes, and the extent of the globe. I
feel more like a citizen of the world at the
sight of the palm-leaf which will cover so
many flaxen New England heads the next
summer, the Manilla hemp and cocoa-nut
husks, the old junk, gunny bags, scrap iron,
and rusty nails. This car-load of torn sails
is more legible and interesting now than
if they should be wrought into paper and

printed books. Who can write so graph-
ically the history of the storms they have
weathered as these rents have done ? They
are proof-sheets which need no correction.
Here goes lumber from the Maine woods,
which did not go out to sea in the last
freshet, risen four dollars on the thousand
because of what did go out or was split up ;
pine, spruce, cedar, — first, second, third and
fourth qualities, so lately all of one quality,
to wave over the bear, and moose, and cari-
bou. Next rolls Thomaston lime, a prime
lot, which will get far among the hills before
it gets slacked. These rags in bales, of all
hues and qualities, the lowest condition to
which cotton and linen descend, the final
result of dress, — of patterns which are now
no longer cried up, unless it be in Milwaukee,
as those splendid articles, English, French,
or American prints, ginghams, muslins, etc.,
gathered from all quarters both of fashion
and poverty, going to become paper of one
color or a few shades only, on which forsooth
will be written tales of real life, high and
low, and founded on fact! This closed car
smells of salt fish, the strong New England
and commercial scent, reminding me of the
Grand Banks and the fisheries. Who has

not seen a salt fish, thoroughly cured for
this world, so that nothing can spoil it, and
putting the perseverance of the saints to the
blush? with which you may sweep or pave
the streets, and split your kindlings, and
the teamster shelter himself and his lading
against sun wind and rain behind it, — and
the trader, as a Concord trader once did,
hang it up by his door for a sign when he
commences business, until at last his oldest
customer cannot tell surely whether it be
animal, vegetable, or mineral, and yet it shall
be as pure as a snowflake, and if it be put
into a pot and boiled, will come out an excellent dun fish for a Saturday's dinner.
Next Spanish hides, with the tails still pre-
serving their twist and the angle of elevation
they had when the oxen that wore them were
careering over the pampas of the Spanish
main, — a type of all obstinacy, and evin-
cing how almost hopeless and incurable are
all constitutional vices. I confess, that practically speaking, when I have learned a
man's real disposition, I have no hopes of
changing it for the better or worse in this
state of existence. As the Orientals say,
" A cur's tail may be warmed, and pressed,
and bound round with ligatures, and after a

twelve years' labor bestowed upon it, still it will retain its natural form." The only effectual cure for such inveteracies as these tails exhibit is to make glue of them, which I believe is what is usually done with them, and then they will stay put and stick. Here is a hogshead of molasses or of brandy directed to John Smith, Cuttingsville, Vermont, some trader among the Green Mountains, who imports for the farmers near his clearing, and now perchance stands over his bulk-head and thinks of the last arrivals on the coast, how they may affect the price for him, telling his customers this moment, as he has told them twenty times before this morning, that he expects some by the next train of prime quality. It is advertised in the Cuttingsville Times.

While these things go up other things come down. Warned by the whizzing sound, I look up from my book and see some tall pine, hewn on far northern hills, which has winged its way over the Green Mountains and the Connecticut, shot like an arrow through the township within ten minutes, and scarce another eye beholds it; going

" to be the mast
Of some great ammiral."

And hark! here comes the cattle-train bearing the cattle of a thousand hills, sheepcots, stables, and cow-yards in the air, drovers with their sticks, and shepherd boys in the midst of their flocks, all but the mountain pastures, whirled along like leaves blown from the mountains by the September gales. The air is filled with the bleating of calves and sheep, and the hustling of oxen, as if a pastoral valley were going by. When the old bell-weather at the head rattles his bell, the mountains do indeed skip like rams and the little hills like lambs. A car-load of drovers, too, in the midst, on a level with their droves now, their vocation gone, but still clinging to their useless sticks as their badge of office. But their dogs, where are they? It is a stampede to them; they are quite thrown out; they have lost the scent. Methinks I hear them barking behind the Peterboro' Hills, or panting up the western slope of the Green Mountains. They will not be in at the death. Their vocation, too, is gone. Their fidelity and sagacity are below par now. They will slink back to their kennels in disgrace, or perchance run wild and strike a league with the wolf and the fox. So is your pastoral life whirled

past and away. But the bell rings, and I
must get off the track and let the cars go
by ; —

> What's the railroad to me ?
> I never go to see
> Where it ends.
> It fills a few hollows,
> And makes banks for the swallows,
> It sets the sand a-blowing,
> And the blackberries a-growing,

but I cross it like a cart-path in the woods.
I will not have my eyes put out and my ears
spoiled by its smoke and steam and hissing.

Now that the cars are gone by and all the
restless world with them, and the fishes in
the pond no longer feel their rumbling, I am
more alone than ever. For the rest of the
long afternoon, perhaps, my meditations are
interrupted only by the faint rattle of a carriage or team along the distant highway.

Sometimes, on Sundays, I heard the bells,
the Lincoln, Acton, Bedford, or Concord
bell, when the wind was favorable, a faint,
sweet, and, as it were, natural melody, worth
importing into the wilderness. At a sufficient distance over the woods this sound acquires a certain vibratory hum, as if the
pine needles in the horizon were the strings

of a harp which it swept. All sound heard
at the greatest possible distance produces
one and the same effect, a vibration of the
universal lyre, just as the intervening atmosphere makes a distant ridge of earth interesting to our eyes by the azure tint it imparts
to it. There came to me in this case a melody which the air had strained, and which
had conversed with every leaf and needle of
the wood, that portion of the sound which
the elements had taken up and modulated
and echoed from vale to vale. The echo is,
to some extent, an original sound, and therein is the magic and charm of it. It is not
merely a repetition of what was worth repeating in the bell, but partly the voice of
the wood the same trivial words and notes
sung by a wood-nymph.

At evening, the distant lowing of some
cow in the horizon beyond the woods sounded
sweet and melodious, and at first I would
mistake it for the voices of certain minstrels
by whom I was sometimes serenaded, who
might be straying over hill and dale ; but
soon I was not unpleasantly disappointed
when it was prolonged into the cheap and
natural music of the cow. I do not mean to
be satirical, but to express my appreciation

of those youths' singing, when I state that I
perceived clearly that it was akin to the
music of the cow, and they were at length
one articulation of Nature.

Regularly at half past seven, in one part
of the summer, after the evening train had
gone by, the whippoorwills chanted their
vespers for half an hour, sitting on a stump
by my door, or upon the ridge-pole of the
house. They would begin to sing almost
with as much precision as a clock, within
five minutes of a particular time, referred
to the setting of the sun, every evening. I
had a rare opportunity to become acquainted
with their habits. Sometimes I heard four
or five at once in different parts of the
wood, by accident one a bar behind another,
and so near me that I distinguished not
only the cluck after each note, but often
that singular buzzing sound like a fly in a
spider's web, only proportionally louder.
Sometimes one would circle round and
round me in the woods a few feet distant
as if tethered by a string, when probably I
was near its eggs. They sang at intervals
throughout the night, and were again as
musical as ever just before and about dawn.

When other birds are still the screech

owls take up the strain, like mourning women their ancient u-lu-lu. Their dismal
scream is truly Ben Jonsonian. Wise midnight hags! It is no honest and blunt tu-
whit tu-who of the poets, but, without jesting, a most solemn graveyard ditty, the
mutual consolations of suicide lovers remembering the pangs and the delights of
supernal love in the infernal groves. Yet
I love to hear their wailing, their doleful
responses, trilled along the woodside ; reminding me sometimes of music and singing birds ; as if it were the dark and tear-
ful side of music, the regrets and sighs that
would fain be sung. They are the spirits,
the low spirits and melancholy forebodings,
of fallen souls that once in human shape
night-walked the earth and did the deeds of
darkness, now expiating their sins with their
wailing hymns or threnodies in the scenery
of their transgressions. They give me a
new sense of the variety and capacity of
that nature which is our common dwelling.
Oh-o-o-o-o that I never had been bor-r-r-r-n !
sighs one on this side of the pond, and circles with the restlessness of despair to some
new perch on the gray oaks. Then — *that
I never had been bor-r-r-r-n !* echoes another

on the farther side with tremulous sincerity,
and — *bor-r-r-r-n !* comes faintly from far in
the Lincoln woods.

I was also serenaded by a hooting owl.
Near at hand you could fancy it the most
melancholy sound in Nature, as if she meant
by this to stereotype and make permanent
in her choir the dying moans of a human
being, — some poor weak relic of mortality
who has left hope behind, and howls like an
animal, yet with human sobs, on entering
the dark valley, made more awful by a certain gurgling melodiousness, — I find myself
beginning with the letters gl when I try to
imitate it, — expressive of a mind which has
reached the gelatinous mildewy stage in the
mortification of all healthy and courageous
thought. It reminded me of ghouls and
idiots and insane howlings. But now one
answers from far woods in a strain made
really melodious by distance, — *Hoo hoo
hoo, hoorer hoo ;* and indeed for the most
part it suggested only pleasing associations,
whether heard by day or night, summer or
winter.

I rejoice that there are owls. Let them
do the idiotic and maniacal hooting for men.
It is a sound admirably suited to swamps and

twilight woods which no day illustrates, sug-
gesting a vast and undeveloped nature which
men have not recognized. They represent
the stark twilight and unsatisfied thoughts
which all have. All day the sun has shone
on the surface of some savage swamp, where
the single spruce stands hung with usnea
lichens, and small hawks circulate above,
and the chicadee lisps amid the evergreens,
and the partridge and rabbit skulk beneath; but now a more dismal and fitting
day dawns, and a different race of creatures
awakes to express the meaning of Nature
there.

Late in the evening I heard the distant
rumbling of wagons over bridges, — a sound
heard farther than almost any other at night,
— the baying of dogs, and sometimes again
the lowing of some disconsolate cow in a distant barn-yard. In the mean while all the
shore rang with the trump of bullfrogs, the
sturdy spirits of ancient wine-bibbers and
wassailers, still unrepentant, trying to sing
a catch in their Stygian lake, — if the Walden nymphs will pardon the comparison, for
though there are almost no weeds, there are
frogs there, — who would fain keep up the
hilarious rules of their old festal tables,

though their voices have waxed hoarse and solemnly grave, mocking at mirth, and the wine has lost its flavor, and become only liquor to distend their paunches, and sweet intoxication never comes to drown the memory of the past, but mere saturation and waterloggedness and distention. The most aldermanic, with his chin upon a heart-leaf, which serves for a napkin to his drooling chaps, under this northern shore quaffs a deep draught of the once scorned water, and passes round the cup with the ejaculation *tr-r-r-oonk, tr-r-r-oonk, tr-r-r-oonk!* and straightway comes over the water from some distant cove the same password repeated, where the next in seniority and girth has gulped down to his mark; and when this observance has made the circuit of the shores, then ejaculates the master of ceremonies, with satisfaction, *tr-r-r-oonk!* and each in his turn repeats the same down to the least distended, leakiest, and flabbiest paunched, that there be no mistake; and then the bowl goes round again and again, until the sun disperses the morning mist, and only the patriarch is not under the pond, but vainly bellowing *troonk* from time to time, and pausing for a reply.

I am not sure that I ever heard the sound of cock - crowing from my clearing, and I thought that it might be worth the while to keep a cockerel for his music merely, as a singing bird. The note of this once wild Indian pheasant is certainly the most remarkable of any bird's, and if they could be naturalized without being domesticated, it would soon become the most famous sound in our woods, surpassing the clangor of the goose and the hooting of the owl; and then imagine the cackling of the hens to fill the pauses when their lords' clarions rested ! No wonder that man added this bird to his tame stock, — to say nothing of the eggs and drumsticks. To walk in a winter morning in a wood where these birds abounded, their native woods, and hear the wild cockerels crow on the trees, clear and shrill for miles over the resounding earth, drowning the feebler notes of other birds, — think of it ! It would put nations on the alert. Who would not be early to rise, and rise earlier and earlier every successive day of his life, till he became unspeakably healthy, wealthy, and wise ? This foreign bird's note is celebrated by the poets of all countries along with the notes of their native songsters.

All climates agree with brave Chanticleer. He is more indigenous even than the natives. His health is ever good, his lungs are sound, his spirits never flag. Even the sailor on the Atlantic and Pacific is awakened by his voice; but its shrill sound never roused me from my slumbers. I kept neither dog, cat, cow, pig, nor hens, so that you would have said there was a deficiency of domestic sounds; neither the churn, nor the spinning-wheel, nor even the singing of the kettle, nor the hissing of the urn, nor children crying, to comfort one. An old-fashioned man would have lost his senses or died of ennui before this. Not even rats in the wall, for they were starved out, or rather were never baited in, — only squirrels on the roof and under the floor, a whippoorwill on the ridge-pole, a blue-jay screaming beneath the window, a hare or woodchuck under the house, a screech-owl or a cat-owl behind it, a flock of wild geese or a laughing loon on the pond, and a fox to bark in the night. Not even a lark or an oriole, those mild plantation birds, ever visited my clearing. No cockerels to crow nor hens to cackle in the yard. No yard! but unfenced Nature reaching up to your very sills. A

young forest growing up under your windows, and wild sumachs and blackberry
vines breaking through into your cellar;
sturdy pitch - pines rubbing and creaking
against the shingles for want of room, their
roots reaching quite under the house. Instead of a scuttle or a blind blown off in the
gale, — a pine tree snapped off or torn up
by the roots behind your house for fuel.
Instead of no path to the front-yard gate in
the Great Snow, — no gate — no front-yard,
— and no path to the civilized world.

V.

SOLITUDE.

THIS is a delicious evening, when the whole body is one sense, and imbibes delight through every pore. I go and come with a strange liberty in Nature, a part of herself. As I walk along the stony shore of the pond in my shirt sleeves, though it is cool as well as cloudy and windy, and I see nothing special to attract me, all the elements are unusually congenial to me. The bullfrogs trump to usher in the night, and the note of the whippoorwill is borne on the rippling wind from over the water. Sympathy with the fluttering alder and poplar leaves almost takes away my breath; yet, like the lake, my serenity is rippled but not ruffled. These small waves raised by the evening wind are as remote from storm as the smooth reflecting surface. Though it is now dark, the wind still blows and roars in the wood, the waves still dash, and some creatures lull the rest with their notes. The repose is never

complete. The wildest animals do not repose, but seek their prey now ; the fox, and
skunk, and rabbit, now roam the fields and
woods without fear. They are Nature's
watchmen, — links which connect the days
of animated life.

When I return to my house I find that
visitors have been there and left their cards,
either a bunch of flowers, or a wreath of
evergreen, or a name in pencil on a yellow
walnut leaf or a chip. They who come
rarely to the woods take some little piece of
the forest into their hands to play with by
the way, which they leave, either intention-
ally or accidentally. One has peeled a willow wand, woven it into a ring, and dropped
it on my table. I could always tell if visitors had called in my absence, either by the
bended twigs or grass, or the print of their
shoes, and generally of what sex or age or
quality they were by some slight trace left,
as a flower dropped, or a bunch of grass
plucked and thrown away, even as far off as
the railroad, half a mile distant, or by the
lingering odor of a cigar or pipe. Nay, I
was frequently notified of the passage of a
traveller along the highway sixty rods off by
the scent of his pipe.

There is commonly sufficient space about us. Our horizon is never quite at our elbows. The thick wood is not just at our door, nor the pond, but somewhat is always clearing, familiar and worn by us, appropriated and fenced in some way, and reclaimed from Nature. For what reason have I this vast range and circuit, some square miles of unfrequented forest, for my privacy, abandoned to me by men? My nearest neighbor is a mile distant, and no house is visible from any place but the hill-tops within half a mile of my own. I have my horizon bounded by woods all to myself; a distant view of the railroad where it touches the pond on the one hand, and of the fence which skirts the woodland road on the other. But for the most part it is as solitary where I live as on the prairies. It is as much Asia or Africa as New England. I have, as it were, my own sun and moon and stars, and a little world all to myself. At night there was never a traveller passed my house, or knocked at my door, more than if I were the first or last man; unless it were in the spring, when at long intervals some came from the village to fish for pouts, — they plainly fished much more in the Walden

Pond of their own natures, and baited their hooks with darkness, — but they soon retreated, usually with light baskets, and left " the world to darkness and to me," and the black kernel of the night was never profaned by any human neighborhood. I believe that men are generally still a little afraid of the dark, though the witches are all hung, and Christianity and candles have been introduced.

Yet I experienced sometimes that the most sweet and tender, the most innocent and encouraging society may be found in any natural object, even for the poor misanthrope and most melancholy man. There can be no very black melancholy to him who lives in the midst of Nature and has his senses still. There was never yet such a storm but it was Æolian music to a healthy and innocent ear. Nothing can rightly compel a simple and brave man to a vulgar sadness. While I enjoy the friendship of the seasons I trust that nothing can make life a burden to me. The gentle rain which waters my beans and keeps me in the house to-day is not drear and melancholy, but good for me too. Though it prevents my hoeing them, it is of far more worth than my hoeing. If it should continue so long as to cause the seeds to rot in the ground and destroy the potatoes in the low lands, it would still be good for the grass on the uplands, and, being good for the grass, it would be good for me. Sometimes, when I compare myself with other men, it seems as if I were more favored by the gods than they, beyond any deserts that I am conscious of ; as if I had a warrant and surety at their hands which my fellows have not, and were especially guided and guarded. I do not flatter myself, but if it be possible they flatter me. I have never felt lonesome, or in the least oppressed by a sense of solitude, but once, and that was a few weeks after I came to the woods, when, for an hour, I doubted if the near neighborhood of man was not essential to a serene and healthy life. To be alone was something unpleasant. But I was at the same time conscious of a slight insanity in my mood, and seemed to foresee my recovery. In the midst of a gentle rain while these thoughts prevailed, I was suddenly sensible of such sweet and beneficent society in Nature, in the very pattering of the drops, and in every sound and sight around my house, an infinite and unaccountable friend-

liness all at once like an atmosphere sustaining me, as made the fancied advantages of
human neighborhood insignificant, and I
have never thought of them since. Every
little pine needle expanded and swelled with
sympathy and befriended me. I was so distinctly made aware of the presence of something kindred to me, even in scenes which
we are accustomed to call wild and dreary,
and also that the nearest of blood to me and
humanest was not a person nor a villager,
that I thought no place could ever be strange
to me again. —

"Mourning untimely consumes the sad;
   Few are their days in the land of the living,
   Beautiful daughter of Toscar."

Some of my pleasantest hours were during
the long rain storms in the spring or fall,
which confined me to the house for the afternoon as well as the forenoon, soothed by
their ceaseless roar and pelting; when an
early twilight ushered in a long evening in
which many thoughts had time to take root
and unfold themselves. In those driving
north - east rains which tried the village
houses so, when the maids stood ready with
mop and pail in front entries to keep the
deluge out, I sat behind my door in my lit-

tle house, which was all entry, and thoroughly enjoyed its protection. In one heavy thunder shower the lightning struck a large pitch-pine across the pond, making a very conspicuous and perfectly regular spiral groove from top to bottom, an inch or more deep, and four or five inches wide, as you would groove a walking-stick. I passed it again the other day, and was struck with awe on looking up and beholding that mark, now more distinct than ever, where a terrific and resistless bolt came down out of the harmless sky eight years ago. Men frequently say to me, " I should think you would feel lonesome down there, and want to be nearer to folks, rainy and snowy days and nights especially." I am tempted to reply to such, — This whole earth which we inhabit is but a point in space. How far apart, think you, dwell the two most distant inhabitants of yonder star, the breadth of whose disk cannot be appreciated by our instruments? Why should I feel lonely? is not our planet in the Milky Way? This which you put seems to me not to be the most important question. What sort of space is that which separates a man from his fellows and makes him solitary? I have found that no exertion of the legs can bring two minds much nearer to one another. What do we want most to dwell near to? Not to many men surely, the depot, the post - office, the bar - room, the meeting-house, the school-house, the grocery, Beacon Hill, or the Five Points, where men most congregate, but to the perennial source of our life, whence in all our experience we have found that to issue, as the willow stands near the water and sends out its roots in that direction. This will vary with different natures, but this is the place where a wise man will dig his cellar. . . . I one evening overtook one of my townsmen, who has accumulated what is called " a handsome property," — though I never got a *fair* view of it, — on the Walden road, driving a pair of cattle to market, who inquired of me how I could bring my mind to give up so many of the comforts of life. I answered that I was very sure I liked it passably well; I was not joking. And so I went home to my bed, and left him to pick his way through the darkness and the mud to Brighton, — or Bright-town, — which place he would reach some time in the morning.

Any prospect of awakening or coming to life to a dead man makes indifferent all times and places. The place where that may occur is always the same, and indescribably pleasant to all our senses. For the most part we allow only outlying and transient circumstances to make our occasions. They are, in fact, the cause of our distraction. Nearest to all things is that power which fashions their being. *Next* to us the grandest laws are continually being executed. *Next* to us is not the workman whom we have hired, with whom we love so well to talk, but the workman whose work we are.

" How vast and profound is the influence of the subtile powers of Heaven and of Earth ! "

" We seek to perceive them, and we do not see them ; we seek to hear them, and we do not hear them ; identified with the substance of things, they cannot be separated from them."

" They cause that in all the universe men purify and sanctify their hearts, and clothe themselves in their holiday garments to offer sacrifices and oblations to their ancestors. It is an ocean of subtile intelligences. They are everywhere, above us, on our left, on our right ; they environ us on all sides."

We are the subjects of an experiment which is not a little interesting to me. Can

we not do without the society of our gossips
a little while under these circumstances, —
have our own thoughts to cheer us? Confucius says truly, " Virtue does not remain as
an abandoned orphan; it must of necessity
have neighbors."

With thinking we may be beside ourselves
in a sane sense. By a conscious effort of
the mind we can stand aloof from actions
and their consequences; and all things, good
and bad, go by us like a torrent. We are
not wholly involved in Nature. I may be
either the drift-wood in the stream, or Indra
in the sky looking down on it. I *may* be
affected by a theatrical exhibition; on the
other hand, I *may not* be affected by an actual event which appears to concern me much
more. I only know myself as a human en-
tity; the scene, so to speak, of thoughts and
affections; and am sensible of a certain
doubleness by which I can stand as remote
from myself as from another. However in-
tense my experience, I am conscious of the
presence and criticism of a part of me, which,
as it were, is not a part of me, but spectator,
sharing no experience, but taking note of it;
and that is no more I than it is you. When
the play, it may be the tragedy, of life is

over, the spectator goes his way. It was a kind of fiction, a work of the imagination only, so far as he was concerned. This doubleness may easily make us poor neighbors and friends sometimes.

I find it wholesome to be alone the greater part of the time. To be in company, even with the best, is soon wearisome and dissipating. I love to be alone. I never found the companion that was so companionable as solitude. We are for the most part more lonely when we go abroad among men than when we stay in our chambers. A man thinking or working is always alone, let him be where he will. Solitude is not measured by the miles of space that intervene between a man and his fellows. The really diligent student in one of the crowded hives of Cambridge College is as solitary as a dervis in the desert. The farmer can work alone in the field or the woods all day, hoeing or chopping, and not feel lonesome, because he is employed; but when he comes home at night he cannot sit down in a room alone, at the mercy of his thoughts, but must be where he can " see the folks," and recreate, and as he thinks remunerate, himself for his day's solitude; and hence he wonders how the student can sit alone in the house all night and most of the day without ennui and " the blues ; " but he does not realize that the student, though in the house, is still at work in *his* field, and chopping in *his* woods, as the farmer in his, and in turn seeks the same recreation and society that the latter does, though it may be a more condensed form of it.

Society is commonly too cheap. We meet at very short intervals, not having had time to acquire any new value for each other. We meet at meals three times a day, and give each other a new taste of that old musty cheese that we are. We have had to agree on a certain set of rules, called etiquette and politeness, to make this frequent meeting tolerable and that we need not come to open war. We meet at the post-office, and at the sociable, and about the fireside every night ; we live thick and are in each other's way, and stumble over one another, and I think that we thus lose some respect for one another. Certainly less frequency would suffice for all important and hearty communications. Consider the girls in a factory, — never alone, hardly in their dreams. It would be better if there were but one inhabitant to a square mile, as where I live. The value of a man is not in his skin, that we should touch him.

I have heard of a man lost in the woods and dying of famine and exhaustion at the foot of a tree, whose loneliness was relieved by the grotesque visions with which, owing to bodily weakness, his diseased imagination surrounded him, and which he believed to be real. So also, owing to bodily and mental health and strength, we may be continually cheered by a like but more normal and natural society, and come to know that we are never alone.

I have a great deal of company in my house ; especially in the morning, when nobody calls. Let me suggest a few comparisons, that some one may convey an idea of my situation. I am no more lonely than the loon in the pond that laughs so loud, or than Walden Pond itself. What company has that lonely lake, I pray ? And yet it has not the blue devils, but the blue angels in it, in the azure tint of its waters. The sun is alone, except in thick weather, when there sometimes appear to be two, but one is a mock sun. God is alone, — but the devil, he is far from being alone ; he sees a great

deal of company; he is legion. I am no
more lonely than a single mullein or dande-
lion in a pasture, or a bean leaf, or sorrel,
or a horse-fly, or a humble-bee. I am no
more lonely than the Mill Brook, or a
weathercock, or the north star, or the south
wind, or an April shower, or a January
thaw, or the first spider in a new house.

I have occasional visits in the long winter
evenings, when the snow falls fast and the
wind howls in the wood, from an old settler
and original proprietor, who is reported to
have dug Walden Pond, and stoned it, and
fringed it with pine woods; who tells me
stories of old time and of new eternity; and
between us we manage to pass a cheerful
evening with social mirth and pleasant views
of things, even without apples or cider, — a
most wise and humorous friend, whom I love
much, who keeps himself more secret than
ever did Goffe or Whalley; and though he
is thought to be dead, none can show where
he is buried. An elderly dame, too, dwells
in my neighborhood, invisible to most persons, in whose odorous herb garden I love
to stroll sometimes, gathering simples and
listening to her fables; for she has a genius
of unequalled fertility, and her memory runs

back farther than mythology, and she can tell me the original of every fable, and on what fact every one is founded, for the incidents occurred when she was young. A ruddy and lusty old dame, who delights in all weathers and seasons, and is likely to outlive all her children yet.

The indescribable innocence and beneficence of Nature, — of sun and wind and rain, of summer and winter, — such health, such cheer, they afford forever! and such sympathy have they ever with our race, that all Nature would be affected, and the sun's brightness fade, and the winds would sigh humanely, and the clouds rain tears, and the woods shed their leaves and put on mourning in midsummer, if any man should ever for a just cause grieve. Shall I not have intelligence with the earth? Am I not partly leaves and vegetable mould myself?

What is the pill which will keep us well, serene, contented? Not my or thy great-grandfather's, but our great - grandmother Nature's universal, vegetable, botanic medicines, by which she has kept herself young always, outlived so many old Parrs in her day, and fed her health with their decaying fatness. For my panacea, instead of one of

those quack vials of a mixture dipped from
Acheron and the Dead Sea, which come out
of those long shallow black-schooner looking
wagons which we sometimes see made to
carry bottles, let me have a draught of un-
diluted morning air. Morning air! If men
will not drink of this at the fountain-head
of the day, why, then, we must even bottle
up some and sell it in the shops, for the
benefit of those who have lost their subscription ticket to morning time in this
world. But remember, it will not keep
quite till noonday even in the coolest cellar, but drive out the stopples long ere that
and follow westward the steps of Aurora.
I am no worshipper of Hygeia, who was the
daughter of that old herb-doctor Æsculapius, and who is represented on monuments
holding a serpent in one hand, and in the
other a cup out of which the serpent some
times drinks; but rather of Hebe, cup-
bearer to Jupiter, who was the daughter of
Juno and wild lettuce, and who had the
power of restoring gods and men to the
vigor of youth. She was probably the only
thoroughly sound-conditioned, healthy, and
robust young lady that ever walked the
globe, and wherever she came it was spring.

VI.

VISITORS.

I THINK that I love society as much as
most, and am ready enough to fasten myself
like a bloodsucker for the time to any full-
blooded man that comes in my way. I am
naturally no hermit, but might possibly sit
out the sturdiest frequenter of the bar-room,
if my business called me thither.

I had three chairs in my house; one for
solitude, two for friendship, three for society.
When visitors came in larger and unexpected
numbers there was but the third chair for
them all, but they generally economized the
room by standing up. It is surprising how
many great men and women a small house
will contain. I have had twenty-five or
thirty souls, with their bodies, at once under
my roof, and yet we often parted without
being aware that we had come very near to
one another. Many of our houses, both public and private, with their almost innumerable apartments, their huge halls and their

cellars for the storage of wines and other munitions of peace, appear to me extravagantly large for their inhabitants. They are so vast and magnificent that the latter seem to be only vermin which infest them. I am surprised when the herald blows his summons before some Tremont or Astor or Middlesex House, to see come creeping out over the piazza for all inhabitants a ridiculous mouse, which soon again slinks into some hole in the pavement.

One inconvenience I sometimes experienced in so small a house, the difficulty of getting to a sufficient distance from my guest when we began to utter the big thoughts in big words. You want room for your thoughts to get into sailing trim and run a course or two before they make their port. The bullet of your thought must have overcome its lateral and ricochet motion and fallen into its last and steady course before it reaches the ear of the hearer, else it may plough out again through the side of his head. Also, our sentences wanted room to unfold and form their columns in the interval. Individuals, like nations, must have suitable broad and natural boundaries, even a considerable neutral ground, between them.

I have found it a singular luxury to talk
across the pond to a companion on the opposite side.   In my house we were so near that
we could not begin to hear, — we could not
speak low enough to be heard ; as when you
throw two stones into calm water so near
that they break each other's undulations.
If we are merely loquacious and loud talkers,
then we can afford to stand very near together, cheek by jowl, and feel each other's
breath ; but if we speak reservedly and
thoughtfully, we want to be farther apart,
that all animal heat and moisture may have
a chance to evaporate.   If we would enjoy
the most intimate society with that in each
of us which is without, or above, being
spoken to, we must not only be silent, but
commonly so far apart bodily that we cannot possibly hear each other's voice in any
case.   Referred to this standard, speech is
for the convenience of those who are hard of
hearing ; but there are many fine things
which we cannot say if we have to shout.
As the conversation began to assume a loftier
and grander tone, we gradually shoved our
chairs farther apart till they touched the
wall in opposite corners, and then commonly
there was not room enough.

My "best" room, however, my withdraw-ing room, always ready for company, on whose carpet the sun rarely fell, was the pine wood behind my house. Thither in summer days, when distinguished guests came, I took them, and a priceless domestic swept the floor and dusted the furniture and kept the things in order.

If one guest came he sometimes partook of my frugal meal, and it was no interrup-tion to conversation to be stirring a hasty-pudding, or watching the rising and matur-ing of a loaf of bread in the ashes, in the mean while. But if twenty came and sat in my house there was nothing said about dinner, though there might be bread enough for two, more than if eating were a forsaken habit; but we naturally practised abstinence; and this was never felt to be an offence against hospitality, but the most proper and consid-erate course. The waste and decay of phys-ical life, which so often needs repair, seemed miraculously retarded in such a case, and the vital vigor stood its ground. I could enter-tain thus a thousand as well as twenty; and if any ever went away disappointed or hun-gry from my house when they found me at home, they may depend upon it that I sympathized with them at least. So easy is it, though many housekeepers doubt it, to establish new and better customs in the place of the old. You need not rest your reputation on the dinners you give. For my own part, I was never so effectually deterred from frequenting a man's house, by any kind of Cerberus whatever, as by the parade one made about dining me, which I took to be a very polite and roundabout hint never to trouble him so again. I think I shall never revisit those scenes. I should be proud to have for the motto of my cabin those lines of Spenser which one of my visitors inscribed on a yellow walnut leaf for a card : —

> " Arrivéd there, the little house they fill,
> Ne looke for entertainment where none was ;
> Rest is their feast, and all things at their will :
> The noblest mind the best contentment has."

When Winslow, afterward governor of the Plymouth Colony, went with a companion on a visit of ceremony to Massasoit on foot through the woods, and arrived tired and hungry at his lodge, they were well received by the king, but nothing was said about eating that day. When the night arrived, to quote their own words, — " He laid us on the bed with himself and his wife, they

at the one end and we at the other, it being
only plank, laid a foot from the ground, and
a thin mat upon them. Two more of his
chief men, for want of room, pressed by and
upon us; so that we were worse weary of
our lodging than of our journey." At one
o'clock the next day Massasoit "brought
two fishes that he had shot," about thrice as
big as a bream; "these being boiled, there
were at least forty looked for a share in
them. The most ate of them. This meal
only we had in two nights and a day; and
had not one of us bought a partridge, we
had taken our journey fasting." Fearing
that they would be light-headed for want of
food and also sleep, owing to "the savages'
barbarous singing, (for they used to sing
themselves asleep,)" and that they might get
home while they had strength to travel, they
departed. As for lodging, it is true they
were but poorly entertained, though what
they found an inconvenience was no doubt
intended for an honor; but as far as eating
was concerned, I do not see how the Indians
could have done better. They had nothing
to eat themselves, and they were wiser than
to think that apologies could supply the place
of food to their guests; so they drew their

belts tighter and said nothing about it. Another time when Winslow visited them, it being a season of plenty with them, there was no deficiency in this respect.

As for men, they will hardly fail one anywhere. I had more visitors while I lived in the woods at than any other period of my life; I mean that I had some. I met several there under more favorable circumstances than I could anywhere else. But fewer came to see me on trivial business. In this respect, my company was winnowed by my mere distance from town. I had withdrawn so far within the great ocean of solitude, into which the rivers of society empty, that for the most part, so far as my needs were concerned, only the finest sediment was deposited around me. Beside, there were wafted to me evidences of unexplored and uncultivated continents on the other side.

Who should come to my lodge this morning but a true Homeric or Paphlagonian man, — he had so suitable and poetic a name that I am sorry I cannot print it here, — a Canadian, a wood-chopper and post-maker, who can hole fifty posts in a day, who made his last supper on a woodchuck which his dog caught. He, too, has heard

of Homer, and, " if it were not for books,"
would " not know what to do rainy days,"
though perhaps he has not read one wholly
through for many rainy seasons.   Some
priest who could pronounce the Greek itself
taught him to read his verse in the testament
in his native parish far away ; and now I
must translate to him, while he holds the
book, Achilles' reproof to Patroclus for his
sad countenance. — " Why are you in tears,
Patroclus, like a young girl ? " —

" Or have you alone heard some news from Phthia ?
They say that Menœtius lives yet, son of Actor,
And Peleus lives, son of Æacus, among the Myrmidons,
Either of whom having died, we should greatly grieve."

He says, " That 's good." He has a great
bundle of white-oak bark under his arm for
a sick man, gathered this Sunday morning.
" I suppose there 's no harm in going after
such a thing to-day," says he.   To him
Homer was a great writer, though what his
writing was about he did not know. A more
simple and natural man it would be hard to
find.   Vice and disease, which cast such a
sombre moral hue over the world, seemed
to have hardly any existence for him. He
was about twenty-eight years old, and had
left Canada and his father's house a dozen

years before to work in the States, and earn
money to buy a farm with at last, perhaps
in his native country. He was cast in the
coarsest mould ; a stout but sluggish body,
yet gracefully carried, with a thick sun-
burnt neck, dark bushy hair, and dull sleepy
blue eyes, which were occasionally lit up
with expression. He wore a flat gray cloth
cap, a dingy wool-colored great-coat, and
cowhide boots. He was a great consumer
of meat, usually carrying his dinner to his
work a couple of miles past my house, — for
he chopped all summer, — in a tin pail ;
cold meats, often cold woodchucks, and coffee in a stone bottle which dangled by a
string from his belt ; and sometimes he offered me a drink. He came along early,
crossing my bean-field, though without anxiety or haste to get to his work, such as Yan-
kees exhibit. He was n't a-going to hurt
himself. He did n't care if he only earned
his board. Frequently he would leave his
dinner in the bushes, when his dog had
caught a woodchuck by the way, and go back
a mile and a half to dress it and leave it in
the cellar of the house where he boarded,
after deliberating first for half an hour
whether he could not sink it in the pond

safely till nightfall, — loving to dwell long
upon these themes. He would say, as he
went by in the morning, " How thick the
pigeons are ! If working every day were
not my trade, I could get all the meat I
should want by hunting, — pigeons, woodchucks, rabbits, partridges, — by gosh ! I
could get all I should want for a week in
one day."

He was a skilful chopper, and indulged
in some flourishes and ornaments in his art.
He cut his trees level and close to the
ground, that the sprouts which came up afterward might be more vigorous and a sled
might slide over the stumps ; and instead of
leaving a whole tree to support his corded
wood, he would pare it away to a slender
stake or splinter which you could break off
with your hand at last.

He interested me because he was so quiet
and solitary and so happy withal ; a well of
good humor and contentment which overflowed at his eyes. His mirth was without
alloy. Sometimes I saw him at his work in
the woods, felling trees, and he would greet
me with a laugh of inexpressible satisfaction,
and a salutation in Canadian French, though
he spoke English as well. When I ap-

proached him he would suspend his work, and with half-suppressed mirth lie along the trunk of a pine which he had felled, and, peeling off the inner bark, roll it up into a ball and chew it while he laughed and talked.   Such an exuberance of animal spirits had he that he sometimes tumbled down and rolled on the ground with laughter at anything which made him think and tickled him.   Looking round upon the trees he would exclaim, — " By George ! I can enjoy myself well enough here chopping ; I want no better sport."   Sometimes, when at leisure, he amused himself all day in the woods with a pocket pistol, firing salutes to himself at regular intervals as he walked.   In the winter he had a fire by which at noon he warmed his coffee in a kettle ; and as he sat on a log to eat his dinner the chicadees would sometimes come round and alight on his arm and peck at the potato in his fingers ; and he said that he " liked to have the little *fellers* about him."

In him the animal man chiefly was developed.   In physical endurance and contentment he was cousin to the pine and the rock.   I asked him once if he was not sometimes tired at night, after working all day ;

and he answered, with a sincere and serious
look, " Gorrappit, I never was tired in my
life." But the intellectual and what is
called spiritual man in him were slumbering as in an infant. He had been instructed
only in that innocent and ineffectual way in
which the Catholic priests teach the aborigines, by which the pupil is never educated
to the degree of consciousness, but only to
the degree of trust and reverence, and a
child is not made a man, but kept a child.
When Nature made him, she gave him a
strong body and contentment for his portion, and propped him on every side with
reverence and reliance, that he might live
out his threescore years and ten a child.
He was so genuine and unsophisticated that
no introduction would serve to introduce
him, more than if you introduced a woodchuck to your neighbor. He had got to find
him out as you did. He would not play any
part. Men paid him wages for work, and
so helped to feed and clothe him ; but he
never exchanged opinions with them. He
was so simply and naturally humble — if he
can be called humble who never aspires —
that humility was no distinct quality in him,
nor could he conceive of it. Wiser men

were demigods to him. If you told him
that such a one was coming, he did as if he
thought that anything so grand would expect nothing of himself, but take all the re-
sponsibility on itself, and let him be forgotten still. He never heard the sound
of praise. He particularly reverenced the
writer and the preacher. Their performances were miracles. When I told him that
I wrote considerably, he thought for a long
time that it was merely the handwriting
which I meant, for he could write a remarkably good hand himself. I sometimes found
the name of his native parish handsomely
written in the snow by the highway, with
the proper French accent, and knew that he
had passed. I asked him if he ever wished
to write his thoughts. He said that he had
read and written letters for those who could
not, but he never tried to write thoughts, —
no, he could not, he could not tell what to
put first, it would kill him, and then there
was spelling to be attended to at the same
time!

I heard that a distinguished wise man and
reformer asked him if he did not want the
world to be changed; but he answered with
a chuckle of surprise in his Canadian ac-

cent, not knowing that the question had ever been entertained before, " No, I like it well enough." It would have suggested many things to a philosopher to have dealings with him. To a stranger he appeared to know nothing of things in general; yet I sometimes saw in him a man whom I had not seen before, and I did not know whether he was as wise as Shakespeare or as simply ignorant as a child, whether to suspect him of a fine poetic consciousness or of stupidity. A townsman told me that when he met him sauntering through the village in his small close-fitting cap, and whistling to himself, he reminded him of a prince in disguise.

His only books were an almanac and an arithmetic, in which last he was considerably expert. The former was a sort of cyclopædia to him, which he supposed to contain an abstract of human knowledge, as indeed it does to a considerable extent. I loved to sound him on the various reforms of the day, and he never failed to look at them in the most simple and practical light. He had never heard of such things before. Could he do without factories? I asked. He had worn the home-made Vermont gray, he said, and that was good. Could he dispense

with tea and coffee? Did this country afford any beverage beside water? He had
soaked hemlock leaves in water and drank
it, and thought that was better than water
in warm weather. When I asked him if he
could do without money, he showed the convenience of money in such a way as to suggest and coincide with the most philosophical accounts of the origin of this institution,
and the very derivation of the word *pecunia*.
If an ox were his property, and he wished
to get needles and thread at the store, he
thought it would be inconvenient and impossible soon to go on mortgaging some
portion of the creature each time to that
amount. He could defend many institutions better than any philosopher, because,
in describing them as they concerned him,
he gave the true reason for their prevalence,
and speculation had not suggested to him
any other. At another time, hearing Plato's definition of a man, — a biped without feathers, — and that one exhibited a
cock plucked and called it Plato's man, he
thought it an important difference that the
knees bent the wrong way. He would sometimes exclaim, "How I love to talk! By
George, I could talk all day!" I asked

him once, when I had not seen him for many
months, if he had got a new idea this summer. "Good Lord," said he, "a man that
has to work as I do, if he does not forget
the ideas he has had, he will do well. May
be the man you hoe with is inclined to race;
then, by gorry, your mind must be there;
you think of weeds." He would sometimes
ask me first on such occasions, if I had made
any improvement. One winter day I asked
him if he was always satisfied with himself,
wishing to suggest a substitute within him
for the priest without, and some higher motive for living. "Satisfied!" said he; "some
men are satisfied with one thing, and some
with another. One man, perhaps, if he has
got enough, will be satisfied to sit all day
with his back to the fire and his belly to
the table, by George!" Yet I never, by
any manœuvring, could get him to take the
spiritual view of things; the highest that
he appeared to conceive of was a simple ex-
pediency, such as you might expect an animal to appreciate; and this, practically, is
true of most men. If I suggested any improvement in his mode of life, he merely answered, without expressing any regret, that
it was too late. Yet he thoroughly believed
in honesty and the like virtues.

There was a certain positive originality, however slight, to be detected in him, and I occasionally observed that he was thinking for himself and expressing his own opinion, a phenomenon so rare that I would any day walk ten miles to observe it, and it amounted to the re-origination of many of the institutions of society. Though he hesitated, and perhaps failed to express himself distinctly, he always had a presentable thought behind. Yet his thinking was so primitive and immersed in his animal life, that, though more promising than a merely learned man's, it rarely ripened to anything which can be reported. He suggested that there might be men of genius in the lowest grades of life, however permanently humble and illiterate, who take their own view always, or do not pretend to see at all ; who are as bottomless even as Walden Pond was thought to be, though they may be dark and muddy.

Many a traveller came out of his way to see me and the inside of my house, and, as an excuse for calling, asked for a glass of water. I told them that I drank at the pond, and pointed thither, offering to lend them a dipper. Far off as I lived, I was not exempted from that annual visitation which occurs, methinks, about the first of April, when everybody is on the move; and I had my share of good luck, though there were some curious specimens among my visitors. Half - witted men from the alms-house and elsewhere came to see me; but I endeavored to make them exercise all the wit they had, and make their confessions to me; in such cases making wit the theme of our conversation; and so was compensated. Indeed, I found some of them to be wiser than the so-called *overseers* of the poor and selectmen of the town, and thought it was time that the tables were turned. With re-spect to wit, I learned that there was not much difference between the half and the whole. One day, in particular, an inoffen-sive, simple - minded pauper, whom with others I had often seen used as fencing stuff, standing or sitting on a bushel in the fields to keep cattle and himself from straying, visited me, and expressed a wish to live as I did. He told me, with the utmost simplicity and truth, quite superior, or rather *inferior*, to anything that is called humility, that he was " deficient in intellect." These were his words. The Lord had made him so, yet he supposed the Lord cared as much for him as for another. " I have always been so," said he, "from my childhood; I never had much mind ; I was not like other children ; I am weak in the head. It was the Lord's will, I suppose." And there he was to prove the truth of his words. He was a metaphysical puzzle to me. I have rarely met a fellow-man on such promising ground, — it was so simple and sincere and so true all that he said. And, true enough, in proportion as he appeared to humble himself was he exalted. I did not know at first but it was the result of a wise policy. It seemed that from such a basis of truth and frankness as the poor weak-headed pauper had laid, our intercourse might go forward to something better than the intercourse of sages.

I had some guests from those not reckoned commonly among the town's poor, but who should be; who are among the world's poor, at any rate; guests who appeal, not to your hospitality, but to your *hospitalality ;* who earnestly wish to be helped, and preface their appeal with the information that they are resolved, for one thing, never to help themselves. I require of a visitor that he be not actually starving, though he may have

the very best appetite in the world, however
he got it.   Objects of charity are not guests.
Men who did not know when their visit had
terminated, though I went about my business
again, answering them from greater and
greater remoteness.   Men of almost every
degree of wit called on me in the migrating
season.   Some who had more wits than they
knew what to do with; runaway slaves with
plantation manners, who listened from time
to time, like the fox in the fable, as if they
heard the hounds a-baying on their track,
and looked at me beseechingly, as much as
to say, —

"O Christian, will you send me back ? "

One real runaway slave, among the rest,
whom I helped to forward toward the north-
star.   Men of one idea, like a hen with one
chicken, and that a duckling; men of a
thousand ideas, and unkempt heads, like
those hens which are made to take charge of
a hundred chickens, all in pursuit of one
bug, a score of them lost in every morning's
dew, — and become frizzled and mangy in
consequence ; men of ideas instead of legs, a
sort of intellectual centipede that made you
crawl all over.   One man proposed a book

in which visitors should write their names,
as at the White Mountains; but, alas! I
have too good a memory to make that necessary.

I could not but notice some of the pecu-
liarities of my visitors. Girls and boys and
young women generally seemed glad to be
in the woods. They looked in the pond and
at the flowers, and improved their time.
Men of business, even farmers, thought only
of solitude and employment, and of the
great distance at which I dwelt from something or other; and though they said that
they loved a ramble in the woods occasionally, it was obvious that they did not.
Restless committed men, whose time was all
taken up in getting a living or keeping it;
ministers who spoke of God as if they enjoyed a monopoly of the subject, who could
not bear all kinds of opinions; doctors, law-
yers, uneasy housekeepers who pried into
my cupboard and bed when I was out, —
how came Mrs. —— to know that my sheets
were not as clean as hers? — young men who
had ceased to be young, and had concluded
that it was safest to follow the beaten track
of the professions, — all these generally said
that it was not possible to do so much good

in my position.   Ay! there was the rub.
The old and infirm and the timid, of whatever age or sex, thought most of sickness,
and sudden accident and death ; to them life
seemed full of danger, — what danger is
there if you don't think of any? — and they
thought that a prudent man would carefully
select the safest position, where Dr. B. might
be on hand at a moment's warning.   To
them the village was literally a *com-munity*,
a league for mutual defence, and you would
suppose that they would not go a-huckleberrying without a medicine chest.   The
amount of it is, if a man is alive, there is
always *danger* that he may die, though the
danger must be allowed to be less in proportion as he is dead-and-alive to begin with.   A
man sits as many risks as he runs.   Finally,
there were the self-styled reformers, the greatest bores of all, who thought that I was forever singing, —

> This is the house that I built ;
> This is the man that lives in the house that I built ;

but they did not know that the third line
was, —

> These are the folks that worry the man
> That lives in the house that I built.

I did not fear the hen-harriers, for I kept

no chickens; but I feared the men-harriers rather.

I had more cheering visitors than the last. Children come a-berrying, railroad men taking a Sunday morning walk in clean shirts, fishermen and hunters, poets and philosophers; in short, all honest pilgrims, who came out to the woods for freedom's sake, and really left the village behind, I was ready to greet with, — " Welcome, Englishmen! welcome, Englishmen! " for I had had communication with that race.

VII.

MEANWHILE my beans, the length of whose rows, added together, was seven miles already planted, were impatient to be hoed, for the earliest had grown considerably before the latest were in the ground; indeed they were not easily to be put off. What was the meaning of this so steady and self-respecting, this small Herculean labor, I knew not. I came to love my rows, my beans, though so many more than I wanted. They attached me to the earth, and so I got strength like Antæus. But why should I raise them? Only Heaven knows. This was my curious labor all summer, — to make this portion of the earth's surface, which had yielded only cinquefoil, black-berries, johnswort, and the like, before, sweet wild fruits and pleasant flowers, pro-duce instead this pulse. What shall I learn of beans or beans of me? I cherish them, I hoe them, early and late I have an eye to

them ; and this is my day's work. It is a
fine broad leaf to look on. My auxiliaries
are the dews and rains which water this dry
soil, and what fertility is in the soil itself,
which for the most part is lean and effete.
My enemies are worms, cool days, and most
of all woodchucks. The last have nibbled
for me a quarter of an acre clean. But
what right had I to oust johnswort and the
rest, and break up their ancient herb garden ? Soon, however, the remaining beans
will be too tough for them, and go forward
to meet new foes.

When I was four years old, as I well remember, I was brought from Boston to this
my native town, through these very woods
and this field, to the pond. It is one of the
oldest scenes stamped on my memory. And
now to-night my flute has waked the echoes
over that very water. The pines still stand
here older than I ; or, if some have fallen, I
have cooked my supper with their stumps,
and a new growth is rising all around, preparing another aspect for new infant eyes.
Almost the same johnswort springs from the
same perennial root in this pasture, and
even I have at length helped to clothe that
fabulous landscape of my infant dreams,

and one of the results of my presence and influence is seen in these bean leaves, corn blades, and potato vines.

I planted about two acres and a half of upland ; and as it was only about fifteen years since the land was cleared, and I myself had got out two or three cords of stumps, I did not give it any manure ; but in the course of the summer it appeared by the arrow-heads which I turned up in hoeing, that an extinct nation had anciently dwelt here and planted corn and beans ere white men came to clear the land, and so, to some extent, had exhausted the soil for this very crop.

Before yet any woodchuck or squirrel had run across the road, or the sun had got above the shrub-oaks, while all the dew was on, though the farmers warned me against it, — I would advise you to do all your work if possible while the dew is on, — I began to level the ranks of haughty weeds in my bean-field and throw dust upon their heads. Early in the morning I worked barefooted, dabbling like a plastic artist in the dewy and crumbling sand, but later in the day the sun blistered my feet. There the sun lighted me to hoe beans, pacing slowly back-

ward and forward over that yellow gravelly
upland, between the long green rows, fifteen
rods, the one end terminating in a shrub
oak copse where I could rest in the shade,
the other in a blackberry field where the
green berries deepened their tints by the
time I had made another bout. Removing
the weeds, putting fresh soil about the bean
stems, and encouraging this weed which I
had sown, making the yellow soil express its
summer thought in bean leaves and blos-
soms rather than in wormwood and piper
and millet grass, making the earth say beans
instead of grass, — this was my daily work.
As I had little aid from horses or cattle, or
hired men or boys, or improved implements
of husbandry, I was much slower, and became much more intimate with my beans
than usual. But labor of the hands, even
when pursued to the verge of drudgery, is
perhaps never the worst form of idleness.
It has a constant and imperishable moral,
and to the scholar it yields a classic result.
A very *agricola laboriosus* was I to travellers bound westward through Lincoln and
Wayland to nobody knows where; they sitting at their ease in gigs, with elbows on
knees, and reins loosely hanging in festoons;

I the home-staying, laborious native of the
soil. But soon my homestead was out of
their sight and thought. It was the only
open and cultivated field for a great distance on either side of the road, so they
made the most of it ; and sometimes the man
in the field heard more of travellers' gossip
and comment than was meant for his ear :
" Beans so late ! peas so late ! " — for I continued to plant when others had begun to
hoe, — the ministerial husbandman had not
suspected it. " Corn, my boy, for fodder ;
corn for fodder." " Does he *live* there ? "
asks the black bonnet of the gray coat ; and
the hard-featured farmer reins up his grate-
ful dobbin to inquire what you are doing
where he sees no manure in the furrow, and
recommends a little chip dirt, or any little
waste stuff, or it may be ashes or plaster.
But here were two acres and a half of furrows, and only a hoe for cart and two hands
to draw it, — there being an aversion to
other carts and horses, — and chip dirt far
away. Fellow-travellers as they rattled by
compared it aloud with the fields which they
had passed, so that I came to know how I
stood in the agricultural world. This was
one field not in Mr. Coleman's report. And,

by the way, who estimates the value of the crop which Nature yields in the still wilder fields unimproved by man? The crop of *English* hay is carefully weighed, the moisture calculated, the silicates and the potash; but in all dells and pond holes in the woods and pastures and swamps grows a rich and various crop only unreaped by man. Mine was, as it were, the connecting link between wild and cultivated fields; as some states are civilized, and others half-civilized, and others savage or barbarous, so my field was, though not in a bad sense, a half-cultivated field. They were beans cheerfully returning to their wild and primitive state that I cultivated, and my hoe played the *Ranz des Vaches* for them.

Near at hand, upon the topmost spray of a birch, sings the brown-thrasher — or red mavis, as some love to call him — all the morning, glad of your society, that would find out another farmer's field if yours were not here. While you are planting the seed, he cries, — "Drop it, drop it, — cover it up, cover it up, — pull it up, pull it up, pull it up." But this was not corn, and so it was safe from such enemies as he. You may wonder what his rigmarole, his amateur

Paganini performances on one string or on twenty, have to do with your planting, and yet prefer it to leached ashes or plaster. It was a cheap sort of top dressing in which I had entire faith.

As I drew a still fresher soil about the rows with my hoe, I disturbed the ashes of unchronicled nations who in primeval years lived under these heavens, and their small implements of war and hunting were brought to the light of this modern day. They lay mingled with other natural stones, some of which bore the marks of having been burned by Indian fires, and some by the sun, and also bits of pottery and glass brought hither by the recent cultivators of the soil. When my hoe tinkled against the stones, that music echoed to the woods and the sky, and was an accompaniment to my labor which yielded an instant and immeasurable crop. It was no longer beans that I hoed, nor I that hoed beans; and I remembered with as much pity as pride, if I remembered at all, my acquaintances who had gone to the city to attend the oratorios. The night-hawk circled overhead in the sunny afternoons — for I sometimes made a day of it — like a mote in the eye, or in heaven's

eye, falling from time to time with a swoop
and a sound as if the heavens were rent, torn
at last to very rags and tatters, and yet a
seamless cope remained; small imps that fill
the air and lay their eggs on the ground on
bare sand or rocks on the tops of hills,
where few have found them ; graceful and
slender like ripples caught up from the
pond, as leaves are raised by the wind to
float in the heavens; such kindredship is in
Nature. The hawk is aerial brother of the
wave which he sails over and surveys, those
his perfect air-inflated wings answering to
the elemental unfledged pinions of the sea.
Or sometimes I watched a pair of hen-hawks
circling high in the sky, alternately soaring
and descending, approaching and leaving
one another, as if they were the embodiment
of my own thoughts. Or I was attracted
by the passage of wild pigeons from this
wood to that, with a slight quivering win-
nowing sound and carrier haste ; or from
under a rotten stump my hoe turned up a
sluggish portentous and outlandish spotted
salamander, a trace of Egypt and the Nile,
yet our contemporary. When I paused to
lean on my hoe, these sounds and sights I
heard and saw anywhere in the row, a part

of the inexhaustible entertainment which the country offers.

On gala days the town fires its great guns, which echo like popguns to these woods, and some waifs of martial music occasionally penetrate thus far. To me, away there in my bean-field at the other end of the town, the big guns sounded as if a puff ball had burst; and when there was a military turn-out of which I was ignorant, I have sometimes had a vague sense all the day of some sort of itching and disease in the horizon, as if some eruption would break out there soon, either scarlatina or canker-rash, until at length some more favorable puff of wind, making haste over the fields and up the Wayland road, brought me information of the "trainers." It seemed by the distant hum as if somebody's bees had swarmed, and that the neighbors, according to Virgil's advice, by a faint *tintinnabulum* upon the most sonorous of their domestic utensils, were endeavoring to call them down into the hive again. And when the sound died quite away, and the hum had ceased, and the most favorable breezes told no tale, I knew that they had got the last drone of them all safely into the Middlesex hive, and that now their minds were bent on the honey with which it was smeared.

I felt proud to know that the liberties of Massachusetts and of our fatherland were in such safe keeping; and as I turned to my hoeing again I was filled with an inexpressible confidence, and pursued my labor cheerfully with a calm trust in the future.

When there were several bands of musicians, it sounded as if all the village was a vast bellows, and all the buildings expanded and collapsed alternately with a din. But sometimes it was a really noble and inspiring strain that reached these woods, and the trumpet that sings of fame, and I felt as if I could spit a Mexican with a good relish, — for why should we always stand for trifles? — and looked round for a woodchuck or a skunk to exercise my chivalry upon. These martial strains seemed as far away as Palestine, and reminded me of a march of crusaders in the horizon, with a slight tantivy and tremulous motion of the elm-tree tops which overhang the village. This was one of the *great* days; though the sky had from my clearing only the same everlastingly great look that it wears daily, and I saw no difference in it.

It was a singular experience that long acquaintance which I cultivated with beans, what with planting, and hoeing, and harvesting, and threshing, and picking over and selling them, — the last was the hardest of all, — I might add eating, for I did taste. I was determined to know beans. When they were growing, I used to hoe from five o'clock in the morning till noon, and commonly spent the rest of the day about other affairs. Consider the intimate and curious acquaintance one makes with various kinds of weeds, — it will bear some iteration in the account, for there was no little iteration in the labor, — disturbing their delicate organizations so ruthlessly, and making such invidious distinctions with his hoe, levelling whole ranks of one species, and sedulously cultivating another. That's Roman wormwood, — that's pigweed, — that's sorrel, — that's piper-grass, — have at him, chop him up, turn his roots upward to the sun, don't let him have a fibre in the shade, if you do he'll turn himself t'other side up and be as green as a leek in two days. A long war, not with cranes, but with weeds, those Trojans who had sun and rain and dews on their side. Daily the beans saw me come to their rescue armed with a hoe, and thin the ranks of their enemies, filling up the trenches with weedy dead. Many a lusty crest-waving Hector, that towered a whole foot above his crowding comrades, fell before my weapon and rolled in the dust.

Those summer days which some of my contemporaries devoted to the fine arts in Boston or Rome, and others to contemplation in India, and others to trade in London or New York, I thus, with the other farmers of New England, devoted to husbandry. Not that I wanted beans to eat, for I am by nature a Pythagorean, so far as beans are concerned, whether they mean porridge or voting, and exchanged them for rice; but, perchance, as some must work in fields if only for the sake of tropes and expression, to serve a parable-maker one day. It was on the whole a rare amusement, which, continued too long, might have become a dissipation. Though I gave them no manure, and did not hoe them all once, I hoed them unusually well as far as I went, and was paid for it in the end, " there being in truth," as Evelyn says, " no compost or lætation whatsoever comparable to this continual motion, repastination, and turning of the mould with the spade." "The earth," he adds elsewhere, "especially if fresh, has a certain magnetism in it, by which it attracts the salt, power, or virtue (call it either) which gives it life, and is the logic of all the labor and stir we keep about it, to sustain us ; all dungings and other sordid temperings being but the vicars succedaneous to this improvement." Moreover, this being one of those " worn-out and exhausted lay fields which enjoy their sabbath," had perchance, as Sir Kenelm Digby thinks likely, attracted " vital spirits " from the air. I harvested twelve bushels of beans.

But to be more particular, for it is complained that Mr. Coleman has reported chiefly the expensive experiments of gentlemen farmers, my outgoes were, —

For a hoe, ...	$0 54	
Ploughing, harrowing, and furrowing,	7 50	Too much.
Beans for seed, ...	3 12½	
Potatoes "	1 33	
Peas "	0 40	
Turnip seed, ...	0 06	
White line for crow fence, ...	0 02	
Horse cultivator and boy three hours,	1 00	
Horse and cart to get crop, ...	0 75	
In all, ...	$14 72½	

My income was, (patrem familias venda-
cem, non emacem esse oportet,) from

Nine bushels and twelve quarts of beans sold,		$16 94
Five " large potatoes, ...		2 50
Nine " small, ...		2 25
Grass, ...		1 00
Stalks, ...		0 75
In all, ...		$23 44
Leaving a pecuniary profit, as I have else-		
where said, of		$8 71½.

This is the result of my experience in
raising beans. Plant the common small
white bush bean about the first of June, in
rows three feet by eighteen inches apart,
being careful to select fresh round and unmixed seed. First look out for worms, and
supply vacancies by planting anew. Then
look out for woodchucks, if it is an exposed
place, for they will nibble off the earliest
tender leaves almost clean as they go; and
again, when the young tendrils make their
appearance, they have notice of it, and will
shear them off with both buds and young
pods, sitting erect like a squirrel. But above
all harvest as early as possible, if you would
escape frosts and have a fair and salable
crop; you may save much loss by this
means.

This further experience also I gained. I said to myself, I will not plant beans and corn with so much industry another summer, but such seeds, if the seed is not lost, as sincerity, truth, simplicity, faith, innocence, and the like, and see if they will not grow in this soil, even with less toil and manurance, and sustain me, for surely it has not been exhausted for these crops. Alas! I said this to myself; but now another summer is gone, and another, and another, and I am obliged to say to you, Reader, that the seeds which I planted, if indeed they *were* the seeds of those virtues, were wormeaten or had lost their vitality, and so did not come up. Commonly men will only be brave as their fathers were brave, or timid. This generation is very sure to plant corn and beans each new year precisely as the Indians did centuries ago and taught the first settlers to do, as if there were a fate in it. I saw an old man the other day, to my astonishment, making the holes with a hoe for the seventieth time at least, and not for himself to lie down in! But why should not the New Englander try new adventures, and not lay so much stress on his grain, his potato and grass crop, and his orchards, — raise other crops than these?

Why concern ourselves so much about our beans for seed, and not be concerned at all about a new generation of men? We should really be fed and cheered if when we met a man we were sure to see that some of the qualities which I have named, which we all prize more than those other productions, but which are for the most part broadcast and floating in the air, had taken root and grown in him. Here comes such a subtile and ineffable quality, for instance, as truth or justice, though the slightest amount or new variety of it, along the road. Our ambassadors should be instructed to send home such seeds as these, and Congress help to distribute them over all the land. We should never stand upon ceremony with sincerity. We should never cheat and insult and banish one another by our meanness, if there were present the kernel of worth and friendliness. We should not meet thus in haste. Most men I do not meet at all, for they seem not to have time; they are busy about their beans. We would not deal with a man thus plodding ever, leaning on a hoe or a spade as a staff between his work, not as a mushroom, but partially risen out of the earth, something more than erect, like swallows alighted and walking on the ground: —

" And as he spake, his wings would now and then
   Spread, as he meant to fly, then close again, — "

so that we should suspect that we might be
conversing with an angel. Bread may not
always nourish us; but it always does us
good, it even takes stiffness out of our joints,
and makes us supple and buoyant, when we
knew not what ailed us, to recognize any
generosity in man or Nature, to share any
unmixed and heroic joy.

Ancient poetry and mythology suggest, at
least, that husbandry was once a sacred art;
but it is pursued with irreverent haste and
heedlessness by us, our object being to have
large farms and large crops merely. We
have no festival, nor procession, nor ceremony, not excepting our Cattle-shows and so
called Thanksgivings, by which the farmer
expresses a sense of the sacredness of his
calling, or is reminded of its sacred origin.
It is the premium and the feast which tempt
him. He sacrifices not to Ceres and the
Terrestrial Jove, but to the infernal Plutus
rather. By avarice and selfishness, and a
grovelling habit, from which none of us is
free, of regarding the soil as property, or
the means of acquiring property chiefly, the
landscape is deformed, husbandry is degraded

with us, and the farmer leads the meanest of lives. He knows Nature but as a robber. Cato says that the profits of agriculture are particularly pious or just, (*maximeque pius quæstus,*) and according to Varro the old Romans " called the same earth Mother and Ceres, and thought that they who cultivated it led a pious and useful life, and that they alone were left of the race of King Saturn."

We are wont to forget that the sun looks on our cultivated fields and on the prairies and forests without distinction. They all reflect and absorb his rays alike, and the former make but a small part of the glorious picture which he beholds in his daily course. In his view the earth is all equally cultivated like a garden. Therefore we should receive the benefit of his light and heat with a corresponding trust and magnanimity. What though I value the seed of these beans, and harvest that in the fall of the year? This broad field which I have looked at so long looks not to me as the principal cultivator, but away from me to influences more genial to it, which water and make it green. These beans have results which are not harvested by me. Do they not grow for woodchucks partly? The ear of wheat, (in Latin *spica,* obsoletely *speca,* from *spe,* hope,) should not be the only hope of the husbandman; its kernel or grain (*granum,* from *gerendo,* bearing,) is not all that it bears. How, then, can our harvest fail? Shall I not rejoice also at the abundance of the weeds whose seeds are the granary of the birds? It matters little comparatively whether the fields fill the farmer's barns. The true husbandman will cease from anxiety, as the squirrels manifest no concern whether the woods will bear chestnuts this year or not, and finish his labor with every day, relinquishing all claim to the produce of his fields, and sacrificing in his mind not only his first but his last fruits also.

VIII.

THE VILLAGE.

AFTER hoeing, or perhaps reading and writing, in the forenoon, I usually bathed again in the pond, swimming across one of its coves for a stint, and washed the dust of labor from my person, or smoothed out the last wrinkle which study had made, and for the afternoon was absolutely free. Every day or two I strolled to the village to hear some of the gossip which is incessantly going on there, circulating either from mouth to mouth, or from newspaper to newspaper, and which, taken in homœopathic doses, was really as refreshing in its way as the rustle of leaves and the peeping of frogs. As I walked in the woods to see the birds and squirrels, so I walked in the village to see the men and boys; instead of the wind among

the pines I heard the carts rattle. In one
direction from my house there was a colony
of musk-rats in the river meadows; under the
grove of elms and buttonwoods in the other
horizon was a village of busy men, as curious
to me as if they had been prairie dogs, each
sitting at the mouth of its burrow, or running over to a neighbor's to gossip. I went
there frequently to observe their habits.
The village appeared to me a great news
room ; and on one side, to support it, as
once at Redding & Company's on State
Street, they kept nuts and raisins, or salt
and meal and other groceries. Some have
such a vast appetite for the former com-
modity, that is, the news, and such sound
digestive organs, that they can sit forever in
public avenues without stirring, and let it
simmer and whisper through them like the
Etesian winds, or as if inhaling ether, it
only producing numbness and insensibility
to pain, — otherwise it would often be pain-
ful to hear, — without affecting the consciousness. I hardly ever failed, when I
rambled through the village, to see a row
of such worthies, either sitting on a ladder
sunning themselves, with their bodies inclined forward and their eyes glancing along

the line this way and that, from time to time,
with a voluptuous expression, or else leaning against a barn with their hands in their
pockets, like caryatides, as if to prop it up.
They, being commonly out of doors, heard
whatever was in the wind. These are the
coarsest mills, in which all gossip is first
rudely digested or cracked up before it is
emptied into finer and more delicate hoppers
within doors. I observed that the vitals of
the village were the grocery, the bar-room,
the post-office, and the bank; and, as a necessary part of the machinery, they kept a
bell, a big gun, and a fire-engine, at convenient places; and the houses were so arranged
as to make the most of mankind, in lanes
and fronting one another, so that every traveller had to run the gauntlet, and every man,
woman, and child might get a lick at him.
Of course, those who were stationed nearest
to the head of the line, where they could
most see and be seen, and have the first
blow at him, paid the highest prices for
their places; and the few straggling inhabitants in the outskirts, where long gaps in
the line began to occur, and the traveller
could get over walls or turn aside into cow-
paths, and so escape, paid a very slight

ground or window tax. Signs were hung
out on all sides to allure him; some to catch
him by the appetite, as the tavern and victualling cellar; some by the fancy, as the dry
goods store and the jeweller's; and others
by the hair or the feet or the skirts, as the
barber, the shoemaker, or the tailor. Besides, there was a still more terrible standing
invitation to call at every one of these houses,
and company expected about these times.
For the most part I escaped wonderfully
from these dangers, either by proceeding at
once boldly and without deliberation to the
goal, as is recommended to those who run
the gauntlet, or by keeping my thoughts on
high things, like Orpheus, who, " loudly
singing the praises of the gods to his lyre,
drowned the voices of the Sirens, and kept
out of danger." Sometimes I bolted suddenly, and nobody could tell my whereabouts,
for I did not stand much about gracefulness,
and never hesitated at a gap in a fence. I
was even accustomed to make an irruption
into some houses, where I was well entertained, and after learning the kernels and
very last sieve-ful of news, what had sub-
sided, the prospects of war and peace, and
whether the world was likely to hold to-

gether much longer, I was let out through the rear avenues, and so escaped to the woods again.

It was very pleasant, when I stayed late in town, to launch myself into the night, especially if it was dark and tempestuous, and set sail from some bright village parlor or lecture room, with a bag of rye or Indian meal upon my shoulder, for my snug harbor in the woods, having made all tight without and withdrawn under hatches with a merry crew of thoughts, leaving only my outer man at the helm, or even tying up the helm when it was plain sailing. I had many a genial thought by the cabin fire "as I sailed." I was never cast away nor distressed in any weather, though I encountered some severe storms. It is darker in the woods, even in common nights, than most suppose. I frequently had to look up at the opening between the trees above the path in order to learn my route, and, where there was no cart-path, to feel with my feet the faint track which I had worn, or steer by the known relation of particular trees which I felt with my hands, passing between two pines for instance, not more than eighteen inches apart, in the midst of the woods, invariably in the darkest night. Sometimes, after coming home thus late in a dark and muggy night, when my feet felt the path which my eyes could not see, dreaming and absent - minded all the way, until I was aroused by having to raise my hand to lift the latch, I have not been able to recall a single step of my walk, and I have thought that perhaps my body would find its way home if its master should forsake it, as the hand finds its way to the mouth without assistance. Several times, when a visitor chanced to stay into evening, and it proved a dark night, I was obliged to conduct him to the cart-path in the rear of the house, and then point out to him the direction he was to pursue, and in keeping which he was to be guided rather by his feet than his eyes. One very dark night I directed thus on their way two young men who had been fishing in the pond. They lived about a mile off through the woods, and were quite used to the route. A day or two after one of them told me that they wandered about the greater part of the night, close by their own premises, and did not get home till toward morning, by which time, as there had been several heavy showers in the mean while, and the

leaves were very wet, they were drenched to
their skins. I have heard of many going
astray even in the village streets, when the
darkness was so thick that you could cut it
with a knife, as the saying is. Some who live
in the outskirts, having come to town a-shop-
ping in their wagons, have been obliged to
put up for the night; and gentlemen and
ladies making a call have gone half a mile
out of their way, feeling the sidewalk only
with their feet, and not knowing when they
turned. It is a surprising and memorable,
as well as valuable experience, to be lost in
the woods any time. Often in a snow storm,
even by day, one will come out upon a well-
known road and yet find it impossible to tell
which way leads to the village. Though he
knows that he has travelled it a thousand
times, he cannot recognize a feature in it,
but it is as strange to him as if it were a
road in Siberia. By night, of course, the
perplexity is infinitely greater. In our most
trivial walks, we are constantly, though unconsciously, steering like pilots by certain
well-known beacons and headlands, and if we
go beyond our usual course we still carry in
our minds the bearing of some neighboring
cape ; and not till we are completely lost, or

turned round, — for a man needs only to be turned round once with his eyes shut in this world to be lost, — do we appreciate the vastness and strangeness of Nature. Every man has to learn the points of compass again as often as he awakes, whether from sleep or any abstraction. Not till we are lost, in other words, not till we have lost the world, do we begin to find ourselves, and realize where we are and the infinite extent of our relations.

One afternoon, near the end of the first summer, when I went to the village to get a shoe from the cobbler's, I was seized and put into jail, because, as I have elsewhere related, I did not pay a tax to, or recognize the authority of, the state which buys and sells men, women, and children, like cattle at the door of its senate-house. I had gone down to the woods for other purposes. But, wherever a man goes, men will pursue and paw him with their dirty institutions, and, if they can, constrain him to belong to their desperate odd-fellow society. It is true, I might have resisted forcibly with more or less effect, might have run " amok " against society ; but I preferred that society should run " amok " against me, it being the desper-

ate party. However, I was released the next
day, obtained my mended shoe, and returned
to the woods in season to get my dinner of
huckleberries on Fair Haven Hill. I was
never molested by any person but those who
represented the state. I had no lock nor
bolt but for the desk which held my papers,
not even a nail to put over my latch or windows. I never fastened my door night or
day, though I was to be absent several days;
not even when the next fall I spent a fortnight in the woods of Maine. And yet my
house was more respected than if it had been
surrounded by a file of soldiers. The tired
rambler could rest and warm himself by my
fire, the literary amuse himself with the few
books on my table, or the curious, by opening my closet door, see what was left of my
dinner, and what prospect I had of a supper.
Yet, though many people of every class came
this way to the pond, I suffered no serious
inconvenience from these sources, and I
never missed anything but one small book,
a volume of Homer, which perhaps was im-
properly gilded, and this I trust a soldier of
our camp has found by this time. I am
convinced, that if all men were to live as
simply as I then did, thieving and robbery

would be unknown. These take place only in communities where some have got more than is sufficient while others have not enough. The Pope's Homers would soon get properly distributed —

" Nec bella fuerunt,
Faginus astabat dum scyphus ante dapes."

" Nor wars did men molest,
When only beechen bowls were in request."

"You who govern public affairs, what need have you to employ punishments? Love virtue, and the people will be virtuous. The virtues of a superior man are like the wind; the virtues of a common man are like the grass; the grass, when the wind passes over it, bends."

IX.

THE PONDS.

Sometimes, having had a surfeit of human society and gossip, and worn out all my village friends, I rambled still farther westward than I habitually dwell, into yet more unfrequented parts of the town, "to fresh woods and pastures new," or, while the sun was setting, made my supper of huckleberries and blueberries on Fair Haven Hill, and laid up a store for several days. The fruits do not yield their true flavor to the purchaser of them, nor to him who raises them for the market. There is but one way to obtain it, yet few take that way. If you would know the flavor of huckleberries, ask the cow-boy or the partridge. It is a vulgar error to suppose that you have tasted huckleberries who never plucked them. A huckleberry never reaches Boston; they have not been known there since they grew on her three hills. The ambrosial and essential part of the fruit is lost with the bloom which is rubbed off in the market cart, and they become mere provender. As long as Eternal Justice reigns, not one innocent huckleberry can be transported thither from the country's hills.

Occasionally, after my hoeing was done for the day, I joined some impatient companion who had been fishing on the pond since morning, as silent and motionless as a duck or a floating leaf, and, after practising various kinds of philosophy, had concluded commonly, by the time I arrived, that he belonged to the ancient sect of Cœnobites. There was one older man, an excellent fisher and skilled in all kinds of woodcraft, who was pleased to look upon my house as a building erected for the convenience of fishermen ; and I was equally pleased when he sat in my doorway to arrange his lines. Once in a while we sat together on the pond, he at one end of the boat, and I at the other ; but not many words passed between us, for he had grown deaf in his later years, but he occasionally hummed a psalm, which harmonized well enough with my philosophy. Our intercourse was thus altogether one of unbroken harmony, far more pleasing to remember than if it had been carried on by speech. When, as was commonly the case, I had none to commune with, I used to raise the echoes by striking with a paddle on the side of my boat, filling the surrounding woods with circling and dilating sound, stirring them up as the keeper of a menagerie his wild beasts, until I elicited a growl from every wooded vale and hill-side.

In warm evenings I frequently sat in the boat playing the flute, and saw the perch, which I seem to have charmed, hovering around me, and the moon travelling over the ribbed bottom, which was strewed with the wrecks of the forest. Formerly I had come to this pond adventurously, from time to time, in dark summer nights, with a companion, and making a fire close to the water's edge, which we thought attracted the fishes, we caught pouts with a bunch of worms strung on a thread, and when we had done, far in the night, threw the burning brands high into the air like skyrockets, which, coming down into the pond, were quenched with a loud hissing, and we were suddenly groping in total darkness. Through this, whistling a tune, we took our way to the haunts of men again. But now I had made my home by the shore.

Sometimes, after staying in a village parlor till the family had all retired, I have returned to the woods, and, partly with a view to the next day's dinner, spent the hours of midnight fishing from a boat by moonlight, serenaded by owls and foxes, and hearing, from time to time, the creaking note of some unknown bird close at hand. These experiences were very memorable and valuable to me, — anchored in forty feet of water, and twenty or thirty rods from the shore, surrounded sometimes by thousands of small perch and shiners, dimpling the surface with their tails in the moonlight, and communicating by a long flaxen line with mysterious nocturnal fishes which had their dwelling forty feet below, or sometimes dragging sixty feet of line about the pond as I drifted in the gentle night breeze, now and then feeling a slight vibration along it, indicative of some life prowling about its extremity, of dull uncertain blundering purpose there, and slow to make up its mind. At length you slowly raise, pulling hand over hand, some horned pout squeaking and squirming to the upper air. It was very queer, especially in dark nights, when your thoughts had wandered to vast and cosmogonal themes in other spheres, to feel this faint jerk, which came to interrupt your dreams and link you to Nature again. It seemed as if I might next cast my line upward into the air, as well as downward into this element, which was scarcely more dense. Thus I caught two fishes as it were with one hook.

The scenery of Walden is on a humble scale, and, though very beautiful, does not approach to grandeur, nor can it much concern one who has not long frequented it or lived by its shore; yet this pond is so remarkable for its depth and purity as to merit a particular description. It is a clear and deep green well, half a mile long and a mile and three quarters in circumference, and contains about sixty-one and a half acres; a perennial spring in the midst of pine and oak woods, without any visible inlet or outlet except by the clouds and evaporation. The surrounding hills rise abruptly from the water to the height of forty to eighty feet, though on the south-east and east they attain to about one hundred and one hundred and fifty feet respectively, within a quarter and a third of a mile. They are exclusively woodland. All our Concord waters have

two colors at least; one when viewed at a
distance, and another, more proper, close at
hand. The first depends more on the light,
and follows the sky. In clear weather, in
summer, they appear blue at a little distance,
especially if agitated, and at a great distance
all appear alike. In stormy weather they
are sometimes of a dark slate color. The
sea, however, is said to be blue one day
and green another without any perceptible
change in the atmosphere. I have seen our
river, when, the landscape being covered
with snow, both water and ice were almost
as green as grass. Some consider blue " to
be the color of pure water, whether liquid
or solid." But, looking directly down into
our waters from a boat, they are seen to be
of very different colors. Walden is blue at
one time and green at another, even from
the same point of view. Lying between the
earth and the heavens, it partakes of the
color of both. Viewed from a hill-top it reflects the color of the sky; but near at hand
it is of a yellowish tint next the shore where
you can see the sand, then a light green,
which gradually deepens to a uniform dark
green in the body of the pond. In some
lights, viewed even from a hill-top, it is of a

vivid green next the shore. Some have referred this to the reflection of the verdure;
but it is equally green there against the railroad sand-bank, and in the spring, before
the leaves are expanded, and it may be simply the result of the prevailing blue mixed
with the yellow of the sand. Such is the
color of its iris. This is that portion, also,
where in the spring, the ice being warmed
by the heat of the sun reflected from the
bottom, and also transmitted through the
earth, melts first and forms a narrow canal
about the still frozen middle. Like the rest
of our waters, when much agitated, in clear
weather, so that the surface of the waves
may reflect the sky at the right angle, or
because there is more light mixed with it, it
appears at a little distance of a darker blue
than the sky itself; and at such a time, being on its surface, and looking with divided
vision, so as to see the reflection, I have discerned a matchless and indescribable light
blue, such as watered or changeable silks and
sword blades suggest, more cerulean than
the sky itself, alternating with the original
dark green on the opposite sides of the
waves, which last appeared but muddy in
comparison. It is a vitreous greenish blue,

as I remember it, like those patches of the winter sky seen through cloud vistas in the west before sundown. Yet a single glass of its water held up to the light is as colorless as an equal quantity of air. It is well known that a large plate of glass will have a green tint, owing, as the makers say, to its "body," but a small piece of the same will be colorless. How large a body of Walden water would be required to reflect a green tint I have never proved. The water of our river is black or a very dark brown to one looking directly down on it, and, like that of most ponds, imparts to the body of one bathing in it a yellowish tinge; but this water is of such crystalline purity that the body of the bather appears of an alabaster whiteness, still more unnatural, which, as the limbs are magnified and distorted withal, produces a monstrous effect, making fit studies for a Michael Angelo.

The water is so transparent that the bottom can easily be discerned at the depth of twenty-five or thirty feet. Paddling over it, you may see many feet beneath the surface the schools of perch and shiners, perhaps only an inch long, yet the former easily dis-

tinguished by their transverse bars, and you
think that they must be ascetic fish that find
a subsistence there. Once, in the winter,
many years ago, when I had been cutting
holes through the ice in order to catch pickerel, as I stepped ashore I tossed my axe
back on to the ice, but, as if some evil genius had directed it, it slid four or five rods
directly into one of the holes, where the
water was twenty-five feet deep. Out of
curiosity, I lay down on the ice and looked
through the hole, until I saw the axe a little
on one side, standing on its head, with its
helve erect and gently swaying to and fro
with the pulse of the pond ; and there it
might have stood erect and swaying till in
the course of time the handle rotted off, if
I had not disturbed it. Making another
hole directly over it with an ice chisel which
I had, and cutting down the longest birch
which I could find in the neighborhood with
my knife, I made a slip-noose, which I attached to its end, and, letting it down carefully, passed it over the knob of the handle,
and drew it by a line along the birch, and
so pulled the axe out again.

The shore is composed of a belt of smooth
rounded white stones like paving-stones, ex-

cepting one or two short sand beaches, and
is so steep that in many places a single leap
will carry you into water over your head;
and were it not for its remarkable transparency, that would be the last to be seen of
its bottom till it rose on the opposite side.
Some think it is bottomless. It is nowhere
muddy, and a casual observer would say
that there were no weeds at all in it; and
of noticeable plants, except in the little
meadows recently overflowed, which do not
properly belong to it, a closer scrutiny does
not detect a flag nor a bulrush, nor even a
lily, yellow or white, but only a few small
heart-leaves and potamogetons, and perhaps
a water-target or two; all which however a
bather might not perceive; and these plants
are clean and bright like the element they
grow in. The stones extend a rod or two
into the water, and then the bottom is pure
sand, except in the deepest parts, where
there is usually a little sediment, probably
from the decay of the leaves which have
been wafted on to it so many successive
falls, and a bright green weed is brought up
on anchors even in midwinter.

We have one other pond just like this,
White Pond, in Nine Acre Corner, about

two and a half miles westerly; but, though I am acquainted with most of the ponds within a dozen miles of this centre, I do not know a third of this pure and well-like character. Successive nations perchance have drank at, admired, and fathomed it, and passed away, and still its water is green and pellucid as ever. Not an intermitting spring! Perhaps on that spring morning when Adam and Eve were driven out of Eden Walden Pond was already in existence, and even then breaking up in a gentle spring rain accompanied with mist and a southerly wind, and covered with myriads of ducks and geese, which had not heard of the fall, when still such pure lakes sufficed them. Even then it had commenced to rise and fall, and had clarified its waters and colored them of the hue they now wear, and obtained a patent of Heaven to be the only Walden Pond in the world and distiller of celestial dews. Who knows in how many unremembered nations' literatures this has been the Castalian Fountain? or what nymphs presided over it in the Golden Age? It is a gem of the first water which Concord wears in her coronet.

Yet perchance the first who came to this

well have left some trace of their footsteps. I have been surprised to detect encircling the pond, even where a thick wood has just been cut down on the shore, a narrow shelf-like path in the steep hill-side, alternately rising and falling, approaching and receding from the water's edge, as old probably as the race of man here, worn by the feet of aboriginal hunters, and still from time to time unwittingly trodden by the present occupants of the land. This is particularly distinct to one standing on the middle of the pond in winter, just after a light snow has fallen, appearing as a clear undulating white line, unobscured by weeds and twigs, and very obvious a quarter of a mile off in many places where in summer it is hardly distinguishable close at hand. The snow reprints it, as it were, in clear white type alto-relievo. The ornamented grounds of villas which will one day be built here may still preserve some trace of this.

The pond rises and falls, but whether regularly or not, and within what period, nobody knows, though, as usual, many pretend to know. It is commonly higher in the winter and lower in the summer, though not corresponding to the general wet and dry-

ness. I can remember when it was a foot
or two lower, and also when it was at least
five feet higher, than when I lived by it.
There is a narrow sand-bar running into it,
with very deep water on one side, on which
I helped boil a kettle of chowder, some six
rods from the main shore, about the year
1824, which it has not been possible to do
for twenty - five years; and, on the other
hand, my friends used to listen with incre-
dulity when I told them, that a few years
later I was accustomed to fish from a boat
in a secluded cove in the woods, fifteen rods
from the only shore they knew, which place
was long since converted into a meadow.
But the pond has risen steadily for two
years, and now, in the summer of '52, is just
five feet higher than when I lived there, or
as high as it was thirty years ago, and fishing goes on again in the meadow. This
makes a difference of level, at the outside,
of six or seven feet; and yet the water shed
by the surrounding hills is insignificant in
amount, and this overflow must be referred
to causes which affect the deep springs.
This same summer the pond has begun to
fall again. It is remarkable that this fluctuation, whether periodical or not, appears

thus to require many years for its accomplishment. I have observed one rise and a part of two falls, and I expect that a dozen or fifteen years hence the water will again be as low as I have ever known it. Flints' Pond, a mile eastward, allowing for the disturbance occasioned by its inlets and outlets, and the smaller intermediate ponds also, sympathize with Walden, and recently attained their greatest height at the same time with the latter. The same is true, as far as my observation goes, of White Pond.

This rise and fall of Walden at long intervals serves this use at least; the water standing at this great height for a year or more, though it makes it difficult to walk round it, kills the shrubs and trees which have sprung up about its edge since the last rise, — pitch-pines, birches, alders, aspens, and others,— and, falling again, leaves an unobstructed shore; for, unlike many ponds and all waters which are subject to a daily tide, its shore is cleanest when the water is lowest. On the side of the pond next my house a row of pitch-pines, fifteen feet high, has been killed and tipped over as if by a lever, and thus a stop put to their encroachments; and their size indicates how many years have

elapsed since the last rise to this height. By
this fluctuation the pond asserts its title to a
shore, and thus the *shore* is *shorn*, and the
trees cannot hold it by right of possession.
These are the lips of the lake on which no
beard grows. It licks its chaps from time
to time. When the water is at its height,
the alders, willows, and maples send forth a
mass of fibrous red roots several feet long
from all sides of their stems in the water,
and to the height of three or four feet from
the ground, in the effort to maintain themselves; and I have known the high-blueberry
bushes about the shore, which commonly
produce no fruit, bear an abundant crop
under these circumstances.

Some have been puzzled to tell how the
shore became so regularly paved. My townsmen have all heard the tradition, the oldest
people tell me that they heard it in their
youth, that anciently the Indians were holding a pow-wow upon a hill here, which rose
as high into the heavens as the pond now
sinks deep into the earth, and they used
much profanity, as the story goes, though
this vice is one of which the Indians were
never guilty, and while they were thus engaged the hill shook and suddenly sank, and

only one old squaw, named Walden, escaped, and from her the pond was named. It has been conjectured that when the hill shook these stones rolled down its side and became the present shore. It is very certain, at any rate, that once there was no pond here, and now there is one ; and this Indian fable does not in any respect conflict with the account of that ancient settler whom I have mentioned, who remembers so well when he first came here with his divining rod, saw a thin vapor rising from the sward, and the hazel pointed steadily downward, and he concluded to dig a well here. As for the stones, many still think that they are hardly to be accounted for by the action of the waves on these hills ; but I observe that the surrounding hills are remarkably full of the same kind of stones, so that they have been obliged to pile them up in walls on both sides of the railroad cut nearest the pond ; and, moreover, there are most stones where the shore is most abrupt; so that, unfortunately, it is no longer a mystery to me. I detect the paver. If the name was not derived from that of some English locality, — Saffron Walden, for instance, — one might suppose that it was called originally *Walled-in* Pond.

The pond was my well ready dug. For
four months in the year its water is as cold
as it is pure at all times; and I think that
it is then as good as any, if not the best, in
the town. In the winter, all water which is
exposed to the air is colder than springs and
wells which are protected from it. The temperature of the pond water which had stood
in the room where I sat from five o'clock in
the afternoon till noon the next day, the
sixth of March, 1846, the thermometer having been up to 65° or 70° some of the time,
owing partly to the sun on the roof, was 42°,
or one degree colder than the water of one
of the coldest wells in the village just drawn.
The temperature of the Boiling Spring the
same day was 45°, or the warmest of any
water tried, though it is the coldest that I
know of in summer, when, beside, shallow
and stagnant surface water is not mingled
with it. Moreover, in summer, Walden
never becomes so warm as most water which
is exposed to the sun, on account of its
depth. In the warmest weather I usually
placed a pailful in my cellar, where it became cool in the night, and remained so during the day; though I also resorted to a
spring in the neighborhood. It was as good

when a week old as the day it was dipped,
and had no taste of the pump. Whoever
camps for a week in summer by the shore of
a pond, needs only bury a pail of water a
few feet deep in the shade of his camp to be
independent of the luxury of ice.

There have been caught in Walden pickerel, one weighing seven pounds, — to say
nothing of another which carried off a reel
with great velocity, which the fisherman
safely set down at eight pounds because he
did not see him, — perch and pouts, some
of each weighing over two pounds, shiners,
chivins or roach, (*Leuciscus pulchellus*,) a
very few breams, and a couple of eels, one
weighing four pounds, — I am thus particular because the weight of a fish is commonly
its only title to fame, and these are the only
eels I have heard of here ; — also, I have a
faint recollection of a little fish some five
inches long, with silvery sides and a greenish
back, somewhat dace-like in its character,
which I mention here chiefly to link my
facts to fable. Nevertheless, this pond is
not very fertile in fish. Its pickerel, though
not abundant, are its chief boast. I have
seen at one time lying on the ice pickerel of
at least three different kinds : a long **and**

shallow one, steel-colored, most like those caught in the river ; a bright golden kind, with greenish reflections and remarkably deep, which is the most common here ; and another, golden-colored, and shaped like the last, but peppered on the sides with small dark brown or black spots, intermixed with a few faint blood-red ones, very much like a trout. The specific name *reticulatus* would not apply to this ; it should be *guttatus* rather. These are all very firm fish, and weigh more than their size promises. The shiners, pouts, and perch also, and indeed all the fishes which inhabit this pond, are much cleaner, handsomer, and firmer fleshed than those in the river and most other ponds, as the water is purer, and they can easily be distinguished from them. Probably many ichthyologists would make new varieties of some of them. There are also a clean race of frogs and tortoises, and a few muscles in it ; muskrats and minks leave their traces about it, and occasionally a travelling mud-turtle visits it. Sometimes, when I pushed off my boat in the morning, I disturbed a great mud-turtle which had secreted himself under the boat in the night. Ducks and geese frequent it in the spring and fall, the white-bellied swallows (*Hi-rundo bicolor*) skim over it, and the peet-weets (*Totanus macularius*) "teter" along its stony shores all summer. I have some-times disturbed a fish-hawk sitting on a white-pine over the water ; but I doubt if it is ever profaned by the wing of a gull, like Fair Haven. At most, it tolerates one an-nual loon. These are all the animals of consequence which frequent it now.

You may see from a boat, in calm weather, near the sandy eastern shore, where the water is eight or ten feet deep, and also in some other parts of the pond, some circular heaps half a dozen feet in diameter by a foot in height, consisting of small stones less than a hen's egg in size, where all around is bare sand. At first you wonder if the Indians could have formed them on the ice for any purpose, and so, when the ice melted, they sank to the bottom ; but they are too regu-lar and some of them plainly too fresh for that. They are similar to those found in rivers ; but as there are no suckers nor lam-preys here, I know not by what fish they could be made. Perhaps they are the nests of the chivin. These lend a pleasing mys-tery to the bottom.

The shore is irregular enough not to be monotonous. I have in my mind's eye the western indented with deep bays, the bolder northern, and the beautifully scolloped southern shore, where successive capes overlap each other and suggest unexplored coves between. The forest has never so good a setting, nor is so distinctly beautiful, as when seen from the middle of a small lake amid hills which rise from the water's edge; for the water in which it is reflected not only makes the best foreground in such a case, but, with its winding shore, the most natural and agreeable boundary to it. There is no rawness nor imperfection in its edge there, as where the axe has cleared a part, or a cultivated field abuts on it. The trees have ample room to expand on the water side, and each sends forth its most vigorous branch in that direction. There Nature has woven a natural selvage, and the eye rises by just gradations from the low shrubs of the shore to the highest trees. There are few traces of man's hand to be seen. The water laves the shore as it did a thousand years ago.

A lake is the landscape's most beautiful and expressive feature. It is earth's eye;

looking into which the beholder measures the depth of his own nature. The fluviatile trees next the shore are the slender eyelashes which fringe it, and the wooded hills and cliffs around are its overhanging brows.

Standing on the smooth sandy beach at the east end of the pond, in a calm September afternoon, when a slight haze makes the opposite shore line indistinct, I have seen whence came the expression, " the glassy surface of a lake." When you invert your head, it looks like a thread of finest gossamer stretched across the valley, and gleaming against the distant pine woods, separating one stratum of the atmosphere from another. You would think that you could walk dry under it to the opposite hills, and that the swallows which skim over might perch on it. Indeed, they sometimes dive below the line, as it were by mistake, and are undeceived. As you look over the pond westward you are obliged to employ both your hands to defend your eyes against the reflected as well as the true sun, for they are equally bright ; and if, between the two, you survey its surface critically, it is literally as smooth as glass, except where the skater insects, at equal intervals scattered over its

whole extent, by their motions in the sun
produce the finest imaginable sparkle on it,
or, perchance, a duck plumes itself, or, as I
have said, a swallow skims so low as to touch
it. It may be that in the distance a fish
describes an arc of three or four feet in the
air, and there is one bright flash where it
emerges, and another where it strikes the
water; sometimes the whole silvery arc is
revealed; or here and there, perhaps, is a
thistle-down floating on its surface, which
the fishes dart at and so dimple it again.
It is like molten glass cooled but not congealed, and the few motes in it are pure and
beautiful like the imperfections in glass.
You may often detect a yet smoother and
darker water, separated from the rest as if
by an invisible cobweb, boom of the water
nymphs, resting on it. From a hill-top you
can see a fish leap in almost any part; for
not a pickerel or shiner picks an insect from
this smooth surface but it manifestly disturbs
the equilibrium of the whole lake. It is
wonderful with what elaborateness this
simple fact is advertised, — this piscine murder will out, — and from my distant perch
I distinguish the circling undulations when
they are half a dozen rods in diameter. You

can even detect a water - bug (*Gyrinus*)
ceaselessly progressing over the smooth surface a quarter of a mile off ; for they furrow
the water slightly, making a conspicuous
ripple bounded by two diverging lines, but
the skaters glide over it without rippling it
perceptibly.   When the surface is considerably agitated there are no skaters nor water-
bugs on it, but apparently, in calm days,
they leave their havens and adventurously
glide forth from the shore by short impulses
till they completely cover it.   It is a soothing employment, on one of those fine days in
the fall when all the warmth of the sun is
fully appreciated, to sit on a stump on such
a height as this, overlooking the pond, and
study the dimpling circles which are incessantly inscribed on its otherwise invisible
surface amid the reflected skies and trees.
Over this great expanse there is no disturbance but it is thus at once gently smoothed
away and assuaged, as, when a vase of water
is jarred, the trembling circles seek the shore
and all is smooth again.   Not a fish can
leap or an insect fall on the pond but it is
thus reported in circling dimples, in lines of
beauty, as it were the constant welling up of
its fountain, the gentle pulsing of its life,

the heaving of its breast. The thrills of joy
and thrills of pain are undistinguishable.
How peaceful the phenomena of the lake!
Again the works of man shine as in the
spring. Ay, every leaf and twig and stone
and cobweb sparkles now at mid-afternoon
as when covered with dew in a spring morning. Every motion of an oar or an insect
produces a flash of light; and if an oar falls,
how sweet the echo!

In such a day, in September or October,
Walden is a perfect forest mirror, set round
with stones as precious to my eye as if fewer
or rarer. Nothing so fair, so pure, and at
the same time so large, as a lake, perchance,
lies on the surface of the earth. Sky water.
It needs no fence. Nations come and go
without defiling it. It is a mirror which no
stone can crack, whose quicksilver will never
wear off, whose gilding Nature continually
repairs; no storms, no dust, can dim its surface ever fresh; — a mirror in which all
impurity presented to it sinks, swept and
dusted by the sun's hazy brush, — this the
light dust-cloth, — which retains no breath
that is breathed on it, but sends its own to
float as clouds high above its surface, and
be reflected in its bosom still.

A field of water betrays the spirit that is in the air. It is continually receiving new life and motion from above. It is intermediate in its nature between land and sky. On land only the grass and trees wave, but the water itself is rippled by the wind. I see where the breeze dashes across it by the streaks or flakes of light. It is remarkable that we can look down on its surface. We shall, perhaps, look down thus on the surface of air at length, and mark where a still subtler spirit sweeps over it.

The skaters and water-bugs finally disappear in the latter part of October, when the severe frosts have come; and then and in November, usually, in a calm day, there is absolutely nothing to ripple the surface. One November afternoon, in the calm at the end of a rain storm of several days' duration, when the sky was still completely overcast and the air was full of mist, I observed that the pond was remarkably smooth, so that it was difficult to distinguish its surface; though it no longer reflected the bright tints of October, but the sombre November colors of the surrounding hills. Though I passed over it as gently as possible, the slight undulations produced by my boat extended almost as far as I could see, and gave a ribbed appearance to the reflections. But, as I was looking over the surface, I saw here and there at a distance a faint glimmer, as if some skater insects which had escaped the frosts might be collected there, or, perchance, the surface, being so smooth, betrayed where a spring welled up from the bottom. Paddling gently to one of these places, I was surprised to find myself surrounded by myriads of small perch, about five inches long, of a rich bronze color in the green water, sporting there, and constantly rising to the surface and dimpling it, sometimes leaving bubbles on it. In such transparent and seemingly bottomless water, reflecting the clouds, I seemed to be floating through the air as in a balloon, and their swimming impressed me as a kind of flight or hovering, as if they were a compact flock of birds passing just beneath my level on the right or left, their fins, like sails, set all around them. There were many such schools in the pond, apparently improving the short season before winter would draw an icy shutter over their broad skylight, sometimes giving to the surface an appearance as if a slight breeze struck it, or a few rain-drops fell there. When I approached carelessly and alarmed them, they made a sudden plash and rippling with their tails, as if one had struck the water with a brushy bough, and instantly took refuge in the depths. At length the wind rose, the mist increased, and the waves began to run, and the perch leaped much higher than before, half out of water, a hundred black points, three inches long, at once above the surface. Even as late as the fifth of December, one year, I saw some dimples on the surface, and thinking it was going to rain hard immediately, the air being full of mist, I made haste to take my place at the oars and row homeward; already the rain seemed rapidly increasing, though I felt none on my cheek, and I anticipated a thorough soaking. But suddenly the dimples ceased, for they were produced by the perch, which the noise of my oars had scared into the depths, and I saw their schools dimly disappearing; so I spent a dry afternoon after all.

An old man who used to frequent this pond nearly sixty years ago, when it was dark with surrounding forests, tells me that in those days he sometimes saw it all alive

with ducks and other water fowl, and that
there were many eagles about it. He came
here a-fishing, and used an old log canoe
which he found on the shore. It was made
of two white-pine logs dug out and pinned
together, and was cut off square at the ends.
It was very clumsy, but lasted a great many
years before it became water-logged and
perhaps sank to the bottom. He did not
know whose it was; it belonged to the pond.
He used to make a cable for his anchor of
strips of hickory bark tied together. An
old man, a potter, who lived by the pond
before the Revolution, told him once that
there was an iron chest at the bottom, and
that he had seen it. Sometimes it would
come floating up to the shore; but when you
went toward it, it would go back into deep
water and disappear. I was pleased to hear
of the old log canoe, which took the place
of an Indian one of the same material but
more graceful construction, which perchance
had first been a tree on the bank, and then,
as it were, fell into the water, to float there
for a generation, the most proper vessel for
the lake. I remember that when I first
looked into these depths there were many
large trunks to be seen indistinctly lying on

the bottom, which had either been blown over formerly, or left on the ice at the last cutting, when wood was cheaper ; but now they have mostly disappeared.

When I first paddled a boat on Walden, it was completely surrounded by thick and lofty pine and oak woods, and in some of its coves grape - vines had run over the trees next the water and formed bowers under which a boat could pass. The hills which form its shores are so steep, and the woods on them were then so high, that, as you looked down from the west end, it had the appearance of an amphitheatre for some kind of sylvan spectacle. I have spent many an hour, when I was younger, floating over its surface as the zephyr willed, having paddled my boat to the middle, and lying on my back across the seats, in a summer fore-noon, dreaming awake, until I was aroused by the boat touching the sand, and I arose to see what shore my fates had impelled me to ; days when idleness was the most attrac-tive and productive industry. Many a fore-noon have I stolen away, preferring to spend thus the most valued part of the day ; for I was rich, if not in money, in sunny hours and summer days, and spent them lavishly; nor do I regret that I did not waste more of them in the workshop or the teacher's desk. But since I left those shores the woodchoppers have still further laid them waste, and now for many a year there will be no more rambling through the aisles of the wood, with occasional vistas through which you see the water. My Muse may be excused if she is silent henceforth. How can you expect the birds to sing when their groves are cut down?

Now the trunks of trees on the bottom, and the old log canoe, and the dark surrounding woods, are gone, and the villagers, who scarcely know where it lies, instead of going to the pond to bathe or drink, are thinking to bring its water, which should be as sacred as the Ganges at least, to the village in a pipe, to wash their dishes with! — to earn their Walden by the turning of a cock or drawing of a plug! That devilish Iron Horse, whose ear-rending neigh is heard throughout the town, has muddied the Boiling Spring with his foot, and he it is that has browsed off all the woods on Walden shore, that Trojan horse, with a thousand men in his belly, introduced by mercenary Greeks! Where is the country's champion, the Moore of Moore Hall, to meet him at the Deep Cut and thrust an avenging lance between the ribs of the bloated pest?

Nevertheless, of all the characters I have known, perhaps Walden wears best, and best preserves its purity. Many men have been likened to it, but few deserve that honor. Though the woodchoppers have laid bare first this shore and then that, and the Irish have built their sties by it, and the railroad has infringed on its border, and the ice-men have skimmed it once, it is itself unchanged, the same water which my youthful eyes fell on; all the change is in me. It has not acquired one permanent wrinkle after all its ripples. It is perennially young, and I may stand and see a swallow dip apparently to pick an insect from its surface as of yore. It struck me again to-night, as if I had not seen it almost daily for more than twenty years, — Why, here is Walden, the same woodland lake that I discovered so many years ago; where a forest was cut down last winter another is springing up by its shore as lustily as ever; the same thought is welling up to its surface that was then; it is the same liquid joy and happiness to itself and its Maker, ay, and it *may* be to me.

It is the work of a brave man surely, in whom there was no guile ! He rounded this water with his hand, deepened and clarified it in his thought, and in his will bequeathed it to Concord. I see by its face that it is visited by the same reflection ; and I can almost say, Walden, is it you ?

> It is no dream of mine,
> To ornament a line ;
> I cannot come nearer to God and Heaven
> Than I live to Walden even.
> I am its stony shore,
> And the breeze that passes o'er ;
> In the hollow of my hand
> Are its water and its sand,
> And its deepest resort
> Lies high in my thought.

The cars never pause to look at it ; yet I fancy that the engineers and firemen and brakemen, and those passengers who have a season ticket and see it often, are better men for the sight. The engineer does not forget at night, or his nature does not, that he has beheld this vision of serenity and purity once at least during the day. Though seen but once, it helps to wash out State-street and the engine's soot. One proposes that it be called " God's Drop."

I have said that Walden has no visible in-

let nor outlet, but it is on the one hand dis-
tantly and indirectly related to Flints' Pond,
which is more elevated, by a chain of small
ponds coming from that quarter, and on the
other directly and manifestly to Concord
River, which is lower, by a similar chain of
ponds through which in some other geolog-
ical period it may have flowed, and by a little digging, which God forbid, it can be
made to flow thither again.   If by living
thus reserved and austere, like a hermit in
the woods, so long, it has acquired such wonderful purity, who would not regret that the
comparatively impure waters of Flints' Pond
should be mingled with it, or itself should
ever go to waste its sweetness in the ocean
wave ?

Flints', or Sandy Pond, in Lincoln, our
greatest lake and inland sea, lies about a
mile east of Walden.   It is much larger,
being said to contain one hundred and ninety-seven acres, and is more fertile in fish ;
but it is comparatively shallow, and not remarkably pure.   A walk through the woods
thither was often my recreation.   It was
worth the while, if only to feel the wind
blow on your cheek freely, and see the waves

run, and remember the life of mariners. I went a-chestnutting there in the fall, on windy days, when the nuts were dropping into the water and were washed to my feet; and one day, as I crept along its sedgy shore, the fresh spray blowing in my face, I came upon the mouldering wreck of a boat, the sides gone, and hardly more than the impression of its flat bottom left amid the rushes; yet its model was sharply defined, as if it were a large decayed pad, with its veins. It was as impressive a wreck as one could imagine on the sea-shore, and had as good a moral. It is by this time mere vegetable mould and undistinguishable pond shore, through which rushes and flags have pushed up. I used to admire the ripple marks on the sandy bottom, at the north end of this pond, made firm and hard to the feet of the wader by the pressure of the water, and the rushes which grew in Indian file, in waving lines, corresponding to these marks, rank behind rank, as if the waves had planted them. There also I have found, in considerable quantities, curious balls, composed apparently of fine grass or roots, of pipewort perhaps, from half an inch to four inches in diameter, and perfectly spherical.

These wash back and forth in shallow water
on a sandy bottom, and are sometimes cast
on the shore.   They are either solid grass,
or have a little sand in the middle.   At first
you would say that they were formed by the
action of the waves, like a pebble ; yet the
smallest are made of equally coarse materials, half an inch long, and they are produced
only at one season of the year.   Moreover,
the waves, I suspect, do not so much construct as wear down a material which has
already acquired consistency.   They preserve
their form when dry for an indefinite period.

Flints' Pond!   Such is the poverty of
our nomenclature.   What right had the unclean and stupid farmer, whose farm abutted
on this sky water, whose shores he has ruthlessly laid bare, to give his name to it?
Some skin-flint, who loved better the reflecting surface of a dollar, or a bright cent, in
which he could see his own brazen face;
who regarded even the wild ducks which
settled in it as trespassers; his fingers grown
into crooked and horny talons from the long
habit of grasping harpy-like ; — so it is not
named for me.   I go not there to see him
nor to hear of him ; who never *saw* it, who
never bathed in it, who never loved it, who

never protected it, who never spoke a good
word for it, nor thanked God that he had
made it. Rather let it be named from the
fishes that swim in it, the wild fowl or quadrupeds which frequent it, the wild flowers
which grow by its shores, or some wild man
or child the thread of whose history is inter-
woven with its own; not from him who
could show no title to it but the deed which
a like-minded neighbor or legislature gave
him, — him who thought only of its money
value; whose presence perchance cursed all
the shore; who exhausted the land around
it, and would fain have exhausted the waters
within it; who regretted only that it was
not English hay or cranberry meadow, —
there was nothing to redeem it, forsooth, in
his eyes, — and would have drained and sold
it for the mud at its bottom. It did not
turn his mill, and it was no *privilege* to him
to behold it. I respect not his labors, his
farm where everything has its price, who
would carry the landscape, who would carry
his God, to market, if he could get anything for him; who goes to market *for* his
god as it is; on whose farm nothing grows
free, whose fields bear no crops, whose meadows no flowers, whose trees no fruits, but

dollars; who loves not the beauty of his fruits, whose fruits are not ripe for him till they are turned to dollars. Give me the poverty that enjoys true wealth. Farmers are respectable and interesting to me in proportion as they are poor, — poor farmers. A model farm! where the house stands like a fungus in a muck-heap, chambers for men, horses, oxen, and swine, cleansed and uncleansed, all contiguous to one another! Stocked with men! A great grease-spot, redolent of manures and buttermilk! Under a high state of cultivation, being manured with the hearts and brains of men! As if you were to raise your potatoes in the churchyard! Such is a model farm.

No, no; if the fairest features of the landscape are to be named after men, let them be the noblest and worthiest men alone. Let our lakes receive as true names at least as the Icarian Sea, where "still the shore" a "brave attempt resounds."

Goose Pond, of small extent, is on my way to Flints'; Fair Haven, an expansion of Concord River, said to contain some seventy acres, is a mile south-west; and White Pond, of about forty acres, is a mile and a half be-

yond Fair Haven. This is my lake country.
These, with Concord River, are my water
privileges; and night and day, year in year
out, they grind such grist as I carry to
them.

Since the wood-cutters, and the railroad,
and I myself have profaned Walden, perhaps the most attractive, if not the most
beautiful, of all our lakes, the gem of the
woods, is White Pond; — a poor name from
its commonness, whether derived from the
remarkable purity of its waters or the color
of its sands. In these as in other respects,
however, it is a lesser twin of Walden.
They are so much alike that you would say
they must be connected under ground. It
has the same stony shore, and its waters are
of the same hue. As at Walden, in sultry
dog-day weather, looking down through the
woods on some of its bays which are not so
deep but that the reflection from the bottom
tinges them, its waters are of a misty bluish-
green or glaucous color. Many years since
I used to go there to collect the sand by
cart-loads, to make sand-paper with, and I
have continued to visit it ever since. One
who frequents it proposes to call it Virid
Lake. Perhaps it might be called Yellow-

Pine Lake, from the following circumstance.
About fifteen years ago you could see the
top of a pitch-pine, of the kind called yellow-pine hereabouts, though it is not a distinct species, projecting above the surface in
deep water, many rods from the shore. It
was even supposed by some that the pond
had sunk, and this was one of the primitive
forest that formerly stood there. I find that
even so long ago as 1792, in a " Topograph-
ical Description of the Town of Concord,"
by one of its citizens, in the Collections of
the Massachusetts Historical Society, the
author, after speaking of Walden and White
Ponds, adds : " In the middle of the latter
may be seen, when the water is very low, a
tree which appears as if it grew in the place
where it now stands, although the roots are
fifty feet below the surface of the water ;
the top of this tree is broken off, and at that
place measures fourteen inches in diameter."
In the spring of '49 I talked with the man
who lives nearest the pond in Sudbury, who
told me that it was he who got out this tree
ten or fifteen years before. As near as he
could remember, it stood twelve or fifteen
rods from the shore, where the water was
thirty or forty feet deep. It was in the win-

ter, and he had been getting out ice in the forenoon, and had resolved that in the afternoon, with the aid of his neighbors, he would take out the old yellow-pine. He sawed a channel in the ice toward the shore, and hauled it over and along and out on to the ice with oxen; but, before he had gone far in his work, he was surprised to find that it was wrong end upward, with the stumps of the branches pointing down, and the small end firmly fastened in the sandy bottom. It was about a foot in diameter at the big end, and he had expected to get a good saw-log, but it was so rotten as to be fit only for fuel, if for that. He had some of it in his shed then. There were marks of an axe and of woodpeckers on the butt. He thought that it might have been a dead tree on the shore, but was finally blown over into the pond, and after the top had become water-logged, while the butt-end was still dry and light, had drifted out and sunk wrong end up. His father, eighty years old, could not remember when it was not there. Several pretty large logs may still be seen lying on the bottom, where, owing to the undulation of the surface, they look like huge water snakes in motion.

This pond has rarely been profaned by a boat, for there is little in it to tempt a fisherman. Instead of the white lily, which requires mud, or the common sweet flag, the blue flag (*Iris versicolor*) grows thinly in the pure water, rising from the stony bottom all around the shore, where it is visited by humming birds in June; and the color both of its bluish blades and its flowers and especially their reflections, are in singular harmony with the glaucous water.

White Pond and Walden are great crystals on the surface of the earth, Lakes of Light. If they were permanently congealed, and small enough to be clutched, they would, perchance, be carried off by slaves, like precious stones, to adorn the heads of emperors; but being liquid, and ample, and secured to us and our successors forever, we disregard them, and run after the diamond of Kohinoor. They are too pure to have a market value; they contain no muck. How much more beautiful than our lives, how much more transparent than our characters, are they! We never learned meanness of them. How much fairer than the pool before the farmer's door, in which his ducks swim! Hither the clean wild ducks come. Nature has no human inhabitant who appreciates her. The birds with their plumage and their notes are in harmony with the flowers, but what youth or maiden conspires with the wild luxuriant beauty of Nature? She flourishes most alone, far from the towns where they reside. Talk of heaven! ye disgrace earth.

X.

BAKER FARM.

SOMETIMES I rambled to pine groves, standing like temples, or like fleets at sea, full-rigged, with wavy boughs, and rippling with light, so soft and green and shady that the Druids would have forsaken their oaks to worship in them ; or to the cedar wood beyond Flints' Pond, where the trees, covered with hoary blue berries, spiring higher and higher, are fit to stand before Valhalla, and the creeping juniper covers the ground with wreaths full of fruit; or to swamps where the usnea lichen hangs in festoons from the white-spruce trees, and toadstools, round tables of the swamp gods, cover the ground, and more beautiful fungi adorn the stumps, like butterflies or shells, vegetable winkles ; where the swamp-pink and dogwood grow, the red alder-berry glows like eyes of imps, the waxwork grooves and crushes the hardest woods in its folds, and the wild-holly berries make the beholder for-

get his home with their beauty, and he is
dazzled and tempted by nameless other wild
forbidden fruits, too fair for mortal taste.
Instead of calling on some scholar, I paid
many a visit to particular trees, of kinds
which are rare in this neighborhood, standing far away in the middle of some pasture,
or in the depths of a wood or swamp, or on
a hill-top; such as the black-birch, of which
we have some handsome specimens two feet
in diameter; its cousin, the yellow-birch,
with its loose golden vest, perfumed like the
first; the beech, which has so neat a bole
and beautifully lichen-painted, perfect in all
its details, of which, excepting scattered
specimens, I know but one small grove of
sizable trees left in the township, supposed
by some to have been planted by the pigeons
that were once baited with beech nuts near
by; it is worth the while to see the silver
grain sparkle when you split this wood; the
bass; the hornbeam; the *celtis occidentalis*,
or false elm, of which we have but one well-
grown; some taller mast of a pine, a shingle
tree, or a more perfect hemlock than usual,
standing like a pagoda in the midst of the
woods; and many others I could mention.
These were the shrines I visited both summer and winter.

Once it chanced that I stood in the very abutment of a rainbow's arch, which filled the lower stratum of the atmosphere, tinging the grass and leaves around, and dazzling me as if I looked through colored crystal. It was a lake of rainbow light, in which, for a short while, I lived like a dolphin. If it had lasted longer it might have tinged my employments and life. As I walked on the railroad causeway, I used to wonder at the halo of light around my shadow, and would fain fancy myself one of the elect. One who visited me declared that the shadows of some Irishmen before him had no halo about them, that it was only natives that were so distinguished. Benvenuto Cellini tells us in his memoirs, that, after a certain terrible dream or vision which he had during his confinement in the castle of St. Angelo a resplendent light appeared over the shadow of his head at morning and evening, whether he was in Italy or France, and it was particularly conspicuous when the grass was moist with dew. This was probably the same phenomenon to which I have referred, which is especially observed in the morning, but also at other times, and even by moonlight. Though a constant one, it is not commonly noticed, and, in the case of an excitable imagination like Cellini's, it would be basis enough for superstition. Beside, he tells us that he showed it to very few. But are they not indeed distinguished who are conscious that they are regarded at all?

I set out one afternoon to go a-fishing to Fair Haven, through the woods, to eke out my scanty fare of vegetables. My way led through Pleasant Meadow, an adjunct of the Baker Farm, that retreat of which a poet has since sung, beginning, —

> "Thy entry is a pleasant field,
>   Which some mossy fruit trees yield
>   Partly to a ruddy brook,
>   By gliding musquash undertook,
>   And mercurial trout,
>   Darting about."

I thought of living there before I went to Walden. I "hooked" the apples, leaped the brook, and scared the musquash and the trout. It was one of those afternoons which seem indefinitely long before one, in which many events may happen, a large portion of our natural life, though it was already half spent when I started. By the way there came up a shower, which compelled me to stand half an hour under a pine, piling boughs over my head, and wearing my handkerchief for a shed ; and when at length I had made one cast over the pickerel-weed, standing up to my middle in water, I found myself suddenly in the shadow of a cloud, and the thunder began to rumble with such emphasis that I could do no more than listen to it. The gods must be proud, thought I, with such forked flashes to rout a poor unarmed fisherman. So I made haste for shelter to the nearest hut, which stood half a mile from any road, but so much the nearer to the pond, and had long been uninhabited : —

> "And here a poet builded,
>   In the completed years,
>   For behold a trivial cabin
>   That to destruction steers."

So the Muse fables. But therein, as I found, dwelt now John Field, an Irishman, and his wife, and several children, from the broad-faced boy who assisted his father at his work, and now came running by his side from the bog to escape the rain, to the wrinkled, sibyl-like, cone-headed infant that sat upon its father's knee as in the palaces of nobles, and looked out from its home in the

midst of wet and hunger inquisitively upon
the stranger, with the privilege of infancy,
not knowing but it was the last of a noble
line, and the hope and cynosure of the
world, instead of John Field's poor starve-
ling brat. There we sat together under that
part of the roof which leaked the least, while
it showered and thundered without. I had
sat there many times of old before the ship
was built that floated this family to America.
An honest, hard-working, but shiftless man
plainly was John Field; and his wife, she
too was brave to cook so many successive
dinners in the recesses of that lofty stove;
with round greasy face and bare breast, still
thinking to improve her condition one day;
with the never absent mop in one hand, and
yet no effects of it visible anywhere. The
chickens, which had also taken shelter here
from the rain, stalked about the room like
members of the family, too humanized methought to roast well. They stood and looked
in my eye or pecked at my shoe significantly.
Meanwhile my host told me his story, how
hard he worked " bogging " for a neighboring farmer, turning up a meadow with a
spade or bog hoe at the rate of ten dollars
an acre and the use of the land with manure

for one year, and his little broad-faced son
worked cheerfully at his father's side the
while, not knowing how poor a bargain the
latter had made. I tried to help him with
my experience, telling him that he was one
of my nearest neighbors, and that I too, who
came a-fishing here, and looked like a loafer,
was getting my living like himself; that I
lived in a tight, light, and clean house,
which hardly cost more than the annual rent
of such a ruin as his commonly amounts to ;
and how, if he chose, he might in a month
or two build himself a palace of his own ;
that I did not use tea, nor coffee, nor butter,
nor milk, nor fresh meat, and so did not
have to work to get them ; again, as I did
not work hard, I did not have to eat hard,
and it cost me but a trifle for my food ; but
as he began with tea, and coffee, and butter,
and milk, and beef, he had to work hard to
pay for them, and when he had worked hard
he had to eat hard again to repair the waste
of his system, — and so it was as broad as
it was long, indeed it was broader than it
was long, for he was discontented and wasted
his life into the bargain ; and yet he had
rated it as a gain in coming to America,
that here you could get tea, and coffee, and

meat every day. But the only true America
is that country where you are at liberty to
pursue such a mode of life as may enable
you to do without these, and where the state
does not endeavor to compel you to sustain
the slavery and war and other superfluous
expenses which directly or indirectly result
from the use of such things. For I pur-
posely talked to him as if he were a philosopher, or desired to be one. I should be glad
if all the meadows on the earth were left in
a wild state, if that were the consequence of
men's beginning to redeem themselves. A
man will not need to study history to find
out what is best for his own culture. But
alas! the culture of an Irishman is an enterprise to be undertaken with a sort of
moral bog hoe. I told him, that as he
worked so hard at bogging, he required
thick boots and stout clothing, which yet
were soon soiled and worn out, but I wore
light shoes and thin clothing, which cost not
half so much, though he might think that I
was dressed like a gentleman, (which, however, was not the case,) and in an hour or
two, without labor, but as a recreation, I
could, if I wished, catch as many fish as I
should want for two days, or earn enough

money to support me a week. If he and
his family would live simply, they might all
go a-huckleberrying in the summer for their
amusement. John heaved a sigh at this,
and his wife stared with arms a-kimbo, and
both appeared to be wondering if they had
capital enough to begin such a course with,
or arithmetic enough to carry it through. It
was sailing by dead reckoning to them, and
they saw not clearly how to make their port
so; therefore I suppose they still take life
bravely, after their fashion, face to face,
giving it tooth and nail, not having skill to
split its massive columns with any fine entering wedge, and rout it in detail; — thinking to deal with it roughly, as one should
handle a thistle. But they fight at an over-
whelming disadvantage, — living, John Field,
alas! without arithmetic, and failing so.

"Do you ever fish?" I asked. "O yes,
I catch a mess now and then when I am
lying by; good perch I catch." "What's
your bait?" "I catch shiners with fish-
worms, and bait the perch with them."
"You'd better go now, John," said his
wife, with glistening and hopeful face; but
John demurred.

The shower was now over, and a rainbow

above the eastern woods promised a fair
evening ; so I took my departure. When I
had got without I asked for a dish, hoping
to get a sight of the well bottom, to complete
my survey of the premises ; but there, alas !
are shallows and quicksands, and rope broken withal, and bucket irrecoverable. Meanwhile the right culinary vessel was selected,
water was seemingly distilled, and after con-
sultation and long delay passed out to the
thirsty one, — not yet suffered to cool, not
yet to settle. Such gruel sustains life here,
I thought ; so, shutting my eyes, and exclud-
ing the motes by a skilfully directed under-
current, I drank to genuine hospitality the
heartiest draught I could. I am not squeamish in such cases when manners are concerned.

As I was leaving the Irishman's roof after the rain, bending my steps again to the
pond, my haste to catch pickerel, wading in
retired meadows, in sloughs and bog-holes,
in forlorn and savage places, appeared for
an instant trivial to me who had been sent
to school and college ; but as I ran down
the hill toward the reddening west, with the
rainbow over my shoulder, and some faint
tinkling sounds borne to my ear through the

cleansed air, from I know not what quarter, my Good Genius seemed to say, — Go fish and hunt far and wide day by day, — farther and wider, — and rest thee by many brooks and hearth-sides without misgiving. Remember thy Creator in the days of thy youth. Rise free from care before the dawn, and seek adventures. Let the noon find thee by other lakes, and the night overtake thee everywhere at home. There are no larger fields than these, no worthier games than may here be played. Grow wild according to thy nature, like these sedges and brakes, which will never become English hay. Let the thunder rumble ; what if it threaten ruin to farmers' crops ? that is not its errand to thee. Take shelter under the cloud, while they flee to carts and sheds. Let not to get a living be thy trade, but thy sport. Enjoy the land, but own it not. Through want of enterprise and faith men are where they are, buying and selling, and spending their lives like serfs.

O Baker Farm !

> " Landscape where the richest element
> Is a little sunshine innocent." . . ,

> " No one runs to revel
> On thy rail-fenced lea." . . .

" Debate with no man hast thou,
    With questions art never perplexed,
  As tame at the first sight as now,
    In thy plain russet gabardine dressed." . . .

" Come ye who love,
    And ye who hate,
  Children of the Holy Dove,
    And Guy Faux of the state,
  And hang conspiracies
  From the tough rafters of the trees ! "

Men come tamely home at night only from
the next field or street, where their household echoes haunt, and their life pines because it breathes its own breath over again ;
their shadows morning and evening reach
farther than their daily steps. We should
come home from far, from adventures, and
perils, and discoveries every day, with new
experience and character.

Before I had reached the pond some fresh
impulse had brought out John Field, with
altered mind, letting go " bogging " ere this
sunset. But he, poor man, disturbed only
a couple of fins while I was catching a fair
string, and he said it was his luck ; but
when we changed seats in the boat luck
changed seats too. Poor John Field ! — I
trust he does not read this, unless he will
improve by it, — thinking to live by some

derivative old country mode in this primitive
new country, — to catch perch with shiners.
It is good bait sometimes, I allow. With
his horizon all his own, yet he a poor man,
born to be poor, with his inherited Irish poverty or poor life, his Adam's grandmother
and boggy ways, not to rise in this world, he
nor his posterity, till their wading webbed
bog-trotting feet get *talaria* to their heels.

XI.

As I came home through the woods with my string of fish, trailing my pole, it being now quite dark, I caught a glimpse of a woodchuck stealing across my path, and felt a strange thrill of savage delight, and was strongly tempted to seize and devour him raw; not that I was hungry then, except for that wildness which he represented. Once or twice, however, while I lived at the pond, I found myself ranging the woods, like a half-starved hound, with a strange abandonment, seeking some kind of venison which I might devour, and no morsel could have been too savage for me. The wildest scenes had become unaccountably familiar. I found in myself, and still find, an instinct toward a higher, or, as it is named, spiritual life, as do most men, and another toward a primitive rank and savage one, and I reverence them both. I love the wild not less than the good. The wildness and adventure that are in fishing still recommended it to me. I like sometimes to take rank hold on life and spend my day more as the animals do. Perhaps I have owed to this employment and to hunting, when quite young, my closest acquaintance with Nature. They early introduce us to and detain us in scenery with which otherwise, at that age, we should have little acquaintance. Fishermen, hunters, woodchoppers, and others, spending their lives in the fields and woods, in a peculiar sense a part of Nature themselves, are often in a more favorable mood for observing her, in the intervals of their pursuits, than philosophers or poets even, who approach her with expectation. She is not afraid to exhibit herself to them. The traveller on the prairie is naturally a hunter, on the head waters of the Missouri and Columbia a trapper, and at the Falls of St. Mary a fisherman. He who is only a traveller learns things at second-hand and by the halves, and is poor authority. We are most interested when science reports what those men already know practically or instinctively, for that alone is a true *humanity*, or account of human experience.

They mistake who assert that the Yankee

has few amusements, because he has not so many public holidays, and men and boys do not play so many games as they do in England, for here the more primitive but solitary amusements of hunting, fishing, and the like have not yet given place to the former. Almost every New England boy among my contemporaries shouldered a fowling piece between the ages of ten and fourteen ; and his hunting and fishing grounds were not limited, like the preserves of an English nobleman, but were more boundless even than those of a savage. No wonder, then, that he did not oftener stay to play on the common. But already a change is taking place, owing, not to an increased humanity, but to an increased scarcity of game, for perhaps the hunter is the greatest friend of the animals hunted, not excepting the Humane Society.

Moreover, when at the pond, I wished sometimes to add fish to my fare for variety. I have actually fished from the same kind of necessity that the first fishers did. Whatever humanity I might conjure up against it was all factitious, and concerned my philosophy more than my feelings. I speak of fishing only now, for I had long

felt differently about fowling, and sold my
gun before I went to the woods. Not that
I am less humane than others, but I did not
perceive that my feelings were much affected. I did not pity the fishes nor the
worms. This was habit. As for fowling,
during the last years that I carried a gun
my excuse was that I was studying ornithology, and sought only new or rare birds.
But I confess that I am now inclined to
think that there is a finer way of studying
ornithology than this. It requires so much
closer attention to the habits of the birds,
that, if for that reason only, I have been
willing to omit the gun. Yet notwithstanding the objection on the score of humanity,
I am compelled to doubt if equally valuable
sports are ever substituted for these; and
when some of my friends have asked me
anxiously about their boys, whether they
should let them hunt, I have answered, yes,
— remembering that it was one of the best
parts of my education, — *make* them hunters, though sportsmen only at first, if possible, mighty hunters at last, so that they
shall not find game large enough for them
in this or any vegetable wilderness, — hunters as well as fishers of men. Thus far I
am of the opinion of Chaucer's nun, who

" yave not of the text a pulled hen
That saith that hunters ben not holy men."

There is a period in the history of the individual, as of the race, when the hunters
are the " best men," as the Algonquins
called them. We cannot but pity the boy
who has never fired a gun ; he is no more
humane, while his education has been sadly
neglected. This was my answer with respect to those youths who were bent on
this pursuit, trusting that they would soon
outgrow it. No humane being, past the
thoughtless age of boyhood, will wantonly
murder any creature, which holds its life by
the same tenure that he does. The hare in
its extremity cries like a child. I warn you,
mothers, that my sympathies do not always
make the usual phil-*anthropic* distinctions.

Such is oftenest the young man's introduction to the forest, and the most original
part of himself. He goes thither at first as
a hunter and fisher, until at last, if he has
the seeds of a better life in him, he distinguishes his proper objects, as a poet or
naturalist it may be, and leaves the gun and
fish-pole behind. The mass of men are still
and always young in this respect. In some
countries a hunting parson is no uncommon

sight. Such a one might make a good shepherd's dog, but is far from being the Good
Shepherd. I have been surprised to consider that the only obvious employment, except wood-chopping, ice-cutting, or the like
business, which ever to my knowledge detained at Walden Pond for a whole half day
any of my fellow-citizens, whether fathers or
children of the town, with just one exception, was fishing. Commonly they did not
think that they were lucky, or well paid for
their time, unless they got a long string of
fish, though they had the opportunity of seeing the pond all the while. They might go
there a thousand times before the sediment
of fishing would sink to the bottom and
leave their purpose pure ; but no doubt such
a clarifying process would be going on all
the while. The governor and his council
faintly remember the pond, for they went
a-fishing there when they were boys ; but
now they are too old and dignified to go
a-fishing, and so they know it no more forever. Yet even they expect to go to heaven
at last. If the legislature regards it, it is
chiefly to regulate the number of hooks to
be used there ; but they know nothing about
the hook of hooks with which to angle for

the pond itself, impaling the legislature for a bait. Thus, even in civilized communities, the embryo man passes through the hunter stage of development.

I have found repeatedly, of late years, that I cannot fish without falling a little in self-respect. I have tried it again and again. I have skill at it, and, like many of my fellows, a certain instinct for it, which revives from time to time, but always when I have done I feel that it would have been better if I had not fished. I think that I do not mistake. It is a faint intimation, yet so are the first streaks of morning. There is unquestionably this instinct in me which belongs to the lower orders of creation ; yet with every year I am less a fisherman, though without more humanity or even wisdom ; at present I am no fisherman at all. But I see that if I were to live in a wilderness I should again be tempted to become a fisher and hunter in earnest. Beside, there is something essentially unclean about this diet and all flesh, and I began to see where housework commences, and whence the endeavor, which costs so much, to wear a tidy and respectable appearance each day, to keep the house sweet and free from all ill odors and sights. Having been my own butcher and scullion and cook, as well as the gentleman for whom the dishes were served up, I can speak from an unusually complete experience. The practical objection to animal food in my case was its uncleanness; and besides, when I had caught and cleaned and cooked and eaten my fish, they seemed not to have fed me essentially. It was insignificant and unnecessary, and cost more than it came to. A little bread or a few potatoes would have done as well, with less trouble and filth. Like many of my contemporaries, I had rarely for many years used animal food, or tea, or coffee, etc.; not so much because of any ill effects which I had traced to them, as because they were not agreeable to my imagination. The repugnance to animal food is not the effect of experience, but is an instinct. It appeared more beautiful to live low and fare hard in many respects; and though I never did so, I went far enough to please my imagination. I believe that every man who has ever been earnest to preserve his higher or poetic faculties in the best condition has been particularly inclined to abstain from animal food, and from much food of any kind. It is a significant fact,

stated by entomologists, I find it in Kirby
and Spence, that " some insects in their perfect state, though furnished with organs of
feeding, make no use of them ; " and they
lay it down as " a general rule, that almost
all insects in this state eat much less than
in that of larvæ. The voracious caterpillar
when transformed into a butterfly," . . .
" and the gluttonous maggot when become
a fly," content themselves with a drop or two
of honey or some other sweet liquid. The
abdomen under the wings of the butterfly
still represents the larva. This is the tid-
bit which tempts his insectivorous fate. The
gross feeder is a man in the larva state ; and
there are whole nations in that condition,
nations without fancy or imagination, whose
vast abdomens betray them.

It is hard to provide and cook so simple
and clean a diet as will not offend the imagination ; but this, I think, is to be fed when
we feed the body ; they should both sit down
at the same table. Yet perhaps this may be
done. The fruits eaten temperately need
not make us ashamed of our appetites, nor
interrupt the worthiest pursuits. But put
an extra condiment into your dish, and it
will poison you. It is not worth the while

to live by rich cookery. Most men would feel shame if caught preparing with their own hands precisely such a dinner, whether of animal or vegetable food, as is every day prepared for them by others. Yet till this is otherwise we are not civilized, and, if gentlemen and ladies, are not true men and women. This certainly suggests what change is to be made. It may be vain to ask why the imagination will not be reconciled to flesh and fat. I am satisfied that it is not. Is it not a reproach that man is a carnivorous animal? True, he can and does live, in a great measure, by preying on other animals; but this is a miserable way, — as any one who will go to snaring rabbits, or slaughtering lambs, may learn, — and he will be regarded as a benefactor of his race who shall teach man to confine himself to a more innocent and wholesome diet. Whatever my own practice may be, I have no doubt that it is a part of the destiny of the human race, in its gradual improvement, to leave off eating animals, as surely as the savage tribes have left off eating each other when they came in contact with the more civilized.

If one listens to the faintest but constant

suggestions of his genius, which are certainly
true, he sees not to what extremes, or even
insanity, it may lead him ; and yet that way,
as he grows more resolute and faithful, his
road lies. The faintest assured objection
which one healthy man feels will at length
prevail over the arguments and customs of
mankind. No man ever followed his genius
till it misled him. Though the result were
bodily weakness, yet perhaps no one can say
that the consequences were to be regretted,
for these were a life in conformity to higher
principles. If the day and the night are
such that you greet them with joy, and life
emits a fragrance like flowers and sweet-
scented herbs, is more elastic, more starry,
more immortal, — that is your success. All
nature is your congratulation, and you have
cause momentarily to bless yourself. The
greatest gains and values are farthest from
being appreciated. We easily come to doubt
if they exist. We soon forget them. They
are the highest reality. Perhaps the facts
most astounding and most real are never
communicated by man to man. The true
harvest of my daily life is somewhat as in-
tangible and indescribable as the tints of
morning or evening. It is a little star-dust

caught, a segment of the rainbow which I have clutched.

Yet, for my part, I was never unusually squeamish; I could sometimes eat a fried rat with a good relish, if it were necessary. I am glad to have drunk water so long, for the same reason that I prefer the natural sky to an opium-eater's heaven. I would fain keep sober always; and there are infinite degrees of drunkenness. I believe that water is the only drink for a wise man; wine is not so noble a liquor; and think of dashing the hopes of a morning with a cup of warm coffee, or of an evening with a dish of tea! Ah, how low I fall when I am tempted by them! Even music may be intoxicating. Such apparently slight causes destroyed Greece and Rome, and will destroy England and America. Of all ebriosity, who does not prefer to be intoxicated by the air he breathes? I have found it to be the most serious objection to coarse labors long continued, that they compelled me to eat and drink coarsely also. But to tell the truth, I find myself at present somewhat less particular in these respects. I carry less religion to the table, ask no blessing; not because I am wiser than I was, but, I am

obliged to confess, because, however much it
is to be regretted, with years I have grown
more coarse and indifferent.   Perhaps these
questions are entertained only in youth, as
most believe of poetry.   My practice is
"nowhere," my opinion is here.   Nevertheless I am far from regarding myself as one
of those privileged ones to whom the Ved
refers when it says, that "he who has true
faith in the Omnipresent Supreme Being
may eat all that exists," that is, is not bound
to inquire what is his food, or who prepares
it; and even in their case it is to be observed, as a Hindoo commentator has remarked, that the Vedant limits this privilege to "the time of distress."

Who has not sometimes derived an inexpressible satisfaction from his food in
which appetite had no share?   I have been
thrilled to think that I owed a mental perception to the commonly gross sense of taste,
that I have been inspired through the palate,
that some berries which I had eaten on a
hill-side had fed my genius.   "The soul not
being mistress of herself," says Thseng-tseu,
"one looks, and one does not see; one listens, and one does not hear; one eats, and
one does not know the savor of food."   He

who distinguishes the true savor of his food
can never be a glutton; he who does not
cannot be otherwise. A puritan may go to
his brown-bread crust with as gross an appetite as ever an alderman to his turtle. Not
that food which entereth into the mouth de-
fileth a man, but the appetite with which it
is eaten. It is neither the quality nor the
quantity, but the devotion to sensual savors;
when that which is eaten is not a viand to
sustain our animal, or inspire our spiritual
life, but food for the worms that possess us.
If the hunter has a taste for mud-turtles,
muskrats, and other such savage tid-bits,
the fine lady indulges a taste for jelly made
of a calf's foot, or for sardines from over the
sea, and they are even. He goes to the mill-
pond, she to her preserve-pot. The wonder
is how they, how you and I, can live this
slimy beastly life, eating and drinking.

Our whole life is startlingly moral. There
is never an instant's truce between virtue
and vice. Goodness is the only investment
that never fails. In the music of the harp
which trembles round the world it is the in-
sisting on this which thrills us. The harp
is the travelling patterer for the Universe's
Insurance Company, recommending its laws,

and our little goodness is all the assessment
that we pay. Though the youth at last
grows indifferent, the laws of the universe
are not indifferent, but are forever on the
side of the most sensitive. Listen to every
zephyr for some reproof, for it is surely
there, and he is unfortunate who does not
hear it. We cannot touch a string or move
a stop but the charming moral transfixes us.
Many an irksome noise, go a long way off,
is heard as music, a proud sweet satire on
the meanness of our lives.

We are conscious of an animal in us,
which awakens in proportion as our higher
nature slumbers. It is reptile and sensual,
and perhaps cannot be wholly expelled; like
the worms which, even in life and health,
occupy our bodies. Possibly we may withdraw from it, but never change its nature. I
fear that it may enjoy a certain health of its
own; that we may be well, yet not pure.
The other day I picked up the lower jaw of
a hog, with white and sound teeth and tusks,
which suggested that there was an animal
health and vigor distinct from the spiritual.
This creature succeeded by other means
than temperance and purity. " That in
which men differ from brute beasts," says

Mencius, "is a thing very inconsiderable; the common herd lose it very soon; superior men preserve it carefully." Who knows what sort of life would result if we had attained to purity? If I knew so wise a man as could teach me purity I would go to seek him forthwith. "A command over our passions, and over the external senses of the body, and good acts, are declared by the Ved to be indispensable in the mind's approximation to God." Yet the spirit can for the time pervade and control every member and function of the body, and transmute what in form is the grossest sensuality into purity and devotion. The generative energy, which, when we are loose, dissipates and makes us unclean, when we are continent invigorates and inspires us. Chastity is the flowering of man; and what are called Genius, Heroism, Holiness, and the like, are but various fruits which succeed it. Man flows at once to God when the channel of purity is open. By turns our purity inspires and our impurity casts us down. He is blessed who is assured that the animal is dying out in him day by day, and the divine being established. Perhaps there is none but has cause for shame on account of the inferior and brutish nature to which he is allied. I fear that we are such gods or demigods only as fauns and satyrs, the divine allied to beasts, the creatures of appetite, and that, to some extent, our very life is our disgrace. —

"How happy's he who hath due place assigned
To his beasts and disafforested his mind!

.   .   .   .

Can use his horse, goat, wolf, and ev'ry beast,
And is not ass himself to all the rest!
Else man not only is the herd of swine,
But he's those devils too which did incline
Them to a headlong rage, and made them worse."

All sensuality is one, though it takes many forms; all purity is one. It is the same whether a man eat, or drink, or cohabit, or sleep sensually. They are but one appetite, and we only need to see a person do any one of these things to know how great a sensualist he is. The impure can neither stand nor sit with purity. When the reptile is attacked at one mouth of his burrow, he shows himself at another. If you would be chaste, you must be temperate. What is chastity? How shall a man know if he is chaste? He shall not know it. We have heard of this virtue, but we know not what it is. We speak conformably to the rumor which we have heard. From exertion come wisdom and purity; from sloth ignorance and sensuality. In the student sensuality is a sluggish habit of mind. An unclean person is universally a slothful one, one who sits by a stove, whom the sun shines on prostrate, who reposes without being fatigued. If you would avoid uncleanness, and all the sins, work earnestly, though it be at cleaning a stable. Nature is hard to be overcome, but she must be overcome. What avails it that you are Christian, if you are not purer than the heathen, if you deny yourself no more, if you are not more religious? I know of many systems of religion esteemed heathenish whose precepts fill the reader with shame, and provoke him to new endeavors, though it be to the performance of rites merely.

I hesitate to say these things, but it is not because of the subject, — I care not how obscene my *words* are, — but because I cannot speak of them without betraying my impurity. We discourse freely without shame of one form of sensuality, and are silent about another. We are so degraded that we cannot speak simply of the necessary functions of human nature. In earlier ages, in some countries, every function was reverently spoken of and regulated by law. Nothing was too trivial for the Hindoo lawgiver, however offensive it may be to modern taste. He teaches how to eat, drink, cohabit, void excrement and urine, and the like, elevating what is mean, and does not falsely excuse himself by calling these things trifles.

Every man is the builder of a temple, called his body, to the god he worships, after a style purely his own, nor can he get off by hammering marble instead. We are all sculptors and painters, and our material is our own flesh and blood and bones. Any nobleness begins at once to refine a man's features, any meanness or sensuality to imbrute them.

John Farmer sat at his door one September evening, after a hard day's work, his mind still running on his labor more or less. Having bathed he sat down to recreate his intellectual man. It was a rather cool evening, and some of his neighbors were apprehending a frost. He had not attended to the train of his thoughts long when he heard some one playing on a flute, and that sound harmonized with his mood. Still he thought of his work; but the burden of his thought was, that though this kept running in his head, and he found himself planning and contriving it against his will, yet it concerned him very little. It was no more than the scurf of his skin, which was constantly shuffled off. But the notes of the flute came home to his ears out of a different sphere from that he worked in, and suggested work for certain faculties which slumbered in him. They gently did away with the street, and the village, and the state in which he lived. A voice said to him, — Why do you stay here and live this mean moiling life, when a glorious existence is possible for you? Those same stars twinkle over other fields than these. — But how to come out of this condition and actually migrate thither? All that he could think of was to practise some new austerity, to let his mind descend into his body and redeem it, and treat himself with ever increasing respect.

XII.

BRUTE NEIGHBORS.

SOMETIMES I had a companion in my fishing, who came through the village to my house from the other side of the town, and the catching of the dinner was as much a social exercise as the eating of it.

Hermit. I wonder what the world is doing now. I have not heard so much as a locust over the sweet-fern these three hours. The pigeons are all asleep upon their roosts, — no flutter from them. Was that a farmer's noon horn which sounded from beyond the woods just now? The hands are coming in to boiled salt beef and cider and Indian bread. Why will men worry themselves so? He that does not eat need not work. I wonder how much they have reaped. Who would live there where a body can never think for the barking of Bose? And O, the housekeeping! to keep bright the devil's doorknobs, and scour his tubs this bright day! Better not keep a house. Say, some hollow tree; and then for morning calls and dinner-parties! Only a woodpecker tapping. O, they swarm; the sun is too warm there; they are born too far into life for me. I have water from the spring, and a loaf of brown bread on the shelf. — Hark! I hear a rustling of the leaves. Is it some ill-fed village hound yielding to the instinct of the chase? or the lost pig which is said to be in these woods, whose tracks I saw after the rain? It comes on apace; my sumachs and sweet-briers tremble. — Eh, Mr. Poet, is it you? How do you like the world to-day?

Poet. See those clouds; how they hang! That's the greatest thing I have seen to-day. There's nothing like it in old paintings, nothing like it in foreign lands, — unless when we were off the coast of Spain. That's a true Mediterranean sky. I thought, as I have my living to get, and have not eaten to-day, that I might go a-fishing. That's the true industry for poets. It is the only trade I have learned. Come, let's along.

Hermit. I cannot resist. My brown bread will soon be gone. I will go with you gladly soon, but I am just concluding a serious meditation. I think that I am near the end of it. Leave me alone, then, for a

while. But that we may not be delayed,
you shall be digging the bait meanwhile.
Angle-worms are rarely to be met with in
these parts, where the soil was never fat-
tened with manure ; the race is nearly extinct. The sport of digging the bait is
nearly equal to that of catching the fish,
when one's appetite is not too keen ; and
this you may have all to yourself to-day. I
would advise you to set in the spade down
yonder among the ground-nuts, where you
see the johnswort waving. I think that I
may warrant you one worm to every three
sods you turn up, if you look well in among
the roots of the grass, as if you were weed-
ing. Or, if you choose to go farther, it will
not be unwise, for I have found the increase
of fair bait to be very nearly as the squares
of the distances.

Hermit alone. Let me see ; where was
I ? Methinks I was nearly in this frame
of mind ; the world lay about at this angle.
Shall I go to heaven or a-fishing ? If I
should soon bring this meditation to an end,
would another so sweet occasion be likely to
offer ? I was as near being resolved into
the essence of things as ever I was in my
life. I fear my thoughts will not come back

to me. If it would do any good, I would whistle for them. When they make us an offer, is it wise to say, We will think of it? My thoughts have left no track, and I cannot find the path again. What was it that I was thinking of? It was a very hazy day. I will just try these three sentences of Confut-see; they may fetch that state about again. I know not whether it was the dumps or a budding ecstasy. Mem. There never is but one opportunity of a kind.

Poet. How now, Hermit, is it too soon? I have got just thirteen whole ones, beside several which are imperfect or undersized; but they will do for the smaller fry; they do not cover up the hook so much. Those village worms are quite too large; a shiner may make a meal off one without finding the skewer.

Hermit. Well, then, let's be off. Shall we to the Concord? There's good sport there if the water be not too high.

Why do precisely these objects which we behold make a world? Why has man just these species of animals for his neighbors; as if nothing but a mouse could have filled this crevice? I suspect that Pilpay & Co.

have put animals to their best use, for they are all beasts of burden, in a sense, made to carry some portion of our thoughts.

The mice which haunted my house were not the common ones, which are said to have been introduced into the country, but a wild native kind not found in the village. I sent one to a distinguished naturalist, and it interested him much. When I was building, one of these had its nest underneath the house, and before I had laid the second floor, and swept out the shavings, would come out regularly at lunch time and pick up the crumbs at my feet. It probably had never seen a man before; and it soon became quite familiar, and would run over my shoes and up my clothes. It could readily ascend the sides of the room by short impulses, like a squirrel, which it resembled in its motions. At length, as I leaned with my elbow on the bench one day, it ran up my clothes, and along my sleeve, and round and round the paper which held my dinner, while I kept the latter close, and dodged and played at bo-peep with it; and when at last I held still a piece of cheese between my thumb and finger, it came and nibbled it, sitting in my hand, and afterward cleaned its face and paws, like a fly, and walked away.

A phœbe soon built in my shed, and a
robin for protection in a pine which grew
against the house. In June the partridge,
(*Tetrao umbellus*,) which is so shy a bird,
led her brood past my windows, from the
woods in the rear to the front of my house,
clucking and calling to them like a hen, and
in all her behavior proving herself the hen
of the woods. The young suddenly disperse
on your approach, at a signal from the
mother, as if a whirlwind had swept them
away, and they so exactly resemble the dried
leaves and twigs that many a traveller has
placed his foot in the midst of a brood, and
heard the whir of the old bird as she flew
off, and her anxious calls and mewing, or
seen her trail her wings to attract his attention, without suspecting their neighborhood.
The parent will sometimes roll and spin
round before you in such a dishabille, that
you cannot, for a few moments, detect what
kind of creature it is. The young squat still
and flat, often running their heads under a
leaf, and mind only their mother's directions
given from a distance, nor will your approach
make them run again and betray themselves.
You may even tread on them, or have your
eyes on them for a minute, without discover-

ing them. I have held them in my open
hand at such a time, and still their only care,
obedient to their mother and their instinct,
was to squat there without fear or trembling.
So perfect is this instinct, that once, when I
had laid them on the leaves again, and one
accidentally fell on its side, it was found
with the rest in exactly the same position
ten minutes afterward. They are not callow
like the young of most birds, but more perfectly developed and precocious even than
chickens. The remarkably adult yet innocent expression of their open and serene eyes
is very memorable. All intelligence seems
reflected in them. They suggest not merely
the purity of infancy, but a wisdom clarified
by experience. Such an eye was not born
when the bird was, but is coeval with the sky
it reflects. The woods do not yield another
such a gem. The traveller does not often
look into such a limpid well. The ignorant
or reckless sportsman often shoots the parent
at such a time, and leaves these innocents to
fall a prey to some prowling beast or bird,
or gradually mingle with the decaying leaves
which they so much resemble. It is said
that when hatched by a hen they will directly
disperse on some alarm, and so are lost, for

they never hear the mother's call which gathers them again. These were my hens and chickens.

It is remarkable how many creatures live wild and free though secret in the woods, and still sustain themselves in the neighborhood of towns, suspected by hunters only. How retired the otter manages to live here! He grows to be four feet long, as big as a small boy, perhaps without any human being getting a glimpse of him. I formerly saw the raccoon in the woods behind where my house is built, and probably still heard their whinnering at night. Commonly I rested an hour or two in the shade at noon, after planting, and ate my lunch, and read a little by a spring which was the source of a swamp and of a brook, oozing from under Brister's Hill, half a mile from my field. The approach to this was through a succession of descending grassy hollows, full of young pitch - pines, into a larger wood about the swamp. There, in a very secluded and shaded spot, under a spreading white - pine, there was yet a clean firm sward to sit on. I had dug out the spring and made a well of clear gray water, where I could dip up a pailful without roiling it, and thither I went

for this purpose almost every day in midsummer, when the pond was warmest.
Thither too the wood-cock led her brood, to
probe the mud for worms, flying but a foot
above them down the bank, while they ran
in a troop beneath; but at last, spying me,
she would leave her young and circle round
and round me, nearer and nearer till within
four or five feet, pretending broken wings
and legs, to attract my attention, and get
off her young, who would already have taken
up their march, with faint wiry peep, single
file through the swamp, as she directed. Or
I heard the peep of the young when I could
not see the parent bird. There too the tur-
tle-doves sat over the spring, or fluttered
from bough to bough of the soft white-pines
over my head; or the red squirrel, coursing
down the nearest bough, was particularly
familiar and inquisitive. You only need
sit still long enough in some attractive spot
in the woods that all its inhabitants may exhibit themselves to you by turns.

I was witness to events of a less peaceful
character. One day when I went out to my
wood-pile, or rather my pile of stumps, I
observed two large ants, the one red, the
other much larger, nearly half an inch long,

and black, fiercely contending with one another. Having once got hold they never let go, but struggled and wrestled and rolled on the chips incessantly. Looking farther, I was surprised to find that the chips were covered with such combatants, that it was not a *duellum*, but a *bellum*, a war between two races of ants, the red always pitted against the black, and frequently two red ones to one black. The legions of these Myrmidons covered all the hills and vales in my wood-yard, and the ground was already strewn with the dead and dying, both red and black. It was the only battle which I have ever witnessed, the only battle-field I ever trod while the battle was raging ; internecine war ; the red republicans on the one hand, and the black imperialists on the other. On every side they were engaged in deadly combat, yet without any noise that I could hear, and human soldiers never fought so resolutely. I watched a couple that were fast locked in each other's embraces, in a little sunny valley amid the chips, now at noon-day prepared to fight till the sun went down, or life went out. The smaller red champion had fastened himself like a vice to his adversary's front, and through

all the tumblings on that field never for an
instant ceased to gnaw at one of his feelers near the root, having already caused the
other to go by the board; while the stronger
black one dashed him from side to side, and,
as I saw on looking nearer, had already divested him of several of his members. They
fought with more pertinacity than bull-dogs.
Neither manifested the least disposition to
retreat. It was evident that their battle-
cry was Conquer or die. In the mean while
there came along a single red ant on the hill-
side of this valley, evidently full of excite-
ment, who either had despatched his foe, or
had not yet taken part in the battle; probably the latter, for he had lost none of his
limbs; whose mother had charged him to
return with his shield or upon it. Or perchance he was some Achilles, who had nour-
ished his wrath apart, and had now come to
avenge or rescue his Patroclus. He saw this
unequal combat from afar, — for the blacks
were nearly twice the size of the red, — he
drew near with rapid pace till he stood on
his guard within half an inch of the combatants; then, watching his opportunity, he
sprang upon the black warrior, and commenced his operations near the root of his

right fore-leg, leaving the foe to select among
his own members; and so there were three
united for life, as if a new kind of attraction had been invented which put all other
locks and cements to shame. I should not
have wondered by this time to find that they
had their respective musical bands stationed
on some eminent chip, and playing their na-
tional airs the while, to excite the slow and
cheer the dying combatants. I was myself
excited somewhat even as if they had been
men. The more you think of it, the less
the difference. And certainly there is not
the fight recorded in Concord history, at
least, if in the history of America, that will
bear a moment's comparison with this,
whether for the numbers engaged in it, or
for the patriotism and heroism displayed.
For numbers and for carnage it was an Aus-
terlitz or Dresden. Concord Fight! Two
killed on the patriots' side, and Luther
Blanchard wounded! Why here every ant
was a Buttrick, — " Fire! for God's sake
fire!" — and thousands shared the fate of
Davis and Hosmer. There was not one
hireling there. I have no doubt that it was
a principle they fought for, as much as our
ancestors, and not to avoid a three-penny tax

on their tea ; and the results of this battle
will be as important and memorable to those
whom it concerns as those of the battle of
Bunker Hill, at least.

I took up the chip on which the three I
have particularly described were struggling,
carried it into my house, and placed it under
a tumbler on my window-sill, in order to see
the issue.   Holding a microscope to the first-
mentioned red ant, I saw that, though he
was assiduously gnawing at the near fore-
leg of his enemy, having severed his remaining feeler, his own breast was all torn away,
exposing what vitals he had there to the
jaws of the black warrior, whose breast-
plate was apparently too thick for him to
pierce ; and the dark carbuncles of the suf-
ferer's eyes shone with ferocity such as war
only could excite.   They struggled half an
hour longer under the tumbler, and when 1
looked again the black soldier had severed
the heads of his foes from their bodies, and
the still living heads were hanging on either
side of him like ghastly trophies at his sad-
dle-bow, still apparently as firmly fastened
as ever, and he was endeavoring with feeble
struggles, being without feelers and with
only the remnant of a leg, and I know not

how many other wounds, to divest himself of them ; which at length, after half an hour more, he accomplished. I raised the glass, and he went off over the window-sill in that crippled state. Whether he finally survived that combat, and spent the remainder of his days in some Hotel des Invalides, I do not know ; but I thought that his industry would not be worth much thereafter. I never learned which party was victorious, nor the cause of the war ; but I felt for the rest of that day as if I had had my feelings excited and harrowed by witnessing the struggle, the ferocity and carnage, of a human battle before my door.

Kirby and Spence tell us that the battles of ants have long been celebrated and the date of them recorded, though they say that Huber is the only modern author who appears to have witnessed them. "Æneas Sylvius," say they, " after giving a very circumstantial account of one contested with great obstinacy by a great and small species on the trunk of a pear tree," adds that " ' This action was fought in the pontificate of Eugenius the Fourth, in the presence of Nicholas Pistoriensis, an eminent lawyer, who related the whole history of the battle with

the greatest fidelity.' A similar engagement
between great and small ants is recorded
by Olaus Magnus, in which the small ones,
being victorious, are said to have buried the
bodies of their own soldiers, but left those
of their giant enemies a prey to the birds.
This event happened previous to the expul-
sion of the tyrant Christiern the Second
from Sweden." The battle which I witnessed took place in the Presidency of Polk,
five years before the passage of Webster's
Fugitive-Slave Bill.

Many a village Bose, fit only to course a
mud-turtle in a victualling cellar, sported
his heavy quarters in the woods, without the
knowledge of his master, and ineffectually
smelled at old fox burrows and woodchucks'
holes ; led perchance by some slight cur
which nimbly threaded the wood, and might
still inspire a natural terror in its denizens;
— now far behind his guide, barking like
a canine bull toward some small squirrel
which had treed itself for scrutiny, then,
cantering off, bending the bushes with his
weight, imagining that he is on the track of
some stray member of the jerbilla family.
Once I was surprised to see a cat walking
along the stony shore of the pond, for they

rarely wander so far from home. The surprise was mutual. Nevertheless the most domestic cat, which has lain on a rug all her days, appears quite at home in the woods, and, by her sly and stealthy behavior, proves herself more native there than the regular inhabitants. Once, when berrying, I met with a cat with young kittens in the woods, quite wild, and they all, like their mother, had their backs up and were fiercely spitting at me. A few years before I lived in the woods there was what was called a " winged cat " in one of the farm-houses in Lincoln nearest the pond, Mr. Gilian Baker's. When I called to see her in June, 1842, she was gone a - hunting in the woods, as was her wont, (I am not sure whether it was a male or female, and so use the more common pronoun,) but her mistress told me that she came into the neighborhood a little more than a year before, in April, and was finally taken into their house ; that she was of a dark brownish-gray color, with a white spot on her throat, and white feet, and had a large bushy tail like a fox ; that in the winter the fur grew thick and flatted out along her sides, forming strips ten or twelve inches long by two and a half wide, and under her

chin like a muff, the upper side loose, the
under matted like felt, and in the spring
these appendages dropped off. They gave
me a pair of her "wings," which I keep still.
There is no appearance of a membrane about
them. Some thought it was part flying-
squirrel or some other wild animal, which is
not impossible, for, according to naturalists,
prolific hybrids have been produced by the
union of the marten and domestic cat. This
would have been the right kind of cat for
me to keep, if I had kept any; for why
should not a poet's cat be winged as well as
his horse?

In the fall the loon (*Colymbus glacialis*)
came, as usual, to moult and bathe in the
pond, making the woods ring with his wild
laughter before I had risen. At rumor of
his arrival all the Mill-dam sportsmen are
on the alert, in gigs and on foot, two by
two and three by three, with patent rifles
and conical balls and spy - glasses. They
come rustling through the woods like autumn leaves, at least ten men to one loon.
Some station themselves on this side of the
pond, some on that, for the poor bird cannot
be omnipresent; if he dive here he must
come up there. But now the kind October

wind rises, rustling the leaves and rippling the surface of the water, so that no loon can be heard or seen, though his foes sweep the pond with spy-glasses, and make the woods resound with their discharges. The waves generously rise and dash angrily, taking sides with all waterfowl, and our sportsmen must beat a retreat to town and shop and unfinished jobs. But they were too often successful. When I went to get a pail of water early in the morning I frequently saw this stately bird sailing out of my cove within a few rods. If I endeavored to overtake him in a boat, in order to see how he would manœuvre, he would dive and be completely lost, so that I did not discover him again, sometimes, till the latter part of the day. But I was more than a match for him on the surface. He commonly went off in a rain.

As I was paddling along the north shore one very calm October afternoon, for such days especially they settle on to the lakes, like the milkweed down, having looked in vain over the pond for a loon, suddenly one, sailing out from the shore toward the middle a few rods in front of me, set up his wild laugh and betrayed himself. I pursued with

a paddle and he dived, but when he came up
I was nearer than before. He dived again,
but I miscalculated the direction he would
take, and we were fifty rods apart when he
came to the surface this time, for I had
helped to widen the interval ; and again he
laughed long and loud, and with more reason than before. He manœuvred so cunningly that I could not get within half a
dozen rods of him. Each time, when he
came to the surface, turning his head this
way and that, he coolly surveyed the water
and the land, and apparently chose his course
so that he might come up where there was
the widest expanse of water and at the greatest distance from the boat. It was surprising how quickly he made up his mind and
put his resolve into execution. He led me
at once to the widest part of the pond, and
could not be driven from it. While he was
thinking one thing in his brain, I was endeavoring to divine his thought in mine. It was
a pretty game, played on the smooth surface
of the pond, a man against a loon. Suddenly your adversary's checker disappears
beneath the board, and the problem is to
place yours nearest to where his will appear
again. Sometimes he would come up unex-

pectedly on the opposite side of me, having apparently passed directly under the boat. So long-winded was he and so unweariable, that when he had swum farthest he would immediately plunge again, nevertheless; and then no wit could divine where in the deep pond, beneath the smooth surface, he might be speeding his way like a fish, for he had time and ability to visit the bottom of the pond in its deepest part. It is said that loons have been caught in the New York lakes eighty feet beneath the surface, with hooks set for trout, — though Walden is deeper than that. How surprised must the fishes be to see this ungainly visitor from another sphere speeding his way amid their schools! Yet he appeared to know his course as surely under water as on the surface, and swam much faster there. Once or twice I saw a ripple where he approached the surface, just put his head out to reconnoitre, and instantly dived again. I found that it was as well for me to rest on my oars and wait his reappearing as to endeavor to calculate where he would rise; for again and again, when I was straining my eyes over the surface one way, I would suddenly be startled by his unearthly laugh behind me. But

why, after displaying so much cunning, did
he invariably betray himself the moment he
came up by that loud laugh? Did not his
white breast enough betray him? He was
indeed a silly loon, I thought. I could commonly hear the plash of the water when he
came up, and so also detected him. But
after an hour he seemed as fresh as ever,
dived as willingly, and swam yet farther
than at first. It was surprising to see how
serenely he sailed off with unruffled breast
when he came to the surface, doing all the
work with his webbed feet beneath. His
usual note was this demoniac laughter, yet
somewhat like that of a water-fowl; but occasionally, when he had balked me most
successfully and come up a long way off, he
uttered a long-drawn unearthly howl, probably more like that of a wolf than any bird;
as when a beast puts his muzzle to the
ground and deliberately howls. This was
his looning, — perhaps the wildest sound
that is ever heard here, making the woods
ring far and wide. I concluded that he
laughed in derision of my efforts, confident
of his own resources. Though the sky was
by this time overcast, the pond was so
smooth that I could see where he broke the
surface when I did not hear him. His

white breast, the stillness of the air, and the smoothness of the water were all against him. At length, having come up fifty rods off, he uttered one of those prolonged howls, as if calling on the god of loons to aid him, and immediately there came a wind from the east and rippled the surface, and filled the whole air with misty rain, and I was impressed as if it were the prayer of the loon answered, and his god was angry with me; and so I left him disappearing far away on the tumultuous surface.

For hours, in fall days, I watched the ducks cunningly tack and veer and hold the middle of the pond, far from the sportsman; tricks which they will have less need to practise in Louisiana bayous. When compelled to rise they would sometimes circle round and round and over the pond at a considerable height, from which they could easily see to other ponds and the river, like black motes in the sky; and, when I thought they had gone off thither long since, they would settle down by a slanting flight of a quarter of a mile on to a distant part which was left free; but what beside safety they got by sailing in the middle of Walden I do not know, unless they love its water for the same reason that I do.

XIII.

HOUSE-WARMING.

In October I went a-graping to the river
meadows, and loaded myself with clusters
more precious for their beauty and fragrance
than for food. There too I admired, though
I did not gather, the cranberries, small
waxen gems, pendants of the meadow grass,
pearly and red, which the farmer plucks
with an ugly rake, leaving the smooth meadow in a snarl, heedlessly measuring them
by the bushel and the dollar only, and sells
the spoils of the meads to Boston and New
York; destined to be *jammed*, to satisfy the
tastes of lovers of Nature there. So butch-
ers rake the tongues of bison out of the
prairie grass, regardless of the torn and
drooping plant. The barberry's brilliant
fruit was likewise food for my eyes merely;
but I collected a small store of wild apples
for coddling, which the proprietor and travellers had overlooked. When chestnuts were
ripe I laid up half a bushel for winter. It

was very exciting at that season to roam the
then boundless chestnut woods of Lincoln,
— they now sleep their long sleep under the
railroad, — with a bag on my shoulder, and
a stick to open burrs with in my hand, for I
did not always wait for the frost, amid the
rustling of leaves and the loud reproofs of
the red-squirrels and the jays, whose half-
consumed nuts I sometimes stole, for the
burrs which they had selected were sure to
contain sound ones. Occasionally I climbed
and shook the trees. They grew also behind my house, and one large tree, which almost overshadowed it, was, when in flower,
a bouquet which scented the whole neighborhood, but the squirrels and the jays got most
of its fruit; the last coming in flocks early
in the morning and picking the nuts out of
the burrs before they fell. I relinquished
these trees to them and visited the more
distant woods composed wholly of chestnut.
These nuts, as far as they went, were a good
substitute for bread. Many other substitutes might, perhaps, be found. Digging
one day for fish-worms I discovered the
ground-nut (*Apios tuberosa*) on its string,
the potato of the aborigines, a sort of fabulous fruit, which I had begun to doubt if I

had ever dug and eaten in childhood, as I had told, and had not dreamed it. I had often since seen its crimpled red velvety blossom supported by the stems of other plants without knowing it to be the same. Cultivation has well-nigh exterminated it. It has a sweetish taste, much like that of a frost-bitten potato, and I found it better boiled than roasted. This tuber seemed like a faint promise of Nature to rear her own children and feed them simply here at some future period. In these days of fatted cattle and waving grain-fields this humble root, which was once the *totem* of an Indian tribe, is quite forgotten, or known only by its flowering vine; but let wild Nature reign here once more, and the tender and luxurious English grains will probably disappear before a myriad of foes, and without the care of man the crow may carry back even the last seed of corn to the great corn-field of the Indian's God in the south-west, whence he is said to have brought it; but the now almost exterminated ground-nut will perhaps revive and flourish in spite of frosts and wildness, prove itself indigenous, and resume its ancient importance and dignity as the diet of the hunter tribe. Some Indian Ceres or Minerva must have been the inventor and bestower of it ; and when the reign of poetry commences here, its leaves and string of nuts may be represented on our works of art.

Already, by the first of September, I had seen two or three small maples turned scarlet across the pond, beneath where the white stems of three aspens diverged, at the point of a promontory, next the water. Ah, many a tale their color told ! And gradually from week to week the character of each tree came out, and it admired itself reflected in the smooth mirror of the lake. Each morning the manager of this gallery substituted some new picture, distinguished by more brilliant or harmonious coloring, for the old upon the walls.

The wasps came by thousands to my lodge in October, as to winter quarters, and settled on my windows within and on the walls overhead, sometimes deterring visitors from entering. Each morning, when they were numbed with cold, I swept some of them out, but I did not trouble myself much to get rid of them ; I even felt complimented by their regarding my house as a desirable shelter. They never molested me seriously,

though they bedded with me; and they
gradually disappeared, into what crevices I
do not know, avoiding winter and unspeak-
able cold.

Like the wasps, before I finally went into
winter quarters in November, I used to re-
sort to the north-east side of Walden, which
the sun, reflected from the pitch-pine woods
and the stony shore, made the fireside of
the pond; it is so much pleasanter and
wholesomer to be warmed by the sun while
you can be, than by an artificial fire. I thus
warmed myself by the still glowing embers
which the summer, like a departed hunter,
had left.

When I came to build my chimney I studied masonry. My bricks being second-hand
ones required to be cleaned with a trowel, so
that I learned more than usual of the qualities of bricks and trowels. The mortar on
them was fifty years old, and was said to be
still growing harder; but this is one of those
sayings which men love to repeat whether
they are true or not. Such sayings themselves grow harder and adhere more firmly
with age, and it would take many blows with
a trowel to clean an old wiseacre of them.

Many of the villages of Mesopotamia are built of second-hand bricks of a very good quality, obtained from the ruins of Babylon, and the cement on them is older and probably harder still. However that may be, I was struck by the peculiar toughness of the steel which bore so many violent blows without being worn out. As my bricks had been in a chimney before, though I did not read the name of Nebuchadnezzar on them, I picked out as many fireplace bricks as I could find, to save work and waste, and I filled the spaces between the bricks about the fireplace with stones from the pond shore, and also made my mortar with the white sand from the same place. I lingered most about the fireplace, as the most vital part of the house. Indeed, I worked so deliberately, that though I commenced at the ground in the morning, a course of bricks raised a few inches above the floor served for my pillow at night; yet I did not get a stiff neck for it that I remember; my stiff neck is of older date. I took a poet to board for a fortnight about those times, which caused me to be put to it for room. He brought his own knife, though I had two, and we used to scour them by thrusting them into the earth. He shared with me the labors of cooking. I was pleased to see my work rising so square and solid by degrees, and reflected, that, if it proceeded slowly, it was calculated to endure a long time. The chimney is to some extent an independent structure, standing on the ground, and rising through the house to the heavens; even after the house is burned it still stands sometimes, and its importance and independence are apparent. This was toward the end of summer. It was now November.

The north wind had already begun to cool the pond, though it took many weeks of steady blowing to accomplish it, it is so deep. When I began to have a fire at evening, before I plastered my house, the chimney carried smoke particularly well, because of the numerous chinks between the boards. Yet I passed some cheerful evenings in that cool and airy apartment, surrounded by the rough brown boards full of knots, and rafters with the bark on high overhead. My house never pleased my eye so much after it was plastered, though I was obliged to confess that it was more comfortable. Should not every apartment in which man dwells be

lofty enough to create some obscurity overhead, where flickering shadows may play at
evening about the rafters? These forms are
more agreeable to the fancy and imagination than fresco paintings or other the most
expensive furniture. I now first began to
inhabit my house, I may say, when I began
to use it for warmth as well as shelter. I
had got a couple of old fire-dogs to keep the
wood from the hearth, and it did me good to
see the soot form on the back of the chimney which I had built, and I poked the fire
with more right and more satisfaction than
usual. My dwelling was small, and I could
hardly entertain an echo in it; but it seemed
larger for being a single apartment and remote from neighbors. All the attractions of
a house were concentrated in one room; it
was kitchen, chamber, parlor, and keeping-
room; and whatever satisfaction parent or
child, master or servant, derive from living
in a house, I enjoyed it all. Cato says, the
master of a family (*patremfamilias*) must
have in his rustic villa "cellam oleariam,
vinariam, dolia multa, uti lubeat caritatem
expectare, et rei, et virtuti, et gloriæ erit,"
that is, "an oil and wine cellar, many casks,
so that it may be pleasant to expect hard

times; it will be for his advantage, and virtue, and glory." I had in my cellar a firkin of potatoes, about two quarts of peas with the weevil in them, and on my shelf a little rice, a jug of molasses, and of rye and Indian meal a peck each.

I sometimes dream of a larger and more populous house, standing in a golden age, of enduring materials, and without gingerbread work, which shall still consist of only one room, a vast, rude, substantial, primitive hall, without ceiling or plastering, with bare rafters and purlins supporting a sort of lower heaven over one's head, — useful to keep off rain and snow, where the king and queen posts stand out to receive your homage, when you have done reverence to the prostrate Saturn of an older dynasty on stepping over the sill; a cavernous house, wherein you must reach up a torch upon a pole to see the roof; where some may live in the fireplace, some in the recess of a window, and some on settles, some at one end of the hall, some at another, and some aloft on rafters with the spiders, if they choose; a house which you have got into when you have opened the outside door, and the ceremony is over; where the weary traveller

may wash, and eat, and converse, and sleep,
without further journey; such a shelter as
you would be glad to reach in a tempestuous night, containing all the essentials of
a house, and nothing for house-keeping;
where you can see all the treasures of the
house at one view, and everything hangs
upon its peg that a man should use; at
once kitchen, pantry, parlor, chamber, store-
house, and garret; where you can see so
necessary a thing as a barrel or a ladder, so
convenient a thing as a cupboard, and hear
the pot boil, and pay your respects to the
fire that cooks your dinner, and the oven
that bakes your bread, and the necessary
furniture and utensils are the chief ornaments; where the washing is not put out,
nor the fire, nor the mistress, and perhaps
you are sometimes requested to move from
off the trap-door, when the cook would descend into the cellar, and so learn whether
the ground is solid or hollow beneath you
without stamping. A house whose inside is
as open and manifest as a bird's nest, and
you cannot go in at the front door and out
at the back without seeing some of its inhabitants; where to be a guest is to be presented with the freedom of the house, and

not to be carefully excluded from seven eighths of it, shut up in a particular cell, and told to make yourself at home there, — in solitary confinement. Nowadays the host does not admit you to *his* hearth, but has got the mason to build one for yourself somewhere in his alley, and hospitality is the art of *keeping* you at the greatest distance. There is as much secrecy about the cooking as if he had a design to poison you. I am aware that I have been on many a man's premises, and might have been legally ordered off, but I am not aware that I have been in many men's houses. I might visit in my old clothes a king and queen who lived simply in such a house as I have described, if I were going their way ; but backing out of a modern palace will be all that I shall desire to learn, if ever I am caught in one.

It would seem as if the very language of our parlors would lose all its nerve and degenerate into *parlaver* wholly, our lives pass at such remoteness from its symbols, and its metaphors and tropes are necessarily so far fetched, through slides and dumb-waiters, as it were ; in other words, the parlor is so far from the kitchen and workshop. The dinner even is only the parable of a dinner, commonly. As if only the savage dwelt near enough to Nature and Truth to borrow a trope from them. How can the scholar, who dwells away in the North West Territory or the Isle of Man, tell what is parliamentary in the kitchen?

However, only one or two of my guests were ever bold enough to stay and eat a hasty-pudding with me; but when they saw that crisis approaching they beat a hasty retreat rather, as if it would shake the house to its foundations. Nevertheless, it stood through a great many hasty-puddings.

I did not plaster till it was freezing weather. I brought over some whiter and cleaner sand for this purpose from the opposite shore of the pond in a boat, a sort of conveyance which would have tempted me to go much farther if necessary. My house had in the mean while been shingled down to the ground on every side. In lathing I was pleased to be able to send home each nail with a single blow of the hammer, and it was my ambition to transfer the plaster from the board to the wall neatly and rapidly. I remembered the story of a conceited fellow, who, in fine clothes, was wont to lounge about the village once, giving advice to workmen. Venturing one day to substitute deeds for words, he turned up his cuffs, seized a plasterer's board, and having loaded his trowel without mishap, with a complacent look toward the lathing overhead, made a bold gesture thitherward; and straightway, to his complete discomfiture, received the whole contents in his ruffled bosom. I admired anew the economy and convenience of plastering, which so effectually shuts out the cold and takes a handsome finish, and I learned the various casualties to which the plasterer is liable. I was surprised to see how thirsty the bricks were which drank up all the moisture in my plaster before I had smoothed it, and how many pailfuls of water it takes to christen a new hearth. I had the previous winter made a small quantity of lime by burning the shells of the *Unio fluviatilis*, which our river affords, for the sake of the experiment; so that I knew where my materials came from. I might have got good limestone within a mile or two and burned it myself, if I had cared to do so.

The pond had in the mean while skimmed over in the shadiest and shallowest coves, some days or even weeks before the general freezing. The first ice is especially interesting and perfect, being hard, dark, and transparent, and affords the best opportunity that ever offers for examining the bottom where it is shallow; for you can lie at your length on ice only an inch thick, like a skater insect on the surface of the water, and study the bottom at your leisure, only two or three inches distant, like a picture behind a glass, and the water is necessarily always smooth then. There are many furrows in the sand where some creature has travelled about and doubled on its tracks; and, for wrecks, it is strewn with the cases of caddis worms made of minute grains of white quartz. Perhaps these have creased it, for you find some of their cases in the furrows, though they are deep and broad for them to make. But the ice itself is the object of most interest, though you must improve the earliest opportunity to study it. If you examine it closely the morning after it freezes, you find that the greater part of the bubbles, which at first appeared to be within it, are against its under surface, and that more are continually rising from the bottom; while the ice is as yet comparatively solid and dark, that is,

you see the water through it. These bubbles are from an eightieth to an eighth of
an inch in diameter, very clear and beautiful, and you see your face reflected in them
through the ice. There may be thirty or
forty of them to a square inch. There are
also already within the ice narrow oblong
perpendicular bubbles about half an inch
long, sharp cones with the apex upward; or
oftener, if the ice is quite fresh, minute
spherical bubbles one directly above another, like a string of beads. But these
within the ice are not so numerous nor obvious as those beneath. I sometimes used
to cast on stones to try the strength of the
ice, and those which broke through carried
in air with them, which formed very large
and conspicuous white bubbles beneath.
One day when I came to the same place
forty-eight hours afterward, I found that
those large bubbles were still perfect, though
an inch more of ice had formed, as I could
see distinctly by the seam in the edge of a
cake. But as the last two days had been
very warm, like an Indian summer, the ice
was not now transparent, showing the dark
green color of the water, and the bottom,
but opaque and whitish or gray, and though

twice as thick was hardly stronger than before, for the air bubbles had greatly expanded under this heat and run together,
and lost their regularity; they were no
longer one directly over another, but often
like silvery coins poured from a bag, one
overlapping another, or in thin flakes, as if
occupying slight cleavages. The beauty of
the ice was gone, and it was too late to study
the bottom. Being curious to know what
position my great bubbles occupied with regard to the new ice, I broke out a cake containing a middling sized one, and turned it
bottom upward. The new ice had formed
around and under the bubble, so that it
was included between the two ices. It was
wholly in the lower ice, but close against
the upper, and was flattish, or perhaps
slightly lenticular, with a rounded edge, a
quarter of an inch deep by four inches in
diameter; and I was surprised to find that
directly under the bubble the ice was melted
with great regularity in the form of a saucer reversed, to the height of five eighths of
an inch in the middle, leaving a thin parti-
tion there between the water and the bubble,
hardly an eighth of an inch thick; and in
many places the small bubbles in this parti-

tion had burst out downward, and probably
there was no ice at all under the largest
bubbles, which were a foot in diameter. I
inferred that the infinite number of minute
bubbles which I had first seen against the
under surface of the ice were now frozen in
likewise, and that each, in its degree, had
operated like a burning glass on the ice beneath to melt and rot it. These are the
little air-guns which contribute to make the
ice crack and whoop.

At length the winter set in in good earnest, just as I had finished plastering, and
the wind began to howl around the house
as if it had not had permission to do so till
then. Night after night the geese came lumbering in in the dark with a clangor and a
whistling of wings, even after the ground
was covered with snow, some to alight in
Walden, and some flying low over the woods
toward Fair Haven, bound for Mexico. Several times, when returning from the village
at ten or eleven o'clock at night, I heard the
tread of a flock of geese, or else ducks, on
the dry leaves in the woods by a pond-hole
behind my dwelling, where they had come
up to feed, and the faint honk or quack of

their leader as they hurried off. In 1845
Walden froze entirely over for the first time
on the night of the 22d of December, Flints'
and other shallower ponds and the river having been frozen ten days or more ; in '46,
the 16th ; in '49, about the 31st ; and in '50,
about the 27th of December ; in '52, the 5th
of January ; in '53, the 31st of December.
The snow had already covered the ground
since the 25th of November, and surrounded
me suddenly with the scenery of winter. I
withdrew yet farther into my shell, and endeavored to keep a bright fire both within
my house and within my breast. My employment out of doors now was to collect the
dead wood in the forest, bringing it in my
hands or on my shoulders, or sometimes trailing a dead pine-tree under each arm to my
shed. An old forest fence which had seen
its best days was a great haul for me. I
sacrificed it to Vulcan, for it was past serving the god Terminus. How much more interesting an event is that man's supper who
has just been forth in the snow to hunt, nay,
you might say, steal, the fuel to cook it with !
His bread and meat are sweet. There are
enough fagots and waste wood of all kinds
in the forests of most of our towns to sup-

port many fires, but which at present warm
none, and, some think, hinder the growth of
the young wood. There was also the drift-
wood of the pond. In the course of the
summer I had discovered a raft of pitch-
pine logs with the bark on, pinned together
by the Irish when the railroad was built.
This I hauled up partly on the shore. After
soaking two years and then lying high six
months it was perfectly sound, though wa-
terlogged past drying. I amused myself
one winter day with sliding this piece-meal
across the pond, nearly half a mile, skating
behind with one end of a log fifteen feet
long on my shoulder, and the other on the
ice ; or I tied several logs together with a
birch withe, and then, with a longer birch or
alder which had a hook at the end, dragged
them across. Though completely water-
logged and almost as heavy as lead, they
not only burned long, but made a very hot
fire ; nay, I thought that they burned better
for the soaking, as if the pitch, being confined by the water, burned longer as in a
lamp.

Gilpin, in his account of the forest bor-
derers of England, says that " the encroachments of trespassers, and the houses and

fences thus raised on the borders of the forest," were " considered as great nuisances by the old forest law, and were severely punished under the name of *purprestures*, as tending *ad terrorem ferarum — ad nocumentum forestæ*, etc.," to the frightening of the game and the detriment of the forest. But I was interested in the preservation of the venison and the vert more than the hunters or wood-choppers, and as much as though I had been the Lord Warden himself ; and if any part was burned, though I burned it myself by accident, I grieved with a grief that lasted longer and was more inconsolable than that of the proprietors ; nay, I grieved when it was cut down by the proprietors themselves. I would that our farmers when they cut down a forest felt some of that awe which the old Romans did when they came to thin, or let in the light to, a consecrated grove, (*lucum conlucare*,) that is, would believe that it is sacred to some god. The Roman made an expiatory offering, and prayed, Whatever god or goddess thou art to whom this grove is sacred, be propitious to me, my family, and children, etc.

It is remarkable what a value is still put

upon wood even in this age and in this new
country, a value more permanent and universal than that of gold. After all our discoveries and inventions no man will go by a
pile of wood. It is as precious to us as it
was to our Saxon and Norman ancestors.
If they made their bows of it, we make our
gun-stocks of it. Michaux, more than thirty
years ago, says that the price of wood for
fuel in New York and Philadelphia " nearly
equals, and sometimes exceeds, that of the
best wood in Paris, though this immense
capital annually requires more than three
hundred thousand cords, and is surrounded
to the distance of three hundred miles by
cultivated plains." In this town the price
of wood rises almost steadily, and the only
question is, how much higher it is to be this
year than it was the last. Mechanics and
tradesmen who come in person to the forest
on no other errand, are sure to attend the
wood auction, and even pay a high price for
the privilege of gleaning after the wood-
chopper. It is now many years that men
have resorted to the forest for fuel and the
materials of the arts : the New Englander
and the New Hollander, the Parisian and
the Celt, the farmer and Robinhood, Goody

Blake and Harry Gill; in most parts of the world the prince and the peasant, the scholar and the savage, equally require still a few sticks from the forest to warm them and cook their food. Neither could I do without them.

Every man looks at his wood-pile with a kind of affection. I loved to have mine before my window, and the more chips the better to remind me of my pleasing work. I had an old axe which nobody claimed, with which by spells in winter days, on the sunny side of the house, I played about the stumps which I had got out of my bean-field. As my driver prophesied when I was ploughing, they warmed me twice, — once while I was splitting them, and again when they were on the fire, so that no fuel could give out more heat. As for the axe, I was advised to get the village blacksmith to "jump" it; but I jumped him, and, putting a hickory helve from the woods into it, made it do. If it was dull, it was at least hung true.

A few pieces of fat pine were a great treasure. It is interesting to remember how much of this food for fire is still concealed in the bowels of the earth. In previous years I had often gone "prospecting" over

some bare hill side, where a pitch-pine wood
had formerly stood, and got out the fat
pine roots. They are almost indestructible.
Stumps thirty or forty years old, at least,
will still be sound at the core, though the
sapwood has all become vegetable mould, as
appears by the scales of the thick bark forming a ring level with the earth four or five
inches distant from the heart. With axe
and shovel you explore this mine, and follow
the marrowy store, yellow as beef tallow, or
as if you had struck on a vein of gold, deep
into the earth. But commonly I kindled my
fire with the dry leaves of the forest, which
I had stored up in my shed before the snow
came. Green hickory finely split makes the
wood - chopper's kindlings, when he has a
camp in the woods. Once in a while I got
a little of this. When the villagers were
lighting their fires beyond the horizon, I too
gave notice to the various wild inhabitants
of Walden vale, by a smoky streamer from
my chimney, that I was awake. —

> Light-winged Smoke, Icarian bird,
> Melting thy pinions in thy upward flight,
> Lark without song, and messenger of dawn,
> Circling above the hamlets as thy nest;
> Or else, departing dream, and shadowy form
> Of midnight vision, gathering up thy skirts;

By night star-veiling, and by day
Darkening the light and blotting out the sun;
Go thou my incense upward from this hearth,
And ask the gods to pardon this clear flame.

Hard green wood just cut, though I used but little of that, answered my purpose better than any other. I sometimes left a good fire when I went to take a walk in a winter afternoon; and when I returned, three or four hours afterward, it would be still alive and glowing. My house was not empty though I was gone. It was as if I had left a cheerful housekeeper behind. It was I and Fire that lived there; and commonly my housekeeper proved trustworthy. One day, however, as I was splitting wood, I thought that I would just look in at the window and see if the house was not on fire; it was the only time I remember to have been particularly anxious on this score; so I looked and saw that a spark had caught my bed, and I went in and extinguished it when it had burned a place as big as my hand. But my house occupied so sunny and sheltered a position, and its roof was so low, that I could afford to let the fire go out in the middle of almost any winter day.

The moles nested in my cellar, nibbling

every third potato, and making a snug bed
even there of some hair left after plastering
and of brown paper; for even the wildest
animals love comfort and warmth as well as
man, and they survive the winter only because they are so careful to secure them.
Some of my friends spoke as if I was coming to the woods on purpose to freeze myself. The animal merely makes a bed, which
he warms with his body, in a sheltered place;
but man, having discovered fire, boxes up
some air in a spacious apartment, and warms
that, instead of robbing himself, makes that
his bed, in which he can move about divested
of more cumbrous clothing, maintain a kind
of summer in the midst of winter, and by
means of windows even admit the light, and
with a lamp lengthen out the day. Thus he
goes a step or two beyond instinct, and saves
a little time for the fine arts. Though, when
I had been exposed to the rudest blasts a
long time, my whole body began to grow
torpid, when I reached the genial atmosphere of my house I soon recovered my
faculties and prolonged my life. But the
most luxuriously housed has little to boast
of in this respect, nor need we trouble ourselves to speculate how the human race may

be at last destroyed. It would be easy to
cut their threads any time with a little
sharper blast from the north. We go on
dating from Cold Fridays and Great Snows ;
but a little colder Friday, or greater snow
would put a period to man's existence on
the globe.

The next winter I used a small cooking-
stove for economy, since I did not own the
forest ; but it did not keep fire so well as
the open fireplace. Cooking was then, for
the most part, no longer a poetic, but merely
a chemic process. It will soon be forgotten,
in these days of stoves, that we used to
roast potatoes in the ashes, after the Indian
fashion. The stove not only took up room
and scented the house, but it concealed the
fire, and I felt as if I had lost a companion.
You can always see a face in the fire. The
laborer, looking into it at evening, purifies
his thoughts of the dross and earthiness
which they have accumulated during the
day. But I could no longer sit and look
into the fire, and the pertinent words of a
poet recurred to me with new force. —

> " Never, bright flame, may be denied to me
> Thy dear, life imaging, close sympathy.
> What but my hopes shot upward e'er so bright ?
> What but my fortunes sunk so low in night ?

Why art thou banished from our hearth and hall,
Thou who art welcomed and beloved by all ?
Was thy existence then too fanciful
For our life's common light, who are so dull ?
Did thy bright gleam mysterious converse hold
With our congenial souls ? secrets too bold ?

Well, we are safe and strong, for now we sit
Beside a hearth where no dim shadows flit,
Where nothing cheers nor saddens, but a fire
Warms feet and hands — nor does to more aspire ;
By whose compact utilitarian heap
The present may sit down and go to sleep,
Nor fear the ghosts who from the dim past walked,
And with us by the unequal light of the old wood
     fire talked."

XIV.

FORMER INHABITANTS ; AND WINTER VISITORS.

I WEATHERED some merry snow storms, and spent some cheerful winter evenings by my fireside, while the snow whirled wildly without, and even the hooting of the owl was hushed. For many weeks I met no one in my walks but those who came occasionally to cut wood and sled it to the village. The elements, however, abetted me in making a path through the deepest snow in the woods, for when I had once gone through the wind blew the oak leaves into my tracks, where they lodged, and by absorbing the rays of the sun melted the snow, and so not only made a dry bed for my feet, but in the night their dark line was my guide. For human society I was obliged to conjure up the former occupants of these woods. Within the memory of many of my townsmen the road near which my house stands resounded with the laugh and gossip of inhabitants, and the woods which border it were notched and dotted here and there with their little gardens and dwellings, though it was then much more shut in by the forest than now. In some places, within my own remembrance, the pines would scrape both sides of a chaise at once, and women and children who were compelled to go this way to Lincoln alone and on foot did it with fear, and often ran a good part of the distance. Though mainly but a humble route to neighboring villages, or for the woodman's team, it once amused the traveller more than now by its variety, and lingered longer in his memory. Where now firm open fields stretch from the village to the woods, it then ran through a maple swamp on a foundation of logs, the remnants of which, doubtless, still underlie the present dusty highway, from the Stratten, now the Alms House, Farm, to Brister's Hill.

East of my bean-field, across the road, lived Cato Ingraham, slave of Duncan Ingraham, Esquire, gentleman, of Concord village, who built his slave a house, and gave him permission to live in Walden Woods; — Cato, not Uticensis, but Concordiensis. Some say that he was a Guinea Negro. There are a few who remember his little patch among the walnuts, which he let grow up till he should be old and need them ; but a younger and whiter speculator got them at last. He too, however, occupies an equally narrow house at present. Cato's half - obliterated cellar hole still remains, though known to few, being concealed from the traveller by a fringe of pines. It is now filled with the smooth sumach, (*Rhus glabra,*) and one of the earliest species of goldenrod (*Solidago stricta*) grows there luxuriantly.

Here, by the very corner of my field, still nearer to town, Zilpha, a colored woman, had her little house, where she spun linen for the townsfolk, making the Walden Woods ring with her shrill singing, for she had a loud and notable voice. At length, in the war of 1812, her dwelling was set on fire by English soldiers, prisoners on parole, when she was away, and her cat and dog and hens were all burned up together. She led a hard life, and somewhat inhumane. One old frequenter of these woods remembers, that as he passed her house one noon he heard her muttering to herself over her gurgling pot, — " Ye are all bones, bones ! " I have seen bricks amid the oak copse there.

Down the road, on the right hand, on
Brister's Hill, lived Brister Freeman, "a
handy Negro," slave of Squire Cummings
once, — there where grow still the apple-
trees which Brister planted and tended ;
large old trees now, but their fruit still wild
and ciderish to my taste.　Not long since
I read his epitaph in the old Lincoln burying-ground, a little on one side, near the
unmarked graves of some British grenadiers
who fell in the retreat from Concord, —
where he is styled "Sippio Brister," — Sci-
pio Africanus he had some title to be called,
— "a man of color," as if he were discol-
ored.　It also told me, with staring emphasis, when he died ; which was but an indirect
way of informing me that he ever lived.
With him dwelt Fenda, his hospitable wife,
who told fortunes, yet pleasantly, — large,
round, and black, blacker than any of the
children of night, such a dusky orb as never
rose on Concord before or since.

Farther down the hill, on the left, on the
old road in the woods, are marks of some
homestead of the Stratten family ; whose
orchard once covered all the slope of Brister's Hill, but was long since killed out by
pitch-pines, excepting a few stumps, whose

old roots furnish still the wild stocks of many a thrifty village tree.

Nearer yet to town, you come to Breed's location, on the other side of the way, just on the edge of the wood ; ground famous for the pranks of a demon not distinctly named in old mythology, who has acted a prominent and astounding part in our New England life, and deserves, as much as any mythological character, to have his biography written one day ; who first comes in the guise of a friend or hired man, and then robs and murders the whole family, — New-England Rum. But history must not yet tell the tragedies enacted here ; let time intervene in some measure to assuage and lend an azure tint to them. Here the most indistinct and dubious tradition says that once a tavern stood ; the well the same, which tempered the traveller's beverage and refreshed his steed. Here then men saluted one another, and heard and told the news, and went their ways again.

Breed's hut was standing only a dozen years ago, though it had long been unoccupied. It was about the size of mine. It was set on fire by mischievous boys, one Election night, if I do not mistake. I lived on the

edge of the village then, and had just lost
myself over Davenant's Gondibert, that winter that I labored with a lethargy, — which,
by the way, I never knew whether to regard as a family complaint, having an uncle
who goes to sleep shaving himself, and is
obliged to sprout potatoes in a cellar Sundays, in order to keep awake and keep the
Sabbath, or as the consequence of my attempt to read Chalmers' collection of English poetry without skipping. It fairly over-
came my Nervii. I had just sunk my head
on this when the bells rung fire, and in hot
haste the engines rolled that way, led by
a straggling troop of men and boys, and I
among the foremost, for I had leaped the
brook. We thought it was far south over
the woods, — we who had run to fires before, — barn, shop, or dwelling-house, or all
together. "It's Baker's barn," cried one.
"It is the Codman Place," affirmed another.
And then fresh sparks went up above the
wood, as if the roof fell in, and we all
shouted "Concord to the rescue!" Wagons
shot past with furious speed and crushing
loads, bearing, perchance, among the rest,
the agent of the Insurance Company, who
was bound to go however far; and ever and

anon the engine bell tinkled behind, more slow and sure; and rearmost of all, as it was afterward whispered, came they who set the fire and gave the alarm. Thus we kept on like true idealists, rejecting the evidence of our senses, until at a turn in the road we heard the crackling and actually felt the heat of the fire from over the wall, and realized, alas! that we were there. The very nearness of the fire but cooled our ardor. At first we thought to throw a frog-pond on to it; but concluded to let it burn, it was so far gone and so worthless. So we stood round our engine, jostled one another, expressed our sentiments through speaking-trumpets, or in lower tone referred to the great conflagrations which the world has witnessed, including Bascom's shop, and, between ourselves, we thought that, were we there in season with our "tub," and a full frog-pond by, we could turn that threatened last and universal one into another flood. We finally retreated without doing any mischief, — returned to sleep and Gondibert. But as for Gondibert, I would except that passage in the preface about wit being the soul's powder, — "but most of mankind are strangers to wit, as Indians are to powder."

It chanced that I walked that way across
the fields the following night, about the
same hour, and hearing a low moaning at
this spot, I drew near in the dark, and discovered the only survivor of the family that
I know, the heir of both its virtues and its
vices, who alone was interested in this burning, lying on his stomach and looking over
the cellar wall at the still smouldering cin-
ders beneath, muttering to himself, as is his
wont. He had been working far off in the
river meadows all day, and had improved
the first moments that he could call his own
to visit the home of his fathers and his
youth. He gazed into the cellar from all
sides and points of view by turns, always
lying down to it, as if there was some treasure, which he remembered, concealed between the stones, where there was absolutely
nothing but a heap of bricks and ashes.
The house being gone, he looked at what
there was left. He was soothed by the sympathy which my mere presence implied, and
showed me, as well as the darkness permitted, where the well was covered up; which,
thank Heaven, could never be burned; and
he groped long about the wall to find the
well - sweep which his father had cut and

mounted, feeling for the iron hook or staple by which a burden had been fastened to the heavy end, — all that he could now cling to, — to convince me that it was no common "rider." I felt it, and still remark it almost daily in my walks, for by it hangs the history of a family.

Once more, on the left, where are seen the well and lilac bushes by the wall, in the now open field, lived Nutting and Le Grosse. But to return toward Lincoln.

Farther in the woods than any of these, where the road approaches nearest to the pond, Wyman the potter squatted, and furnished his townsmen with earthen ware, and left descendants to succeed him. Neither were they rich in worldly goods, holding the land by sufferance while they lived; and there often the sheriff came in vain to collect the taxes, and " attached a chip," for form's sake, as I have read in his accounts, there being nothing else that he could lay his hands on. One day in midsummer, when I was hoeing, a man who was carrying a load of pottery to market stopped his horse against my field and inquired concerning Wyman the younger. He had long ago bought a potter's wheel of him, and wished

to know what had become of him. I had
read of the potter's clay and wheel in Scripture, but it had never occurred to me that
the pots we use were not such as had come
down unbroken from those days, or grown
on trees like gourds somewhere, and I was
pleased to hear that so fictile an art was
ever practised in my neighborhood.

The last inhabitant of these woods before
me was an Irishman, Hugh Quoil, (if I
have spelt his name with coil enough,) who
occupied Wyman's tenement, — Col. Quoil,
he was called. Rumor said that he had been
a soldier at Waterloo. If he had lived I
should have made him fight his battles over
again. His trade here was that of a ditcher.
Napoleon went to St. Helena ; Quoil came
to Walden Woods. All I know of him is
tragic. He was a man of manners, like one
who had seen the world, and was capable of
more civil speech than you could well attend
to. He wore a great coat in midsummer, being affected with the trembling delirium, and
his face was the color of carmine. He died in
the road at the foot of Brister's Hill shortly
after I came to the woods, so that I have
not remembered him as a neighbor. Before
his house was pulled down, when his com-

rades avoided it as "an unlucky castle," I
visited it. There lay his old clothes curled
up by use, as if they were himself, upon his
raised plank bed. His pipe lay broken on
the hearth, instead of a bowl broken at the
fountain. The last could never have been
the symbol of his death, for he confessed to
me that, though he had heard of Brister's
Spring, he had never seen it; and soiled
cards, kings of diamonds spades and hearts,
were scattered over the floor. One black
chicken which the administrator could not
catch, black as night and as silent, not even
croaking, awaiting Reynard, still went to
roost in the next apartment. In the rear
there was the dim outline of a garden, which
had been planted but had never received its
first hoeing, owing to those terrible shaking
fits, though it was now harvest time. It was
overrun with Roman wormwood and beggar-
ticks, which last stuck to my clothes for all
fruit. The skin of a woodchuck was freshly
stretched upon the back of the house, a trophy of his last Waterloo; but no warm cap
or mittens would he want more.

　Now only a dent in the earth marks the
site of these dwellings, with buried cellar
stones, and strawberries, raspberries, thim-

ble-berries, hazel-bushes, and sumachs growing in the sunny sward there; some pitch-
pine or gnarled oak occupies what was the
chimney nook, and a sweet-scented black-
birch, perhaps, waves where the door-stone
was. Sometimes the well dent is visible,
where once a spring oozed; now dry and tear-
less grass; or it was covered deep, — not to
be discovered till some late day, — with a flat
stone under the sod, when the last of the
race departed. What a sorrowful act must
that be, — the covering up of wells! coinci-
dent with the opening of wells of tears.
These cellar dents, like deserted fox burrows,
old holes, are all that is left where once
were the stir and bustle of human life, and
" fate, free-will, foreknowledge absolute," in
some form and dialect or other were by
turns discussed. But all I can learn of their
conclusions amounts to just this, that " Cato
and Brister pulled wool;" which is about
as edifying as the history of more famous
schools of philosophy.

Still grows the vivacious lilac a generation after the door and lintel and the sill
are gone, unfolding its sweet-scented flowers
each spring, to be plucked by the musing
traveller; planted and tended once by chil-

dren's hands, in front-yard plots, — now standing by wall-sides in retired pastures, and giving place to new-rising forests ; — the last of that stirp, sole survivor of that family. Little did the dusky children think that the puny slip with its two eyes only, which they stuck in the ground in the shadow of the house and daily watered, would root itself so, and outlive them, and house itself in the rear that shaded it, and grown man's garden and orchard, and tell their story faintly to the lone wanderer a half century after they had grown up and died, — blossoming as fair, and smelling as sweet, as in that first spring. I mark its still tender, civil, cheerful, lilac colors.

But this small village, germ of something more, why did it fail while Concord keeps its ground? Were there no natural advantages, — no water privileges, forsooth? Ay, the deep Walden Pond and cool Brister's Spring, — privilege to drink long and healthy draughts at these, all unimproved by these men but to dilute their glass. They were universally a thirsty race. Might not the basket, stable-broom, mat-making, corn-parching, linen-spinning, and pottery business have thrived here, making the wilderness to blossom like the rose, and a numerous posterity have inherited the land of their fathers ? The sterile soil would at least have been proof against a low-land degeneracy. Alas! how little does the memory of these human inhabitants enhance the beauty of the landscape ! Again, perhaps, Nature will try, with me for a first settler, and my house raised last spring to be the oldest in the hamlet.

I am not aware that any man has ever built on the spot which I occupy. Deliver me from a city built on the site of a more ancient city, whose materials are ruins, whose gardens cemeteries. The soil is blanched and accursed there, and before that becomes necessary the earth itself will be destroyed. With such reminiscences I repeopled the woods and lulled myself asleep.

At this season I seldom had a visitor. When the snow lay deepest no wanderer ventured near my house for a week or fortnight at a time, but there I lived as snug as a meadow mouse, or as cattle and poultry which are said to have survived for a long time buried in drifts, even without food ; or like that early settler's family in the town of

Sutton, in this state, whose cottage was completely covered by the great snow of 1717 when he was absent, and an Indian found it only by the hole which the chimney's breath made in the drift, and so relieved the family. But no friendly Indian concerned himself about me; nor needed he, for the master of the house was at home. The Great Snow! How cheerful it is to hear of! When the farmers could not get to the woods and swamps with their teams, and were obliged to cut down the shade trees before their houses, and when the crust was harder cut off the trees in the swamps ten feet from the ground, as it appeared the next spring.

In the deepest snows, the path which I used from the highway to my house, about half a mile long, might have been represented by a meandering dotted line, with wide intervals between the dots. For a week of even weather I took exactly the same number of steps, and of the same length, coming and going, stepping deliberately and with the precision of a pair of dividers in my own deep tracks, — to such routine the winter reduces us, — yet often they were filled with heaven's own blue. But no weather interfered fatally with my walks, or rather

my going abroad, for I frequently tramped
eight or ten miles through the deepest snow
to keep an appointment with a beech-tree, or
a yellow-birch, or an old acquaintance among
the pines; when the ice and snow causing
their limbs to droop, and so sharpening their
tops, had changed the pines into fir-trees;
wading to the tops of the highest hills when
the snow was nearly two feet deep on a
level, and shaking down another snow-storm
on my head at every step; or sometimes
creeping and floundering thither on my
hands and knees, when the hunters had
gone into winter quarters. One afternoon
I amused myself by watching a barred owl
(*Strix nebulosa*) sitting on one of the lower
dead limbs of a white-pine, close to the
trunk, in broad daylight, I standing within
a rod of him. He could hear me when I
moved and cronched the snow with my feet,
but could not plainly see me. When I
made most noise he would stretch out his
neck, and erect his neck feathers, and open
his eyes wide; but their lids soon fell again,
and he began to nod. I too felt a slum-
berous influence after watching him half an
hour, as he sat thus with his eyes half open,
like a cat, winged brother of the cat. There

was only a narrow slit left between their lids, by which he preserved a peninsular relation to me ; thus, with half-shut eyes, looking out from the land of dreams, and endeavoring to realize me, vague object or mote that interrupted his visions. At length, on some louder noise or my nearer approach, he would grow uneasy and sluggishly turn about on his perch, as if impatient at having his dreams disturbed ; and when he launched himself off and flapped through the pines, spreading his wings to unexpected breadth, I could not hear the slightest sound from them. Thus, guided amid the pine boughs rather by a delicate sense of their neighborhood than by sight, feeling his twilight way as it were with his sensitive pinions, he found a new perch, where he might in peace await the dawning of his day.

As I walked over the long causeway made for the railroad through the meadows, I encountered many a blustering and nipping wind, for nowhere has it freer play ; and when the frost had smitten me on one cheek, heathen as I was, I turned to it the other also. Nor was it much better by the carriage road from Brister's Hill. For I came to town still, like a friendly Indian, when

the contents of the broad open fields were
all piled up between the walls of the Walden
road, and half an hour sufficed to obliterate
the tracks of the last traveller. And when
I returned new drifts would have formed,
through which I floundered, where the busy
north-west wind had been depositing the
powdery snow round a sharp angle in the
road, and not a rabbit's track, nor even the
fine print, the small type, of a meadow
mouse was to be seen. Yet I rarely failed
to find, even in midwinter, some warm and
springy swamp where the grass and the
skunk-cabbage still put forth with perennial
verdure, and some hardier bird occasionally
awaited the return of spring.

Sometimes, notwithstanding the snow,
when I returned from my walk at evening
I crossed the deep tracks of a wood-chopper
leading from my door, and found his pile
of whittlings on the hearth, and my house
filled with the odor of his pipe. Or on a
Sunday afternoon, if I chanced to be at
home, I heard the cronching of the snow
made by the step of a long-headed farmer,
who from far through the woods sought my
house, to have a social "crack;" one of
the few of his vocation who are "men on

their farms;" who donned a frock instead of a professor's gown, and is as ready to extract the moral out of church or state as to haul a load of manure from his barn-yard. We talked of rude and simple times, when men sat about large fires in cold bracing weather, with clear heads; and when other dessert failed, we tried our teeth on many a nut which wise squirrels have long since abandoned, for those which have the thickest shells are commonly empty.

The one who came from farthest to my lodge, through deepest snows and most dismal tempests, was a poet. A farmer, a hunter, a soldier, a reporter, even a philosopher, may be daunted; but nothing can deter a poet, for he is actuated by pure love. Who can predict his comings and goings? His business calls him out at all hours, even when doctors sleep. We made that small house ring with boisterous mirth and resound with the murmur of much sober talk, making amends then to Walden vale for the long silences. Broadway was still and deserted in comparison. At suitable intervals there were regular salutes of laughter, which might have been referred indifferently to the last uttered or the forth-coming jest.

We made many a "bran new" theory of
life over a thin dish of gruel, which com-
bined the advantages of conviviality with
the clear - headedness which philosophy requires.

I should not forget that during my last
winter at the pond there was another welcome visitor, who at one time came through
the village, through snow and rain and darkness, till he saw my lamp through the trees,
and shared with me some long winter evenings. One of the last of the philosophers,
— Connecticut gave him to the world, — he
peddled first her wares, afterwards, as he
declares, his brains. These he peddles still,
prompting God and disgracing man, bearing
for fruit his brain only, like the nut its kernel. I think that he must be the man of
the most faith of any alive. His words and
attitude always suppose a better state of
things than other men are acquainted with,
and he will be the last man to be disappointed as the ages revolve. He has no
venture in the present. But though comparatively disregarded now, when his day
comes, laws unsuspected by most will take
effect, and masters of families and rulers
will come to him for advice. —

"How blind that cannot see serenity!"

A true friend of man; almost the only
friend of human progress. An Old Mortality, say rather an Immortality, with unwearied patience and faith making plain the
image engraven in men's bodies, the God
of whom they are but defaced and leaning
monuments. With his hospitable intellect
he embraces children, beggars, insane, and
scholars, and entertains the thought of all,
adding to it commonly some breadth and
elegance. I think that he should keep a car-
avansary on the world's highway, where philosophers of all nations might put up, and
on his sign should be printed, "Entertainment for man, but not for his beast. Enter
ye that have leisure and a quiet mind, who
earnestly seek the right road." He is perhaps
the sanest man and has the fewest crotchets
of any I chance to know; the same yesterday and to-morrow. Of yore we had saun-
tered and talked, and effectually put the
world behind us; for he was pledged to
no institution in it, freeborn, *ingenuus*.
Whichever way we turned, it seemed that
the heavens and the earth had met together,
since he enhanced the beauty of the landscape. A blue-robed man, whose fittest

roof is the overarching sky which reflects his serenity. I do not see how he can ever die; Nature cannot spare him.

Having each some shingles of thought well dried, we sat and whittled them, trying our knives, and admiring the clear yellowish grain of the pumpkin pine. We waded so gently and reverently, or we pulled together so smoothly, that the fishes of thought were not scared from the stream, nor feared any angler on the bank, but came and went grandly, like the clouds which float through the western sky, and the mother-o'-pearl flocks which sometimes form and dissolve there. There we worked, revising mythology, rounding a fable here and there, and building castles in the air for which earth offered no worthy foundation. Great Looker! Great Expecter! to converse with whom was a New England Night's Entertainment. Ah! such discourse we had, hermit and philosopher, and the old settler I have spoken of, — we three, — it expanded and racked my little house; I should not dare to say how many pounds' weight there was above the atmospheric pressure on every circular inch; it opened its seams so that they had to be calked with much dulness

thereafter to stop the consequent leak ; —
but I had enough of that kind of oakum already picked.

There was one other with whom I had
" solid seasons," long to be remembered, at
his house in the village, and who looked in
upon me from time to time ; but I had no
more for society there.

There too, as everywhere, I sometimes expected the Visitor who never comes. The
Vishnu Purana says, " The house-holder is
to remain at eventide in his court-yard as
long as it takes to milk a cow, or longer if
he pleases, to await the arrival of a guest."
I often performed this duty of hospitality,
waited long enough to milk a whole herd of
cows, but did not see the man approaching
from the town.

XV.

WINTER ANIMALS.

WHEN the ponds were firmly frozen, they afforded not only new and shorter routes to many points, but new views from their surfaces of the familiar landscape around them. When I crossed Flints' Pond, after it was covered with snow, though I had often paddled about and skated over it, it was so unexpectedly wide and so strange that I could think of nothing but Baffin's Bay. The Lincoln hills rose up around me at the extremity of a snowy plain, in which I did not remember to have stood before; and the fishermen, at an indeterminable distance over the ice, moving slowly about with their wolfish dogs, passed for sealers or Esquimaux, or in misty weather loomed like fabulous creatures, and I did not know whether they were giants or pygmies. I took this course when I went to lecture in Lincoln in the evening, travelling in no road and passing no house between my own hut and the lecture room. In Goose Pond, which lay in my way, a colony of muskrats dwelt, and raised their cabins high above the ice, though none could be seen abroad when I crossed it. Walden, being like the rest usually bare of snow, or with only shallow and interrupted drifts on it, was my yard where I could walk freely when the snow was nearly two feet deep on a level elsewhere and the villagers were confined to their streets. There, far from the village street, and except at very long intervals, from the jingle of sleigh-bells, I slid and skated, as in a vast moose-yard well trodden, overhung by oak woods and solemn pines bent down with snow or bristling with icicles.

For sounds in winter nights, and often in winter days, I heard the forlorn but melodious note of a hooting owl indefinitely far; such a sound as the frozen earth would yield if struck with a suitable plectrum, the very *lingua vernacula* of Walden Wood, and quite familiar to me at last, though I never saw the bird while it was making it. I seldom opened my door in a winter evening without hearing it; *Hoo hoo hoo, hoorer hoo,* sounded sonorously, and the first three syllables accented somewhat like *how der do ;*

or sometimes *hoo hoo* only. One night in the beginning of winter, before the pond froze over, about nine o'clock, I was startled by the loud honking of a goose, and, stepping to the door, heard the sound of their wings like a tempest in the woods as they flew low over my house. They passed over the pond toward Fair Haven, seemingly deterred from settling by my light, their commodore honking all the while with a regular beat. Suddenly an unmistakable cat-owl from very near me, with the most harsh and tremendous voice I ever heard from any inhabitant of the woods, responded at regular intervals to the goose, as if determined to expose and disgrace this intruder from Hudson's Bay by exhibiting a greater compass and volume of voice in a native, and *boo-hoo* him out of Concord horizon. What do you mean by alarming the citadel at this time of night consecrated to me? Do you think I am ever caught napping at such an hour, and that I have not got lungs and a larynx as well as yourself? *Boo-hoo, boo-hoo, boo-hoo!* It was one of the most thrilling discords I ever heard. And yet, if you had a discriminating ear, there were in it the elements of a concord such as these plains never saw nor heard.

I also heard the whooping of the ice in the pond, my great bed-fellow in that part of Concord, as if it were restless in its bed and would fain turn over, were troubled with flatulency and bad dreams; or I was waked by the cracking of the ground by the frost, as if some one had driven a team against my door, and in the morning would find a crack in the earth a quarter of a mile long and a third of an inch wide.

Sometimes I heard the foxes as they ranged over the snow crust, in moonlight nights, in search of a partridge or other game, barking raggedly and demoniacally like forest dogs, as if laboring with some anxiety, or seeking expression, struggling for light and to be dogs outright and run freely in the streets; for if we take the ages into our account, may there not be a civilization going on among brutes as well as men? They seemed to me to be rudimental, burrowing men, still standing on their defence, awaiting their transformation. Sometimes one came near to my window, attracted by my light, barked a vulpine curse at me, and then retreated.

Usually the red squirrel (*Sciurus Hudsonius*) waked me in the dawn, coursing

over the roof and up and down the sides of
the house, as if sent out of the woods for
this purpose. In the course of the winter
I threw out half a bushel of ears of sweet-
corn, which had not got ripe, on to the snow
crust by my door, and was amused by watching the motions of the various animals which
were baited by it. In the twilight and the
night the rabbits came regularly and made
a hearty meal. All day long the red squirrels came and went, and afforded me much
entertainment by their manœuvres. One
would approach at first warily through the
shrub-oaks, running over the snow crust by
fits and starts like a leaf blown by the wind,
now a few paces this way, with wonderful
speed and waste of energy, making incon-
ceivable haste with his "trotters," as if it
were for a wager, and now as many paces
that way, but never getting on more than
half a rod at a time ; and then suddenly
pausing with a ludicrous expression and a
gratuitous somerset, as if all the eyes in the
universe were fixed on him, — for all the
motions of a squirrel, even in the most solitary recesses of the forest, imply spectators
as much as those of a dancing girl, — wast-
ing more time in delay and circumspection

than would have sufficed to walk the whole
distance, — I never saw one walk, — and
then suddenly, before you could say Jack
Robinson, he would be in the top of a young
pitch-pine, winding up his clock and chid-
ing all imaginary spectators, soliloquizing
and talking to all the universe at the same
time, — for no reason that I could ever detect, or he himself was aware of, I suspect.
At length he would reach the corn, and se-
lecting a suitable ear, frisk about in the
same uncertain trigonometrical way to the
top-most stick of my wood-pile, before my
window, where he looked me in the face, and
there sit for hours, supplying himself with a
new ear from time to time, nibbling at first
voraciously and throwing the half-naked
cobs about; till at length he grew more
dainty still and played with his food, tast-
ing only the inside of the kernel, and the
ear, which was held balanced over the stick
by one paw, slipped from his careless grasp
and fell to the ground, when he would look
over at it with a ludicrous expression of uncertainty, as if suspecting that it had life,
with a mind not made up whether to get it
again, or a new one, or be off; now thinking
of corn, then listening to hear what was in

the wind. So the little impudent fellow
would waste many an ear in a forenoon; till
at last, seizing some longer and plumper
one, considerably bigger than himself, and
skilfully balancing it, he would set out with
it to the woods, like a tiger with a buffalo,
by the same zigzag course and frequent
pauses, scratching along with it as if it were
too heavy for him and falling all the while,
making its fall a diagonal between a perpendicular and horizontal, being determined to
put it through at any rate; — a singularly
frivolous and whimsical fellow; — and so he
would get off with it to where he lived, perhaps carry it to the top of a pine-tree forty
or fifty rods distant, and I would afterwards
find the cobs strewn about the woods in various directions.

At length the jays arrive, whose discord-
ant screams were heard long before, as they
were warily making their approach an eighth
of a mile off, and in a stealthy and sneaking
manner they flit from tree to tree, nearer
and nearer, and pick up the kernels which
the squirrels have dropped. Then, sitting
on a pitch-pine bough, they attempt to swallow in their haste a kernel which is too big
for their throats and chokes them; and after

great labor they disgorge it, and spend an hour in the endeavor to crack it by repeated blows with their bills. They were manifestly thieves, and I had not much respect for them ; but the squirrels, though at first shy, went to work as if they were taking what was their own.

Meanwhile also came the chicadees in flocks, which, picking up the crumbs the squirrels had dropped, flew to the nearest twig, and, placing them under their claws, hammered away at them with their little bills, as if it were an insect in the bark, till they were sufficiently reduced for their slender throats. A little flock of these tit-mice came daily to pick a dinner out of my woodpile, or the crumbs at my door, with faint flitting lisping notes, like the tinkling of icicles in the grass, or else with sprightly *day day day*, or more rarely, in spring-like days, a wiry summery *phe-be* from the wood-side. They were so familiar that at length one alighted on an armful of wood which I was carrying in, and pecked at the sticks without fear. I once had a sparrow alight upon my shoulder for a moment while I was hoeing in a village garden, and I felt that I was more distinguished by that circumstance

than I should have been by any epaulet I
could have worn. The squirrels also grew
at last to be quite familiar, and occasionally
stepped upon my shoe, when that was the
nearest way.

When the ground was not yet quite covered, and again near the end of winter, when
the snow was melted on my south hill-side
and about my wood-pile, the partridges came
out of the woods morning and evening to
feed there. Whichever side you walk in the
woods the partridge bursts away on whirring
wings, jarring the snow from the dry leaves
and twigs on high, which comes sifting down
in the sunbeams like golden dust, for this
brave bird is not to be scared by winter. It
is frequently covered up by drifts, and, it is
said, " sometimes plunges from on wing into
the soft snow, where it remains concealed
for a day or two." I used to start them in
the open land also, where they had come out
of the woods at sunset to " bud " the wild
apple-trees. They will come regularly every
evening to particular trees, where the cunning sportsman lies in wait for them, and
the distant orchards next the woods suffer
thus not a little. I am glad that the partridge gets fed, at any rate. It is Nature's

own bird which lives on buds and diet-
drink.

In dark winter mornings, or in short winter afternoons, I sometimes heard a pack of
hounds threading all the woods with hounding cry and yelp, unable to resist the instinct
of the chase, and the note of the hunting
horn at intervals, proving that man was in
the rear. The woods ring again, and yet no
fox bursts forth on to the open level of the
pond, nor following pack pursuing their Ac-
tæon. And perhaps at evening I see the
hunters returning with a single brush trailing from their sleigh for a trophy, seeking
their inn. They tell me that if the fox
would remain in the bosom of the frozen
earth he would be safe, or if he would run
in a straight line away no fox-hound could
overtake him; but, having left his pursuers
far behind, he stops to rest and listen till
they come up, and when he runs he circles
round to his old haunts, where the hunters
await him. Sometimes, however, he will run
upon a wall many rods, and then leap off
far to one side, and he appears to know that
water will not retain his scent. A hunter
told me that he once saw a fox pursued by
hounds burst out on to Walden when the

ice was covered with shallow puddles, run
part way across, and then return to the same
shore. Ere long the hounds arrived, but
here they lost the scent. Sometimes a pack
hunting by themselves would pass my door,
and circle round my house, and yelp and
hound without regarding me, as if afflicted
by a species of madness, so that nothing
could divert them from the pursuit. Thus
they circle until they fall upon the recent
trail of a fox, for a wise hound will forsake
everything else for this. One day a man
came to my hut from Lexington to inquire
after his hound that made a large track, and
had been hunting for a week by himself.
But I fear that he was not the wiser for all
I told him, for every time I attempted to
answer his questions he interrupted me by
asking, " What do you do here ? " He had
lost a dog, but found a man.

One old hunter who has a dry tongue, who
used to come to bathe in Walden once every
year when the water was warmest, and at
such times looked in upon me, told me that
many years ago he took his gun one afternoon and went out for a cruise in Walden
Wood ; and as he walked the Wayland road
he heard the cry of hounds approaching,

and ere long a fox leaped the wall into the
road, and as quick as thought leaped the
other wall out of the road, and his swift
bullet had not touched him. Some way behind came an old hound and her three pups
in full pursuit, hunting on their own account, and disappeared again in the woods.
Late in the afternoon, as he was resting in
the thick woods south of Walden, he heard
the voice of the hounds far over toward Fair
Haven still pursuing the fox; and on they
came, their hounding cry which made all the
woods ring sounding nearer and nearer, now
from Well-Meadow, now from the Baker
Farm. For a long time he stood still and
listened to their music, so sweet to a hunter's
ear, when suddenly the fox appeared, threading the solemn aisles with an easy coursing
pace, whose sound was concealed by a sym-
pathetic rustle of the leaves, swift and still,
keeping the ground, leaving his pursuers far
behind; and, leaping upon a rock amid the
woods, he sat erect and listening, with his
back to the hunter. For a moment compassion restrained the latter's arm; but that
was a short-lived mood, and as quick as
thought can follow thought his piece was
levelled, and *whang !* — the fox rolling over

the rock lay dead on the ground. The hunter still kept his place and listened to the
hounds. Still on they came, and now the
near woods resounded through all their aisles
with their demoniac cry. At length the old
hound burst into view with muzzle to the
ground, and snapping the air as if possessed,
and ran directly to the rock; but spying the
dead fox she suddenly ceased her hounding,
as if struck dumb with amazement, and
walked round and round him in silence;
and one by one her pups arrived, and, like
their mother, were sobered into silence by
the mystery. Then the hunter came forward and stood in their midst, and the mystery was solved. They waited in silence
while he skinned the fox, then followed the
brush a while, and at length turned off into
the woods again. That evening a Weston
Squire came to the Concord hunter's cottage
to inquire for his hounds, and told how for
a week they had been hunting on their own
account from Weston woods. The Concord
hunter told him what he knew and offered
him the skin; but the other declined it and
departed. He did not find his hounds that
night, but the next day learned that they
had crossed the river and put up at a farm-

house for the night, whence, having been well fed, they took their departure early in the morning.

The hunter who told me this could remember one Sam Nutting, who used to hunt bears on Fair Haven Ledges, and exchange their skins for rum in Concord village; who told him, even, that he had seen a moose there. Nutting had a famous fox-hound named Burgoyne, —he pronounced it Bugine, — which my informant used to borrow. In the "Wast Book" of an old trader of this town, who was also a captain, town-clerk, and representative, I find the following entry. Jan. 18th, 1742–3, "John Melven Cr. by 1 Grey Fox $0 — 2 — 3$;" they are not now found here; and in his ledger, Feb. 7th, 1743, Hezekiah Stratton has credit "by $\frac{1}{2}$ a Catt skin $0 — 1 — 4\frac{1}{2}$;" of course, a wildcat, for Stratton was a sergeant in the old French war, and would not have got credit for hunting less noble game. Credit is given for deer skins also, and they were daily sold. One man still preserves the horns of the last deer that was killed in this vicinity, and another has told me the particulars of the hunt in which his uncle was engaged. The hunters were formerly a numerous and merry crew here. I remember well one gaunt Nimrod who would catch up a leaf by the road-side and play a strain on it wilder and more melodious, if my memory serves me, than any hunting horn.

At midnight, when there was a moon, I sometimes met with hounds in my path prowling about the woods, which would skulk out of my way, as if afraid, and stand silent amid the bushes till I had passed.

Squirrels and wild mice disputed for my store of nuts. There were scores of pitch-pines around my house, from one to four inches in diameter, which had been gnawed by mice the previous winter, — a Norwegian winter for them, for the snow lay long and deep, and they were obliged to mix a large proportion of pine bark with their other diet. These trees were alive and apparently flourishing at midsummer, and many of them had grown a foot, though completely girdled ; but after another winter such were without exception dead. It is remarkable that a single mouse should thus be allowed a whole pine - tree for its dinner, gnawing round instead of up and down it ; but perhaps it is necessary in order to thin these trees, which are wont to grow up densely.

The hares (*Lepus Americanus*) were very familiar. One had her form under my house all winter, separated from me only by the flooring, and she startled me each morning by her hasty departure when I began to stir, — thump, thump, thump, striking her head against the floor timbers in her hurry. They used to come round my door at dusk to nibble the potato parings which I had thrown out, and were so nearly the color of the ground that they could hardly be distinguished when still. Sometimes in the twilight I alternately lost and recovered sight of one sitting motionless under my window. When I opened my door in the evening, off they would go with a squeak and a bounce. Near at hand they only excited my pity. One evening one sat by my door two paces from me, at first trembling with fear, yet unwilling to move; a poor wee thing, lean and bony, with ragged ears and sharp nose, scant tail and slender paws. It looked as if Nature no longer contained the breed of nobler bloods, but stood on her last toes. Its large eyes appeared young and unhealthy, almost dropsical. I took a step, and lo, away it scud with an elastic spring over the snow crust, straightening its

body and its limbs into graceful length, and
soon put the forest between me and itself, —
the wild free venison, asserting its vigor and
the dignity of Nature. Not without reason
was, its slenderness. Such then was its nature. (*Lepus, levipes,* light-foot some think.)

What is a country without rabbits and
partridges? They are among the most simple and indigenous animal products; ancient and venerable families known to antiquity as to modern times; of the very hue
and substance of Nature, nearest allied to
leaves and to the ground, — and to one another; it is either winged or it is legged.
It is hardly as if you had seen a wild creature when a rabbit or a partridge bursts
away, only a natural one, as much to be
expected as rustling leaves. The partridge
and the rabbit are still sure to thrive, like
true natives of the soil, whatever revolutions
occur. If the forest is cut off, the sprouts
and bushes which spring up afford them
concealment, and they become more numerous than ever. That must be a poor country indeed that does not support a hare.
Our woods teem with them both, and around
every swamp may be seen the partridge or
rabbit walk, beset with twiggy fences and
horse-hair snares, which some cow-boy tends.

XVI.

THE POND IN WINTER.

AFTER a still winter night I awoke with
the impression that some question had been
put to me, which I had been endeavoring in
vain to answer in my sleep, as what — how
— when — where ? But there was dawning
Nature, in whom all creatures live, looking
in at my broad windows with serene and satisfied face, and no question on *her* lips. I
awoke to an answered question, to Nature
and daylight. The snow lying deep on the
earth dotted with young pines, and the very
slope of the hill on which my house is
placed, seemed to say, Forward ! Nature
puts no question and answers none which we
mortals ask. She has long ago taken her
resolution. "O Prince, our eyes contemplate with admiration and transmit to the
soul the wonderful and varied spectacle of
this universe. The night veils without doubt
a part of this glorious creation; but day
comes to reveal to us this great work, which

extends from earth even into the plains of the ether."

Then to my morning work. First I take an axe and pail and go in search of water, if that be not a dream. After a cold and snowy night it needed a divining rod to find it. Every winter the liquid and trembling surface of the pond, which was so sensitive to every breath, and reflected every light and shadow, becomes solid to the depth of a foot or a foot and a half, so that it will support the heaviest teams, and perchance the snow covers it to an equal depth, and it is not to be distinguished from any level field. Like the marmots in the surrounding hills, it closes its eyelids and becomes dormant for three months or more. Standing on the snow-covered plain, as if in a pasture amid the hills, I cut my way first through a foot of snow, and then a foot of ice, and open a window under my feet, where, kneeling to drink, I look down into the quiet parlor of the fishes, pervaded by a softened light as through a window of ground glass, with its bright sanded floor the same as in summer ; there a perennial waveless serenity reigns as in the amber twilight sky, corresponding to the cool and even temperament of the inhabitants. Heaven is under our feet as well as over our heads.

Early in the morning, while all things are crisp with frost, men come with fishing reels and slender lunch, and let down their fine lines through the snowy field to take pickerel and perch ; wild men, who instinctively follow other fashions and trust other authorities than their townsmen, and by their goings and comings stitch towns together in parts where else they would be ripped. They sit and eat their luncheon in stout fear-naughts on the dry oak leaves on the shore, as wise in natural lore as the citizen is in artificial. They never consulted with books, and know and can tell much less than they have done. The things which they practise are said not yet to be known. Here is one fishing for pickerel with grown perch for bait. You look into his pail with wonder as into a summer pond, as if he kept summer locked up at home, or knew where she had retreated. How, pray, did he get these in midwinter ? O, he got worms out of rotten logs since the ground froze, and so he caught them. His life itself passes deeper in Nature than the studies of the naturalist penetrate ; himself a subject for the naturalist. The latter raises the moss and bark gently with his knife in search of insects; the former lays open logs to their core with his axe, and moss and bark fly far and wide. He gets his living by barking trees. Such a man has some right to fish, and I love to see Nature carried out in him. The perch swallows the grub-worm, the pickerel swallows the perch, and the fisherman swallows the pickerel; and so all the chinks in the scale of being are filled.

When I strolled around the pond in misty weather I was sometimes amused by the primitive mode which some ruder fisherman had adopted. He would perhaps have placed alder branches over the narrow holes in the ice, which were four or five rods apart and an equal distance from the shore, and having fastened the end of the line to a stick to prevent its being pulled through, have passed the slack line over a twig of the alder, a foot or more above the ice, and tied a dry oak leaf to it, which, being pulled down, would show when he had a bite. These alders loomed through the mist at regular intervals as you walked half way round the pond.

Ah, the pickerel of Walden! when I see

them lying on the ice, or in the well which
the fisherman cuts in the ice, making a little
hole to admit the water, I am always surprised by their rare beauty, as if they were
fabulous fishes, they are so foreign to the
streets, even to the woods, foreign as Arabia
to our Concord life. They possess a quite
dazzling and transcendent beauty which separates them by a wide interval from the cadav-
erous cod and haddock whose fame is trum-
peted in our streets. They are not green like
the pines, nor gray like the stones, nor blue
like the sky; but they have, to my eyes, if
possible, yet rarer colors, like flowers and
precious stones, as if they were the pearls,
the animalized *nuclei* or crystals of the Walden water. They, of course, are Walden all
over and all through; are themselves small
Waldens in the animal kingdom, Waldenses.
It is surprising that they are caught here, —
that in this deep and capacious spring, far
beneath the rattling teams and chaises and
tinkling sleighs that travel the Walden road,
this great gold and emerald fish swims. I
never chanced to see its kind in any market;
it would be the cynosure of all eyes there.
Easily, with a few convulsive quirks, they
give up their watery ghosts, like a mortal

translated before his time to the thin air of
heaven.

As I was desirous to recover the long lost
bottom of Walden Pond, I surveyed it carefully, before the ice broke up, early in '46,
with compass and chain and sounding line.
There have been many stories told about the
bottom, or rather no bottom, of this pond,
which certainly had no foundation for themselves.   It is remarkable how long men will
believe in the bottomlessness of a pond without taking the trouble to sound it.   I have
visited two such Bottomless Ponds in one
walk in this neighborhood.   Many have believed that Walden reached quite through to
the other side of the globe.   Some who have
lain flat on the ice for a long time, looking
down through the illusive medium, perchance
with watery eyes into the bargain, and driven
to hasty conclusions by the fear of catching
cold in their breasts, have seen vast holes
" into which a load of hay might be driven,"
if there were anybody to drive it, the un-
doubted source of the Styx and entrance to
the Infernal Regions from these parts.   Others have gone down from the village with a
" fifty-six " and a wagon load of inch rope,

but yet have failed to find any bottom ; for while the " fifty - six " was resting by the way, they were paying out the rope in the vain attempt to fathom their truly immeasurable capacity for marvellousness. But I can assure my readers that Walden has a reasonably tight bottom at a not unreasonable, though at an unusual, depth. I fathomed it easily with a cod-line and a stone weighing about a pound and a half, and could tell accurately when the stone left the bottom, by having to pull so much harder before the water got underneath to help me. The greatest depth was exactly one hundred and two feet; to which may be added the five feet which it has risen since, making one hundred and seven. This is a remarkable depth for so small an area ; yet not an inch of it can be spared by the imagination. What if all ponds were shallow ? Would it not react on the minds of men ? I am thankful that this pond was made deep and pure for a symbol. While men believe in the infinite some ponds will be thought to be bottomless.

A factory owner, hearing what depth I had found, thought that it could not be true, for, judging from his acquaintance with dams,

sand would not lie at so steep an angle. But
the deepest ponds are not so deep in proportion to their area as most suppose, and, if
drained, would not leave very remarkable
valleys. They are not like cups between the
hills; for this one, which is so unusually
deep for its area, appears in a vertical section through its centre not deeper than a
shallow plate. Most ponds, emptied, would
leave a meadow no more hollow than we frequently see. William Gilpin, who is so admirable in all that relates to landscapes, and
usually so correct, standing at the head of
Loch Fyne, in Scotland, which he describes
as "a bay of salt water, sixty or seventy
fathoms deep, four miles in breadth," and
about fifty miles long, surrounded by mountains, observes, "If we could have seen it immediately after the diluvian crash, or whatever convulsion of Nature occasioned it,
before the waters gushed in, what a horrid
chasm it must have appeared!

> "So high as heaved the tumid hills, so low
> Down sunk a hollow bottom, broad, and deep,
> Capacious bed of waters ——."

But if, using the shortest diameter of Loch
Fyne, we apply these proportions to Walden, which, as we have seen, appears already

in a vertical section only like a shallow plate,
it will appear four times as shallow. So
much for the *increased* horrors of the chasm
of Loch Fyne when emptied. No doubt
many a smiling valley with its stretching
cornfields occupies exactly such a " horrid
chasm," from which the waters have receded,
though it requires the insight and the far
sight of the geologist to convince the unsus-
pecting inhabitants of this fact. Often an
inquisitive eye may detect the shores of a
primitive lake in the low horizon hills, and
no subsequent elevation of the plain have
been necessary to conceal their history. But
it is easiest, as they who work on the highways know, to find the hollows by the puddles after a shower. The amount of it is,
the imagination, give it the least license,
dives deeper and soars higher than Nature
goes. So, probably, the depth of the ocean
will be found to be very inconsiderable compared with its breadth.

As I sounded through the ice I could de-
termine the shape of the bottom with greater
accuracy than is possible in surveying har-
bors which do not freeze over, and I was
surprised at its general regularity. In the
deepest part there are several acres more

level than almost any field which is exposed to the sun, wind, and plough. In one
instance, on a line arbitrarily chosen, the
depth did not vary more than one foot in
thirty rods; and generally, near the middle,
I could calculate the variation for each one
hundred feet in any direction beforehand
within three or four inches. Some are accustomed to speak of deep and dangerous
holes even in quiet sandy ponds like this,
but the effect of water under these circumstances is to level all inequalities. The regularity of the bottom and its conformity to
the shores and the range of the neighboring
hills were so perfect that a distant promontory betrayed itself in the soundings quite
across the pond, and its direction could be
determined by observing the opposite shore.
Cape becomes bar, and plain shoal, and valley and gorge deep water and channel.

When I had mapped the pond by the
scale of ten rods to an inch, and put down
the soundings, more than a hundred in all, I
observed this remarkable coincidence. Having noticed that the number indicating the
greatest depth was apparently in the centre
of the map, I laid a rule on the map length-
wise, and then breadthwise, and found, to

my surprise, that the line of greatest length intersected the line of greatest breadth *exactly* at the point of greatest depth, notwithstanding that the middle is so nearly level, the outline of the pond far from regular, and the extreme length and breadth were got by measuring into the coves ; and I said to myself, Who knows but this hint would conduct to the deepest part of the ocean as well as of a pond or puddle ? Is not this the rule also for the height of mountains, regarded as the opposite of valleys ? We know that a hill is not highest at its narrowest part.

Of five coves, three, or all which had been sounded, were observed to have a bar quite across their mouths and deeper water within, so that the bay tended to be an expansion of water within the land not only horizontally but vertically, and to form a basin or independent pond, the direction of the two capes showing the course of the bar. Every harbor on the sea-coast, also, has its bar at its entrance. In proportion as the mouth of the cove was wider compared with its length, the water over the bar was deeper compared with that in the basin. Given, then, the length and breadth of the cove, and the character of the surrounding shore, and you have almost elements enough to make out a formula for all cases.

In order to see how nearly I could guess, with this experience, at the deepest point in a pond, by observing the outlines of its surface and the character of its shores alone, I made a plan of White Pond, which contains about forty-one acres, and, like this, has no island in it, nor any visible inlet or outlet; and as the line of greatest breadth fell very near the line of least breadth, where two opposite capes approached each other and two opposite bays receded, I ventured to mark a point a short distance from the latter line, but still on the line of greatest length, as the deepest. The deepest part was found to be within one hundred feet of this, still farther in the direction to which I had inclined, and was only one foot deeper, namely, sixty feet. Of course, a stream running through, or an island in the pond, would make the problem much more complicated.

If we knew all the laws of Nature, we should need only one fact, or the description of one actual phenomenon, to infer all the particular results at that point. Now we know only a few laws, and our result is viti-

ated, not, of course, by any confusion or ir-
regularity in Nature, but by our ignorance
of essential elements in the calculation. Our
notions of law and harmony are commonly
confined to those instances which we detect;
but the harmony which results from a far
greater number of seemingly conflicting, but
really concurring, laws, which we have not
detected, is still more wonderful. The particular laws are as our points of view, as, to
the traveller, a mountain outline varies with
every step, and it has an infinite number
of profiles, though absolutely but one form.
Even when cleft or bored through it is not
comprehended in its entireness.

What I have observed of the pond is no
less true in ethics. It is the law of average.
Such a rule of the two diameters not only
guides us toward the sun in the system and
the heart in man, but draw lines through
the length and breadth of the aggregate of
a man's particular daily behaviors and
waves of life into his coves and inlets, and
where they intersect will be the height or
depth of his character. Perhaps we need
only to know how his shores trend and his
adjacent country or circumstances, to infer
his depth and concealed bottom. If he is

surrounded by mountainous circumstances,
an Achillean shore, whose peaks overshadow
and are reflected in his bosom, they suggest
a corresponding depth in him. But a low
and smooth shore proves him shallow on
that side. In our bodies, a bold projecting
brow falls off to and indicates a corresponding depth of thought. Also there is a bar
across the entrance of our every cove, or
particular inclination; each is our harbor
for a season, in which we are detained and
partially land-locked. These inclinations are
not whimsical usually, but their form, size,
and direction are determined by the prom-
ontories of the shore, the ancient axes of
elevation. When this bar is gradually increased by storms, tides, or currents, or
there is a subsidence of the waters, so that
it reaches to the surface, that which was at
first but an inclination in the shore in which
a thought was harbored becomes an individual lake, cut off from the ocean, wherein
the thought secures its own conditions, —
changes, perhaps, from salt to fresh, becomes
a sweet sea, dead sea, or a marsh. At the
advent of each individual into this life, may
we not suppose that such a bar has risen to
the surface somewhere? It is true, we are

such poor navigators that our thoughts, for the most part, stand off and on upon a harborless coast, are conversant only with the bights of the bays of poesy, or steer for the public ports of entry, and go into the dry docks of science, where they merely refit for this world, and no natural currents concur to individualize them.

As for the inlet or outlet of Walden, I have not discovered any but rain and snow and evaporation, though perhaps, with a thermometer and a line, such places may be found, for where the water flows into the pond it will probably be coldest in summer and warmest in winter. When the ice-men were at work here in '46-7, the cakes sent to the shore were one day rejected by those who were stacking them up there, not being thick enough to lie side by side with the rest ; and the cutters thus discovered that the ice over a small space was two or three inches thinner than elsewhere, which made them think that there was an inlet there. They also showed me in another place what they thought was a " leach hole," through which the pond leaked out under a hill into a neighboring meadow, pushing me out on a cake of ice to see it. It was a small cavity

under ten feet of water; but I think that I
can warrant the pond not to need soldering
till they find a worse leak than that. One
has suggested, that if such a " leach hole "
should be found, its connection with the
meadow, if any existed, might be proved by
conveying some colored powder or sawdust
to the mouth of the hole, and then putting
a strainer over the spring in the meadow,
which would catch some of the particles carried through by the current.

While I was surveying, the ice, which
was sixteen inches thick, undulated under
a slight wind like water. It is well known
that a level cannot be used on ice. At one
rod from the shore its greatest fluctuation,
when observed by means of a level on land
directed toward a graduated staff on the ice,
was three quarters of an inch, though the
ice appeared firmly attached to the shore.
It was probably greater in the middle.
Who knows but if our instruments were delicate enough we might detect an undulation
in the crust of the earth? When two legs
of my level were on the shore and the third
on the ice, and the sights were directed over
the latter, a rise or fall of the ice of an almost infinitesimal amount made a difference

of several feet on a tree across the pond.
When I began to cut holes for sounding
there were three or four inches of water on
the ice under a deep snow which had sunk
it thus far; but the water began immediately to run into these holes, and continued
to run for two days in deep streams, which
wore away the ice on every side, and con-
tributed essentially, if not mainly, to dry
the surface of the pond; for, as the water
ran in, it raised and floated the ice. This
was somewhat like cutting a hole in the bottom of a ship to let the water out. When
such holes freeze, and a rain succeeds, and
finally a new freezing forms a fresh smooth
ice over all, it is beautifully mottled internally by dark figures, shaped somewhat like
a spider's web, what you may call ice ro-
settes, produced by the channels worn by
the water flowing from all sides to a centre.
Sometimes, also, when the ice was covered
with shallow puddles, I saw a double shadow
of myself, one standing on the head of the
other, one on the ice, the other on the trees
or hill-side.

While yet it is cold January, and snow
and ice are thick and solid, the prudent

landlord comes from the village to get ice to
cool his summer drink ; impressively, even
pathetically, wise, to foresee the heat and
thirst of July now in January, — wearing
a thick coat and mittens ! when so many
things are not provided for. It may be that
he lays up no treasures in this world which
will cool his summer drink in the next. He
cuts and saws the solid pond, unroofs the
house of fishes, and carts off their very element and air, held fast by chains and stakes
like corded wood, through the favoring winter air, to wintry cellars, to underlie the
summer there. It looks like solidified azure,
as, far off, it is drawn through the streets.
These ice-cutters are a merry race, full of
jest and sport, and when I went among
them they were wont to invite me to saw
pit - fashion with them, I standing underneath.

In the winter of '46–7 there came a hundred men of Hyperborean extraction swoop
down on to our pond one morning, with
many car-loads of ungainly-looking farming
tools, — sleds, ploughs, drill - barrows, turf-
knives, spades, saws, rakes, and each man
was armed with a double-pointed pike-staff,
such as is not described in the New-England

Farmer or the Cultivator. I did not know
whether they had come to sow a crop of winter rye, or some other kind of grain recently
introduced from Iceland. As I saw no manure, I judged that they meant to skim the
land, as I had done, thinking the soil was
deep and had lain fallow long enough.
They said that a gentleman farmer, who
was behind the scenes, wanted to double his
money, which, as I understood, amounted to
half a million already ; but in order to cover
each one of his dollars with another, he took
off the only coat, ay, the skin itself, of Walden Pond in the midst of a hard winter.
They went to work at once, ploughing, har-
rowing, rolling, furrowing, in admirable order, as if they were bent on making this a
model farm ; but when I was looking sharp
to see what kind of seed they dropped into
the furrow, a gang of fellows by my side
suddenly began to hook up the virgin mould
itself, with a peculiar jerk, clean down to
the sand, or rather the water, — for it was a
very springy soil, — indeed all the *terra firma*
there was, — and haul it away on sleds, and
then I guessed that they must be cutting
peat in a bog. So they came and went
every day, with a peculiar shriek from the

locomotive, from and to some point of the
polar regions, as it seemed to me, like a flock
of arctic snow-birds. But sometimes Squaw
Walden had her revenge, and a hired man,
walking behind his team, slipped through a
crack in the ground down toward Tartarus,
and he who was so brave before suddenly
became but the ninth part of a man, almost
gave up his animal heat, and was glad to
take refuge in my house, and acknowledged
that there was some virtue in a stove; or
sometimes the frozen soil took a piece of
steel out of a ploughshare, or a plough got
set in the furrow and had to be cut out.

To speak literally, a hundred Irishmen,
with Yankee overseers, came from Cambridge every day to get out the ice. They
divided it into cakes by methods too well
known to require description, and these, being sledded to the shore, were rapidly hauled
off on to an ice platform, and raised by grap-
pling irons and block and tackle, worked by
horses, on to a stack, as surely as so many
barrels of flour, and there placed evenly
side by side, and row upon row, as if they
formed the solid base of an obelisk designed
to pierce the clouds. They told me that in
a good day they could get out a thousand

tons, which was the yield of about one acre. Deep ruts and " cradle holes " were worn in the ice, as on *terra firma*, by the passage of the sleds over the same track, and the horses invariably ate their oats out of cakes of ice hollowed out like buckets. They stacked up the cakes thus in the open air in a pile thirty-five feet high on one side and six or seven rods square, putting hay between the outside layers to exclude the air; for when the wind, though never so cold, finds a passage through, it will wear large cavities, leaving slight supports or studs only here and there, and finally topple it down. At first it looked like a vast blue fort or Valhalla; but when they began to tuck the coarse meadow hay into the crevices, and this became covered with rime and icicles, it looked like a venerable moss - grown and hoary ruin, built of azure - tinted marble, the abode of Winter, that old man we see in the almanac, — his shanty, as if he had a design to estivate with us. They calculated that not twenty - five per cent. of this would reach its destination, and that two or three per cent. would be wasted in the cars. However, a still greater part of this heap had a different destiny from what was intended; for, either because

the ice was found not to keep so well as was
expected, containing more air than usual, or
for some other reason, it never got to market. This heap, made in the winter of '46–7
and estimated to contain ten thousand tons,
was finally covered with hay and boards;
and though it was unroofed the following
July, and a part of it carried off, the rest
remaining exposed to the sun, it stood over
that summer and the next winter, and was
not quite melted till September, 1848. Thus
the pond recovered the greater part.

Like the water, the Walden ice, seen near
at hand, has a green tint, but at a distance
is beautifully blue, and you can easily tell
it from the white ice of the river, or the
merely greenish ice of some ponds, a quarter of a mile off. Sometimes one of those
great cakes slips from the ice-man's sled into
the village street, and lies there for a week
like a great emerald, an object of interest to
all passers. I have noticed that a portion
of Walden which in the state of water was
green will often, when frozen, appear from
the same point of view blue. So the hollows
about this pond will, sometimes, in the winter, be filled with a greenish water somewhat
like its own, but the next day will have

frozen blue. Perhaps the blue color of water and ice is due to the light and air they
contain, and the most transparent is the
bluest. Ice is an interesting subject for
contemplation. They told me that they had
some in the ice-houses at Fresh Pond five
years old which was as good as ever. Why
is it that a bucket of water soon becomes
putrid, but frozen remains sweet forever? It
is commonly said that this is the difference
between the affections and the intellect.

Thus for sixteen days I saw from my window a hundred men at work like busy hus-
bandmen, with teams and horses and apparently all the implements of farming, such a
picture as we see on the first page of the almanac ; and as often as I looked out I was
reminded of the fable of the lark and the
reapers, or the parable of the sower, and
the like ; and now they are all gone, and in
thirty days more, probably, I shall look from
the same window on the pure sea-green Walden water there, reflecting the clouds and
the trees, and sending up its evaporations in
solitude, and no traces will appear that a
man has ever stood there. Perhaps I shall
hear a solitary loon laugh as he dives and
plumes himself, or shall see a lonely fisher in

his boat, like a floating leaf, beholding his
form reflected in the waves, where lately a
hundred men securely labored.

Thus it appears that the sweltering inhabitants of Charleston and New Orleans, of
Madras and Bombay and Calcutta, drink at
my well. In the morning I bathe my intellect in the stupendous and cosmogonal philosophy of the Bhagvat Geeta, since whose
composition years of the gods have elapsed,
and in comparison with which our modern
world and its literature seem puny and trivial ; and I doubt if that philosophy is not
to be referred to a previous state of existence, so remote is its sublimity from our conceptions. I lay down the book and go to
my well for water, and lo ! there I meet the
servant of the Bramin, priest of Brahma and
Vishnu and Indra, who still sits in his temple on the Ganges reading the Vedas, or
dwells at the root of a tree with his crust
and water jug. I meet his servant come to
draw water for his master, and our buckets
as it were grate together in the same well.
The pure Walden water is mingled with the
sacred water of the Ganges. With favoring
winds it is wafted past the site of the fabulous islands of Atlantis and the Hesperides,

makes the periplus of Hanno, and, floating by Ternate and Tidore and the mouth of the Persian Gulf, melts in the tropic gales of the Indian seas, and is landed in ports of which Alexander only heard the names.

XVII.

SPRING.

THE opening of large tracts by the ice-cutters commonly causes a pond to break up earlier; for the water, agitated by the wind, even in cold weather, wears away the surrounding ice. But such was not the effect on Walden that year, for she had soon got a thick new garment to take the place of the old. This pond never breaks up so soon as the others in this neighborhood, on account both of its greater depth and its having no stream passing through it to melt or wear away the ice. I never knew it to open in the course of a winter, not excepting that of '52–3, which gave the ponds so severe a trial. It commonly opens about the first of April, a week or ten days later than Flints' Pond and Fair Haven, beginning to melt on the north side and in the shallower parts where it began to freeze. It indicates better than any water hereabouts the absolute progress of the season, being least affected by transient

changes of temperature. A severe cold of a
few days' duration in March may very much
retard the opening of the former ponds, while
the temperature of Walden increases almost
uninterruptedly. A thermometer thrust into
the middle of Walden on the 6th of March,
1847, stood at 32°, or freezing point; near
the shore at 33°; in the middle of Flints'
Pond, the same day, at 32½°; at a dozen
rods from the shore, in shallow water, under
ice a foot thick, at 36°. This difference of
three and a half degrees between the temperature of the deep water and the shallow
in the latter pond, and the fact that a great
proportion of it is comparatively shallow,
show why it should break up so much sooner
than Walden. The ice in the shallowest
part was at this time several inches thinner
than in the middle. In midwinter the middle had been the warmest and the ice thin-
nest there. So, also, every one who has
waded about the shores of a pond in summer must have perceived how much warmer
the water is close to the shore, where only
three or four inches deep, than a little distance out, and on the surface where it is
deep, than near the bottom. In spring the
sun not only exerts an influence through the

increased temperature of the air and earth,
but its heat passes through ice a foot or
more thick, and is reflected from the bottom
in shallow water, and so also warms the water and melts the under side of the ice, at
the same time that it is melting it more directly above, making it uneven, and causing
the air bubbles which it contains to extend
themselves upward and downward until it is
completely honey-combed, and at last disappears suddenly in a single spring rain. Ice
has its grain as well as wood, and when a
cake begins to rot or "comb," that is, assume the appearance of honey-comb, whatever may be its position, the air cells are at
right angles with what was the water surface. Where there is a rock or a log rising
near to the surface the ice over it is much
thinner, and is frequently quite dissolved by
this reflected heat; and I have been told
that in the experiment at Cambridge to
freeze water in a shallow wooden pond,
though the cold air circulated underneath,
and so had access to both sides, the reflection of the sun from the bottom more than
counterbalanced this advantage. When a
warm rain in the middle of the winter melts
off the snow-ice from Walden, and leaves a

hard dark or transparent ice on the middle, there will be a strip of rotten though thicker white ice, a rod or more wide, about the shores, created by this reflected heat. Also, as I have said, the bubbles themselves within the ice operate as burning glasses to melt the ice beneath.

The phenomena of the year take place every day in a pond on a small scale. Every morning, generally speaking, the shallow water is being warmed more rapidly than the deep, though it may not be made so warm after all, and every evening it is being cooled more rapidly until the morning. The day is an epitome of the year. The night is the winter, the morning and evening are the spring and fall, and the noon is the summer. The cracking and booming of the ice indicate a change of temperature. One pleasant morning after a cold night, February 24th, 1850, having gone to Flints' Pond to spend the day, I noticed with surprise, that when I struck the ice with the head of my axe, it resounded like a gong for many rods around, or as if I had struck on a tight drum-head. The pond began to boom about an hour after sunrise, when it felt the influence of the sun's rays slanted upon it

from over the hills ; it stretched itself and
yawned like a waking man with a gradually
increasing tumult, which was kept up three
or four hours. It took a short siesta at
noon, and boomed once more toward night,
as the sun was withdrawing his influence.
In the right stage of the weather a pond
fires its evening gun with great regularity.
But in the middle of the day, being full of
cracks, and the air also being less elastic, it
had completely lost its resonance, and probably fishes and muskrats could not then
have been stunned by a blow on it. The
fishermen say that the " thundering of the
pond " scares the fishes and prevents their
biting. The pond does not thunder every
evening, and I cannot tell surely when to
expect its thundering ; but though I may
perceive no difference in the weather, it
does. Who would have suspected so large
and cold and thick-skinned a thing to be so
sensitive ? Yet it has its law to which it
thunders obedience when it should as surely
as the buds expand in the spring. The
earth is all alive and covered with papillæ.
The largest pond is as sensitive to atmospheric changes as the globule of mercury in
its tube.

One attraction in coming to the woods to live was that I should have leisure and opportunity to see the Spring come in. The ice in the pond at length begins to be honey-combed, and I can set my heel in it as I walk. Fogs and rains and warmer suns are gradually melting the snow; the days have grown sensibly longer; and I see how I shall get through the winter without adding to my wood-pile, for large fires are no longer necessary. I am on the alert for the first signs of spring, to hear the chance note of some arriving bird, or the striped squirrel's chirp, for his stores must be now nearly exhausted, or see the woodchuck venture out of his winter quarters. On the 13th of March, after I had heard the bluebird, song-sparrow, and red-wing, the ice was still nearly a foot thick. As the weather grew warmer it was not sensibly worn away by the water, nor broken up and floated off as in rivers, but, though it was completely melted for half a rod in width about the shore, the middle was merely honey-combed and saturated with water, so that you could put your foot through it when six inches thick; but by the next day evening, perhaps, after a warm rain followed by fog, it would have wholly disappeared, all

gone off with the fog, spirited away. One
year I went across the middle only five days
before it disappeared entirely. In 1845
Walden was first completely open on the
1st of April; in '46, the 25th of March; in
'47, the 8th of April; in '51, the 28th of
March; in '52, the 18th of April; in '53,
the 23d of March; in '54, about the 7th of
April.

Every incident connected with the breaking up of the rivers and ponds and the settling of the weather is particularly interesting to us who live in a climate of so great
extremes. When the warmer days come,
they who dwell near the river hear the ice
crack at night with a startling whoop as loud
as artillery, as if its icy fetters were rent
from end to end, and within a few days see
it rapidly going out. So the alligator comes
out of the mud with quakings of the earth.
One old man, who has been a close observer
of Nature, and seems as thoroughly wise in
regard to all her operations as if she had
been put upon the stocks when he was a boy,
and he had helped to lay her keel, — who
has come to his growth, and can hardly acquire more of natural lore if he should live
to the age of Methuselah, — told me, and I

was surprised to hear him express wonder
at any of Nature's operations, for I thought
that there were no secrets between them,
that one spring day he took his gun and
boat, and thought that he would have a little sport with the ducks. There was ice still
on the meadows, but it was all gone out of
the river, and he dropped down without obstruction from Sudbury, where he lived, to
Fair Haven Pond, which he found, unexpectedly, covered for the most part with a
firm field of ice. It was a warm day, and
he was surprised to see so great a body of
ice remaining. Not seeing any ducks, he
hid his boat on the north or back side of an
island in the pond, and then concealed himself in the bushes on the south side, to await
them. The ice was melted for three or four
rods from the shore, and there was a smooth
and warm sheet of water, with a muddy bottom, such as the ducks love, within, and he
thought it likely that some would be along
pretty soon. After he had lain still there
about an hour he heard a low and seemingly
very distant sound, but singularly grand
and impressive, unlike anything he had ever
heard, gradually swelling and increasing as
if it would have a universal and memorable

ending, a sullen rush and roar, which seemed
to him all at once like the sound of a vast
body of fowl coming in to settle there, and,
seizing his gun, he started up in haste and
excited ; but he found, to his surprise, that
the whole body of the ice had started while
he lay there, and drifted in to the shore,
and the sound he had heard was made by its
edge grating on the shore, — at first gently
nibbled and crumbled off, but at length
heaving up and scattering its wrecks along
the island to a considerable height before it
came to a stand still.

At length the sun's rays have attained the
right angle, and warm winds blow up mist
and rain and melt the snow banks, and the
sun dispersing the mist smiles on a check-
ered landscape of russet and white smoking
with incense, through which the traveller
picks his way from islet to islet, cheered by
the music of a thousand tinkling rills and
rivulets whose veins are filled with the blood
of winter which they are bearing off.

Few phenomena gave me more delight
than to observe the forms which thawing
sand and clay assume in flowing down the
sides of a deep cut on the railroad through
which I passed on my way to the village, a

phenomenon not very common on so large a scale, though the number of freshly exposed banks of the right material must have been greatly multiplied since railroads were invented. The material was sand of every degree of fineness and of various rich colors, commonly mixed with a little clay. When the frost comes out in the spring, and even in a thawing day in the winter, the sand begins to flow down the slopes like lava, sometimes bursting out through the snow and overflowing it where no sand was to be seen before. Innumerable little streams overlap and interlace one with another, exhibiting a sort of hybrid product, which obeys half way the law of currents, and half way that of vegetation. As it flows it takes the forms of sappy leaves or vines, making heaps of pulpy sprays a foot or more in depth, and resembling, as you look down on them, the laciniated, lobed, and imbricated thalluses of some lichens ; or you are reminded of coral, of leopards' paws or birds' feet, of brains or lungs or bowels, and excrements of all kinds. It is a truly *grotesque* vegetation, whose forms and color we see imitated in bronze, a sort of architectural foliage more ancient and typical than acanthus, chiccory, ivy,

vine, or any vegetable leaves; destined perhaps, under some circumstances, to become
a puzzle to future geologists. The whole cut
impressed me as if it were a cave with its
stalactites laid open to the light. The various shades of the sand are singularly rich
and agreeable, embracing the different iron
colors, brown, gray, yellowish, and reddish.
When the flowing mass reaches the drain
at the foot of the bank it spreads out flatter into *strands*, the separate streams losing
their semi - cylindrical form and gradually
becoming more flat and broad, running together as they are more moist, till they form
an almost flat *sand*, still variously and beautifully shaded, but in which you can trace
the original forms of vegetation ; till at
length, in the water itself, they are converted into *banks*, like those formed off the
mouths of rivers, and the forms of vegetation
are lost in the ripple marks on the bottom.

The whole bank, which is from twenty to
forty feet high, is sometimes overlaid with
a mass of this kind of foliage, or sandy rup-
ture, for a quarter of a mile on one or both
sides, the produce of one spring day. What
makes this sand foliage remarkable is its
springing into existence thus suddenly.

When I see on the one side the inert bank, — for the sun acts on one side first, — and on the other this luxuriant foliage, the creation of an hour, I am affected as if in a peculiar sense I stood in the laboratory of the Artist who made the world and me, — had come to where he was still at work, sporting on this bank, and with excess of energy strewing his fresh designs about. I feel as if I were nearer to the vitals of the globe, for this sandy overflow is something such a foliaceous mass as the vitals of the animal body. You find thus in the very sands an anticipation of the vegetable leaf. No wonder that the earth expresses itself outwardly in leaves, it so labors with the idea inwardly. The atoms have already learned this law, and are pregnant by it. The overhanging leaf sees here its prototype. *Internally,* whether in the globe or animal body, it is a moist thick *lobe,* a word especially applicable to the liver and lungs and the *leaves* of fat, (λείβω, *labor, lapsus,* to flow or slip downward, a lapsing; λοβός, *globus,* lobe, globe ; also lap, flap, and many other words,) *externally,* a dry thin *leaf,* even as the *f* and *v* are a pressed and dried *b.* The radicals of lobe are *lb,* the soft mass of the *b* (single

lobed, or B, doubled lobed,) with the liquid
l behind it pressing it forward. In globe,
glb, the guttural *g* adds to the meaning the
capacity of the throat. The feathers and
wings of birds are still drier and thinner
leaves. Thus, also, you pass from the
lumpish grub in the earth to the airy and
fluttering butterfly. The very globe continually transcends and· translates itself, and
becomes winged in its orbit. Even ice begins with delicate crystal leaves, as if it had
flowed into moulds which the fronds of
water plants have impressed on the watery
mirror. The whole tree itself is but one
leaf, and rivers are still vaster leaves whose
pulp is intervening earth, and towns and
cities are the ova of insects in their axils.

When the sun withdraws the sand ceases
to flow, but in the morning the streams will
start once more and branch and branch
again into a myriad of others. You here
see perchance how blood-vessels are formed.
If you look closely you observe that first
there pushes forward from the thawing mass
a stream of softened sand with a drop-like
point, like the ball of the finger, feeling its
way slowly and blindly downward, until at
last with more heat and moisture, as the sun

gets higher, the most fluid portion, in its effort to obey the law to which the most inert also yields, separates from the latter and forms for itself a meandering channel or artery within that, in which is seen a little silvery stream glancing like lightning from one stage of pulpy leaves or branches to another, and ever and anon swallowed up in the sand. It is wonderful how rapidly yet perfectly the sand organizes itself as it flows, using the best material its mass affords to form the sharp edges of its channel. Such are the sources of rivers. In the silicious matter which the water deposits is perhaps the bony system, and in the still finer soil and organic matter the fleshy fibre or cellular tissue. What is man but a mass of thawing clay? The ball of the human finger is but a drop congealed. The fingers and toes flow to their extent from the thawing mass of the body. Who knows what the human body would expand and flow out to under a more genial heaven? Is not the hand a spreading *palm* leaf with its lobes and veins? The ear may be regarded, fancifully, as a lichen, *umbilicaria*, on the side of the head, with its lobe or drop. The lip — *labium*, from *labor* (?) —

laps or lapses from the sides of the cavernous
mouth.   The nose is a manifest congealed
drop or stalactite.   The chin is a still larger
drop, the confluent dripping of the face.
The cheeks are a slide from the brows into
the valley of the face, opposed and diffused
by the cheek bones.   Each rounded lobe of
the vegetable leaf, too, is a thick and now
loitering drop, larger or smaller; the lobes
are the fingers of the leaf; and as many
lobes as it has, in so many directions it
tends to flow, and more heat or other genial
influences would have caused it to flow yet
farther.

Thus it seemed that this one hillside illus-
trated the principle of all the operations of
Nature.   The Maker of this earth but pat-
ented a leaf.   What Champollion will de-
cipher this hieroglyphic for us, that we may
turn over a new leaf at last?   This phenomenon is more exhilarating to me than the
luxuriance and fertility of vineyards.   True,
it is somewhat excrementitious in its character, and there is no end to the heaps of
liver, lights, and bowels, as if the globe were
turned wrong side outward; but this suggests at least that Nature has some bowels,
and there again is mother of humanity.   This

is the frost coming out of the ground; this is Spring. It precedes the green and flowery spring, as mythology precedes regular poetry. I know of nothing more purgative of winter fumes and indigestions. It convinces me that Earth is still in her swaddling clothes, and stretches forth baby fingers on every side. Fresh curls spring from the baldest brow. There is nothing inorganic. These foliaceous heaps lie along the bank like the slag of a furnace, showing that Nature is "in full blast" within. The earth is not a mere fragment of dead history, stratum upon stratum like the leaves of a book, to be studied by geologists and antiquaries chiefly, but living poetry like the leaves of a tree, which precede flowers and fruit, — not a fossil earth, but a living earth; compared with whose great central life all animal and vegetable life is merely parasitic. Its throes will heave our exuviæ from their graves. You may melt your metals and cast them into the most beautiful moulds you can; they will never excite me like the forms which this molten earth flows out into. And not only it, but the institutions upon it are plastic like clay in the hands of the potter.

Ere long, not only on these banks, but on every hill and plain and in every hollow, the frost comes out of the ground like a dormant quadruped from its burrow, and seeks the sea with music, or migrates to other climes in clouds. Thaw with his gentle persuasion is more powerful than Thor with his hammer. The one melts, the other but breaks in pieces.

When the ground was partially bare of snow, and a few warm days had dried its surface somewhat, it was pleasant to compare the first tender signs of the infant year just peeping forth with the stately beauty of the withered vegetation which had withstood the winter, — life - everlasting, golden-rods, pinweeds, and graceful wild grasses, more obvious and interesting frequently than in summer even, as if their beauty was not ripe till then; even cotton - grass, cat- tails, mulleins, johnswort, hard - hack, meadow-sweet, and other strong-stemmed plants, those unexhausted granaries which entertain the earliest birds, — decent weeds, at least, which widowed Nature wears. I am particularly attracted by the arching and sheaf-like top of the wool-grass; it brings back the summer to our winter memories, and is among the forms which art loves to copy, and which, in the vegetable kingdom, have the same relation to types already in the mind of man that astronomy has. It is an antique style, older than Greek or Egyptian. Many of the phenomena of Winter are suggestive of an inexpressible tenderness and fragile delicacy. We are accustomed to hear this king described as a rude and boisterous tyrant; but with the gentleness of a lover he adorns the tresses of Summer.

At the approach of spring the red-squirrels got under my house, two at a time, directly under my feet as I sat reading or writing, and kept up the queerest chuckling and chirruping and vocal pirouetting and gurgling sounds that ever were heard; and when I stamped they only chirruped the louder, as if past all fear and respect in their mad pranks, defying humanity to stop them. No you don't — chickaree — chickaree. They were wholly deaf to my arguments, or failed to perceive their force, and fell into a strain of invective that was irresistible.

The first sparrow of spring! The year beginning with younger hope than ever! The faint silvery warblings heard over the

partially bare and moist fields from the bluebird, the song-sparrow, and the red-wing, as
if the last flakes of winter tinkled as they
fell! What at such a time are histories,
chronologies, traditions, and all written rev-
elations? The brooks sing carols and glees
to the spring. The marsh-hawk sailing low
over the meadow is already seeking the first
slimy life that awakes. The sinking sound
of melting snow is heard in all dells, and
the ice dissolves apace in the ponds. The
grass flames up on the hillsides like a spring
fire, — "et primitus oritur herba imbribus
primoribus evocata," — as if the earth sent
forth an inward heat to greet the returning
sun; not yellow but green is the color of its
flame; — the symbol of perpetual youth, the
grass-blade, like a long green ribbon, streams
from the sod into the summer, checked indeed by the frost, but anon pushing on
again, lifting its spear of last year's hay
with the fresh life below. It grows as steadily as the rill oozes out of the ground. It is
almost identical with that, for in the growing days of June, when the rills are dry,
the grass blades are their channels, and from
year to year the herds drink at this perennial green stream, and the mower draws

from it betimes their winter supply. So our human life but dies down to its root, and still puts forth its green blade to eternity.

Walden is melting apace. There is a canal two rods wide along the northerly and westerly sides, and wider still at the east end. A great field of ice has cracked off from the main body. I hear a song-sparrow singing from the bushes on the shore, — *olit, olit, olit,* — *chip, chip, chip, che char,* — *che wiss, wiss, wiss.* He too is helping to crack it. How handsome the great sweeping curves in the edge of the ice, answering somewhat to those of the shore, but more regular! It is unusually hard, owing to the recent severe but transient cold, and all watered or waved like a palace floor. But the wind slides eastward over its opaque surface in vain, till it reaches the living surface beyond. It is glorious to behold this ribbon of water sparkling in the sun, the bare face of the pond full of glee and youth, as if it spoke the joy of the fishes within it, and of the sands on its shore, — a silvery sheen as from the scales of a *leuciscus,* as it were all one active fish. Such is the contrast between winter and spring. Walden was dead and is alive again. But this spring it broke up more steadily, as I have said.

The change from storm and winter to serene and mild weather, from dark and sluggish hours to bright and elastic ones, is a
memorable crisis which all things proclaim.
It is seemingly instantaneous at last. Suddenly an influx of light filled my house,
though the evening was at hand, and the
clouds of winter still overhung it, and the
eaves were dripping with sleety rain. I
looked out the window, and lo! where yesterday was cold gray ice there lay the transparent pond already calm and full of hope
as in a summer evening, reflecting a summer
evening sky in its bosom, though none was
visible overhead, as if it had intelligence
with some remote horizon. I heard a robin
in the distance, the first I had heard for
many a thousand years, methought, whose
note I shall not forget for many a thousand
more, — the same sweet and powerful song
as of yore. O the evening robin, at the end
of a New England summer day! If I could
ever find the twig he sits upon! I mean *he;*
I mean *the twig*. This at least is not the
Turdus migratorius. The pitch-pines and
shrub-oaks about my house, which had so
long drooped, suddenly resumed their several characters, looked brighter, greener,

and more erect and alive, as if effectually cleansed and restored by the rain. I knew that it would not rain any more. You may tell by looking at any twig of the forest, ay, at your very wood-pile, whether its winter is past or not. As it grew darker, I was startled by the *honking* of geese flying low over the woods, like weary travellers getting in late from southern lakes, and indulging at last in unrestrained complaint and mutual consolation. Standing at my door, I could hear the rush of their wings; when, driving toward my house, they suddenly spied my light, and with hushed clamor wheeled and settled in the pond. So I came in, and shut the door, and passed my first spring night in the woods.

In the morning I watched the geese from the door through the mist, sailing in the middle of the pond, fifty rods off, so large and tumultuous that Walden appeared like an artificial pond for their amusement. But when I stood on the shore they at once rose up with a great flapping of wings at the signal of their commander, and when they had got into rank circled about over my head, twenty-nine of them, and then steered straight to Canada, with a regular *honk* from the leader at intervals, trusting to break their fast in muddier pools. A "plump" of ducks rose at the same time and took the route to the north in the wake of their noisier cousins.

For a week I heard the circling groping clangor of some solitary goose in the foggy mornings, seeking its companion, and still peopling the woods with the sound of a larger life than they could sustain. In April the pigeons were seen again flying express in small flocks, and in due time I heard the martins twittering over my clearing, though it had not seemed that the township contained so many that it could afford me any, and I fancied that they were peculiarly of the ancient race that dwelt in hollow trees ere white men came. In almost all climes the tortoise and the frog are among the precursors and heralds of this season, and birds fly with song and glancing plumage, and plants spring and bloom, and winds blow, to correct this slight oscillation of the poles and preserve the equilibrium of Nature.

As every season seems best to us in its turn, so the coming in of spring is like the creation of Cosmos out of Chaos and the realization of the Golden Age. —

" Eurus ad Auroram, Nabathacaque regna recessit,
  Persidaque, et radiis juga subdita matutinis."

" The East-Wind withdrew to Aurora and the Naba-
      thæan kingdom,
  And the Persian, and the ridges placed under the
      morning rays.

  .   .   .   .

  Man was born. Whether that Artificer of things,
  The origin of a better world, made him from the di-
      vine seed ;
  Or the earth being recent and lately sundered from the ·
      high
  Ether, retained some seeds of cognate heaven."

A single gentle rain makes the grass many
shades greener. So our prospects brighten
on the influx of better thoughts. We should
be blessed if we lived in the present always,
and took advantage of every accident that
befell us, like the grass which confesses the
influence of the slightest dew that falls on
it ; and did not spend our time in atoning
for the neglect of past opportunities, which
we call doing our duty. We loiter in winter while it is already spring. In a pleasant
spring morning all men's sins are forgiven.
Such a day is a truce to vice. While such
a sun holds out to burn, the vilest sinner
may return. Through our own recovered
innocence we discern the innocence of our
neighbors. You may have known your

neighbor yesterday for a thief, a drunkard, or a sensualist, and merely pitied or despised him, and despaired of the world; but the sun shines bright and warm this first spring morning, recreating the world, and you meet him at some serene work, and see how his exhausted and debauched veins expand with still joy and bless the new day, feel the spring influence with the innocence of infancy, and all his faults are forgotten. There is not only an atmosphere of good will about him, but even a savor of holiness groping for expression, blindly and ineffectually perhaps, like a new-born instinct, and for a short hour the south hill-side echoes to no vulgar jest. You see some innocent fair shoots preparing to burst from his gnarled rind and try another year's life, tender and fresh as the youngest plant. Even he has entered into the joy of his Lord. Why the jailer does not leave open his prison doors, — why the judge does not dismiss his case, — why the preacher does not dismiss his congregation! It is because they do not obey the hint which God gives them, nor accept the pardon which he freely offers to all.

" A return to goodness produced each day in the tranquil and beneficent breath of the

morning, causes that in respect to the love
of virtue and the hatred of vice, one approaches a little the primitive nature of man,
as the sprouts of the forest which has been
felled. In like manner the evil which one
does in the interval of a day prevents the
germs of virtues which began to spring up
again from developing themselves and destroys them.

" After the germs of virtue have thus been
prevented many times from developing themselves, then the beneficent breath of evening
does not suffice to preserve them. As soon
as the breath of evening does not suffice
longer to preserve them, then the nature of
man does not differ much from that of the
brute. Men seeing the nature of this man
like that of the brute, think that he has
never possessed the innate faculty of reason.
Are those the true and natural sentiments
of man ? "

"The Golden Age was first created, which without any
    avenger
    Spontaneously without law cherished fidelity and recti-
      tude.
    Punishment and fear were not; nor were threatening
      words read
    On suspended brass; nor did the suppliant crowd fear
    The words of their judge; but were safe without an
      avenger.

Not yet the pine felled on its mountains had descended
To the liquid waves that it might see a foreign world,
And mortals knew no shores but their own.

　　·　　·　　·　　·　　·　　·　　·

There was eternal spring, and placid zephyrs with
　　warm
Blasts soothed the flowers born without seed."

On the 29th of April, as I was fishing
from the bank of the river near the Nine-
Acre-Corner bridge, standing on the quaking
grass and willow roots, where the muskrats
lurk, I heard a singular rattling sound,
somewhat like that of the sticks which boys
play with their fingers, when, looking up, I
observed a very slight and graceful hawk,
like a night-hawk, alternately soaring like a
ripple and tumbling a rod or two over and
over, showing the underside of its wings,
which gleamed like a satin ribbon in the
sun, or like the pearly inside of a shell.
This sight reminded me of falconry and
what nobleness and poetry are associated
with that sport. The Merlin it seemed to
me it might be called: but I care not for its
name. It was the most ethereal flight I
had ever witnessed. It did not simply flutter like a butterfly, nor soar like the larger
hawks, but it sported with proud reliance in
the fields of air ; mounting again and again

with its strange chuckle, it repeated its free
and beautiful fall, turning over and over like
a kite, and then recovering from its lofty
tumbling, as if it had never set its foot on
terra firma. It appeared to have no companion in the universe, — sporting there
alone, — and to need none but the morning
and the ether with which it played. It was
not lonely, but made all the earth lonely
beneath it. Where was the parent which
hatched it, its kindred, and its father in the
heavens? The tenant of the air, it seemed
related to the earth but by an egg hatched
some time in the crevice of a crag; — or was
its native nest made in the angle of a cloud,
woven of the rainbow's trimmings and the
sunset sky, and lined with some soft midsummer haze caught up from earth? Its
eyry now some cliffy cloud.

Beside this I got a rare mess of golden
and silver and bright cupreous fishes, which
looked like a string of jewels. Ah! I have
penetrated to those meadows on the morning
of many a first spring day, jumping from
hummock to hummock, from willow root to
willow root, when the wild river valley and
the woods were bathed in so pure and bright
a light as would have waked the dead, if

they had been slumbering in their graves,
as some suppose. There needs no stronger
proof of immortality. All things must live
in such a light. O Death, where was thy
sting? O Grave, where was thy victory,
then?

Our village life would stagnate if it were
not for the unexplored forests and meadows
which surround it. We need the tonic of
wildness, — to wade sometimes in marshes
where the bittern and the meadow-hen lurk,
and hear the booming of the snipe; to smell
the whispering sedge where only some wilder
and more solitary fowl builds her nest, and
the mink crawls with its belly close to the
ground. At the same time that we are earnest to explore and learn all things, we require that all things be mysterious and unex-
plorable, that land and sea be infinitely wild,
unsurveyed and unfathomed by us because
unfathomable. We can never have enough
of Nature. We must be refreshed by the
sight of inexhaustible vigor, vast and Ti-
tanic features, the sea-coast with its wrecks,
the wilderness with its living and its decaying trees, the thunder cloud, and the rain
which lasts three weeks and produces freshets. We need to witness our own limits

transgressed, and some life pasturing freely where we never wander. We are cheered when we observe the vulture feeding on the carrion, which disgusts and disheartens us, and deriving health and strength from the repast. There was a dead horse in the hollow by the path to my house, which compelled me sometimes to go out of my way, especially in the night when the air was heavy, but the assurance it gave me of the strong appetite and inviolable health of Nature was my compensation for this. I love to see that Nature is so rife with life that myriads can be afforded to be sacrificed and suffered to prey on one another; that tender organizations can be so serenely squashed out of existence like pulp, — tadpoles which herons gobble up, and tortoises and toads run over in the road ; and that sometimes it has rained flesh and blood ! With the liability to accident, we must see how little account is to be made of it. The impression made on a wise man is that of universal innocence. Poison is not poisonous after all, nor are any wounds fatal. Compassion is a very untenable ground. It must be expeditious. Its pleadings will not bear to be stereotyped.

Early in May, the oaks, hickories, maples, and other trees, just putting out amidst the pine woods around the pond, imparted a brightness like sunshine to the landscape, especially in cloudy days, as if the sun were breaking through mists and shining faintly on the hill-sides here and there. On the third or fourth of May I saw a loon in the pond, and during the first week of the month I heard the whippoorwill, the brown-thrasher, the veery, the wood-pewee, the chewink, and other birds. I had heard the wood-thrush long before. The phœbe had already come once more and looked in at my door and window, to see if my house was cavern-like enough for her, sustaining herself on humming wings with clinched talons, as if she held by the air, while she surveyed the premises. The sulphur-like pollen of the pitch-pine soon covered the pond and the stones and rotten wood along the shore, so that you could have collected a barrel-ful. This is the " sulphur showers " we hear of. Even in Calidas' drama of Sacontala, we read of " rills dyed yellow with the golden dust of the lotus." And so the seasons went rolling on into summer, as one rambles into higher and higher grass.

Thus was my first year's life in the woods completed ; and the second year was similar to it.   I finally left Walden September 6th, 1847.

XVIII.

CONCLUSION.

To the sick the doctors wisely recommend
a change of air and scenery. Thank Heaven,
here is not all the world. The buck-eye
does not grow in New England, and the
mocking-bird is rarely heard here. The
wild-goose is more of a cosmopolite than we;
he breaks his fast in Canada, takes a luncheon in the Ohio, and plumes himself for the
night in a southern bayou. Even the bison,
to some extent, keeps pace with the seasons,
cropping the pastures of the Colorado only
till a greener and sweeter grass awaits him
by the Yellowstone. Yet we think that if
rail-fences are pulled down, and stone-walls
piled up on our farms, bounds are henceforth set to our lives and our fates decided.
If you are chosen town-clerk, forsooth, you
cannot go to Tierra del Fuego this summer:
but you may go to the land of infernal fire
nevertheless. The universe is wider than
our views of it.

Yet we should oftener look over the taffered of our craft, like curious passengers, and not make the voyage like stupid sailors picking oakum. The other side of the globe is but the home of our correspondent. Our voyaging is only great-circle sailing, and the doctors prescribe for diseases of the skin merely. One hastens to Southern Africa to chase the giraffe; but surely that is not the game he would be after. How long, pray, would a man hunt giraffes if he could? Snipes and woodcocks also may afford rare sport; but I trust it would be nobler game to shoot one's self. —

> " Direct your eye right inward, and you 'll find
> A thousand regions in your mind
> Yet undiscovered. Travel them, and be
> Expert in home-cosmography."

What does Africa, — what does the West stand for? Is not our own interior white on the chart? black though it may prove, like the coast, when discovered. Is it the source of the Nile, or the Niger, or the Mississippi, or a North-West Passage around this continent, that we would find? Are these the problems which most concern mankind? Is Franklin the only man who is lost, that his wife should be so earnest to find him? Does

Mr. Grinnell know where he himself is ?
Be rather the Mungo Park, the Lewis and
Clarke and Frobisher, of your own streams
and oceans ; explore your own higher latitudes, — with shiploads of preserved meats
to support you, if they be necessary ; and
pile the empty cans sky-high for a sign.
Were preserved meats invented to preserve
meat merely ?   Nay, be a Columbus to whole
new continents and worlds within you, opening new channels, not of trade, but of
thought.   Every man is the lord of a realm
beside which the earthly empire of the Czar
is but a petty state, a hummock left by the
ice.   Yet some can be patriotic who have no
self-respect, and sacrifice the greater to the
less.   They love the soil which makes their
graves, but have no sympathy with the spirit
which may still animate their clay.   Patriotism is a maggot in their heads.   What
was the meaning of that South-Sea Exploring Expedition, with all its parade and expense, but an indirect recognition of the
fact, that there are continents and seas in
the moral world, to which every man is an
isthmus or an inlet, yet unexplored by him,
but that it is easier to sail many thousand
miles through cold and storm and cannibals,

in a government ship, with five hundred men
and boys to assist one, than it is to explore
the private sea, the Atlantic and Pacific
Ocean of one's being alone. —

"Erret, et extremos alter scrutetur Iberos.
Plus habet hic vitæ, plus habet ille viæ."

Let them wander and scrutinize the outlandish Austra-
lians.
I have more of God, they more of the road.

It is not worth the while to go round the
world to count the cats in Zanzibar. Yet
do this even till you can do better, and you
may perhaps find some "Symmes' Hole" by
which to get at the inside at last. England
and France, Spain and Portugal, Gold Coast
and Slave Coast, all front on this private
sea; but no bark from them has ventured
out of sight of land, though it is without
doubt the direct way to India. If you would
learn to speak all tongues and conform to
the customs of all nations, if you would
travel farther than all travellers, be naturalized in all climes, and cause the Sphinx to
dash her head against a stone, even obey the
precept of the old philosopher, and Explore
thyself. Herein are demanded the eye and
the nerve. Only the defeated and deserters
go to the wars, cowards that run away and

enlist. Start now on that farthest western way, which does not pause at the Mississippi or the Pacific, nor conduct toward a worn-out China or Japan, but leads on direct a tangent to this sphere, summer and winter, day and night, sun down, moon down, and at last earth down too.

It is said that Mirabeau took to highway robbery " to ascertain what degree of resolution was necessary in order to place one's self in formal opposition to the most sacred laws of society." He declared that " a soldier who fights in the ranks does not require half so much courage as a foot-pad," — " that honor and religion have never stood in the way of a well-considered and a firm resolve." This was manly, as the world goes ; and yet it was idle, if not desperate. A saner man would have found himself often enough " in formal opposition " to what are deemed " the most sacred laws of society," through obedience to yet more sacred laws, and so have tested his resolution without going out of his way. It is not for a man to put himself in such an attitude to society, but to maintain himself in whatever attitude he find himself through obedience to the laws of his being. which will never be one of opposition to a just government, if he should chance to meet with such.

I left the woods for as good a reason as I went there. Perhaps it seemed to me that I had several more lives to live, and could not spare any more time for that one. It is remarkable how easily and insensibly we fall into a particular route, and make a beaten track for ourselves. I had not lived there a week before my feet wore a path from my door to the pond-side; and though it is five or six years since I trod it, it is still quite distinct. It is true, I fear that others may have fallen into it, and so helped to keep it open. The surface of the earth is soft and impressible by the feet of men; and so with the paths which the mind travels. How worn and dusty, then, must be the highways of the world, how deep the ruts of tradition and conformity! I did not wish to take a cabin passage, but rather to go before the mast and on the deck of the world, for there I could best see the moonlight amid the mountains. I do not wish to go below now.

I learned this, at least, by my experiment; that if one advances confidently in the direction of his dreams, and endeavors to live the life which he has imagined, he will meet with a success unexpected in common hours. He will put some things behind, will pass an invisible boundary; new, universal, and more liberal laws will begin to establish themselves around and within him; or the old laws be expanded, and interpreted in his favor in a more liberal sense, and he will live with the license of a higher order of beings. In proportion as he simplifies his life, the laws of the universe will appear less complex, and solitude will not be solitude, nor poverty poverty, nor weakness weakness. If you have built castles in the air, your work need not be lost; that is where they should be. Now put the foundations under them.

It is a ridiculous demand which England and America make, that you shall speak so that they can understand you. Neither men nor toad-stools grow so. As if that were important, and there were not enough to understand you without them. As if Nature could support but one order of understandings, could not sustain birds as well as quadrupeds, flying as well as creeping things, and *hush* and *who*, which Bright can understand, were the best English. As if there were safety in stupidity alone. I fear chiefly lest

my expression may not be *extra - vagant*
enough, may not wander far enough beyond
the narrow limits of my daily experience, so
as to be adequate to the truth of which I
have been convinced. *Extra vagance!* it
depends on how you are yarded. The migrating buffalo, which seeks new pastures in
another latitude, is not extravagant like the
cow which kicks over the pail, leaps the cow-
yard fence, and runs after her calf, in milk-
ing time. I desire to speak somewhere *without* bounds ; like a man in a waking moment,
to men in their waking moments ; for I am
convinced that I cannot exaggerate enough
even to lay the foundation of a true expression. Who that has heard a strain of music
feared then lest he should speak extravagantly any more forever? In view of the
future or possible, we should live quite laxly
and undefined in front, our outlines dim and
misty on that side ; as our shadows reveal
an insensible perspiration toward the sun.
The volatile truth of our words should continually betray the inadequacy of the re-
sidual statement. Their truth is instantly
translated ; its literal monument alone remains. The words which express our faith
and piety are not definite ; yet they are sig-

nificant and fragrant like frankincense to superior natures.

Why level downward to our dullest perception always, and praise that as common sense? The commonest sense is the sense of men asleep, which they express by snoring. Sometimes we are inclined to class those who are-once-and-a-half witted with the half-witted, because we appreciate only a third part of their wit. Some would find fault with the morning - red, if they ever got up early enough. "They pretend," as I hear, "that the verses of Kabir have four different senses; illusion, spirit, intellect, and the exoteric doctrine of the Vedas;" but in this part of the world it is considered a ground for complaint if a man's writings admit of more than one interpretation. While England endeavors to cure the potato-rot, will not any endeavor to cure the brain-rot, which prevails so much more widely and fatally?

I do not suppose that I have attained to obscurity, but I should be proud if no more fatal fault were found with my pages on this score than was found with the Walden ice. Southern customers objected to its blue color, which is the evidence of its purity, as if it were muddy, and preferred the

Cambridge ice, which is white, but tastes of weeds. The purity men love is like the mists which envelop the earth, and not like the azure ether beyond.

Some are dinning in our ears that we Americans, and moderns generally, are intellectual dwarfs compared with the ancients, or even the Elizabethan men. But what is that to the purpose? A living dog is better than a dead lion. Shall a man go and hang himself because he belongs to the race of pygmies, and not be the biggest pygmy that he can? Let every one mind his own business, and endeavor to be what he was made.

Why should we be in such desperate haste to succeed and in such desperate enterprises? If a man does not keep pace with his companions, perhaps it is because he hears a different drummer. Let him step to the music which he hears, however measured or far away. It is not important that he should mature as soon as an apple-tree or an oak. Shall he turn his spring into summer? If the condition of things which we were made for is not yet, what were any reality which we can substitute? We will not be shipwrecked on a vain reality. Shall we with

pains erect a heaven of blue glass over ourselves, though when it is done we shall be
sure to gaze still at the true ethereal heaven
far above, as if the former were not?

There was an artist in the city of Kouroo
who was disposed to strive after perfection.
One day it came into his mind to make a
staff. Having considered that in an imperfect work time is an ingredient, but into a
perfect work time does not enter, he said to
himself, It shall be perfect in all respects,
though I should do nothing else in my life.
He proceeded instantly to the forest for wood,
being resolved that it should not be made of
unsuitable material; and as he searched for
and rejected stick after stick, his friends
gradually deserted him, for they grew old in
their works and died, but he grew not older
by a moment. His singleness of purpose
and resolution, and his elevated piety, en-
dowed him, without his knowledge, with
perennial youth. As he made no compro-
mise with Time, Time kept out of his way,
and only sighed at a distance because he
could not overcome him. Before he had
found a stock in all respects suitable the
city of Kouroo was a hoary ruin, and he sat
on one of its mounds to peel the stick. Be-

fore he had given it the proper shape the dynasty of the Candahars was at an end, and with the point of the stick he wrote the name of the last of that race in the sand, and then resumed his work. By the time he had smoothed and polished the staff Kalpa was no longer the pole-star; and ere he had put on the ferule and the head adorned with precious stones, Brahma had awoke and slumbered many times. But why do I stay to mention these things? When the finishing stroke was put to his work, it suddenly expanded before the eyes of the astonished artist into the fairest of all the creations of Brahma. He had made a new system in making a staff, a world with full and fair proportions; in which, though the old cities and dynasties had passed away, fairer and more glorious ones had taken their places. And now he saw by the heap of shavings still fresh at his feet, that, for him and his work, the former lapse of time had been an illusion, and that no more time had elapsed than is required for a single scintillation from the brain of Brahma to fall on and inflame the tinder of a mortal brain. The material was pure, and his art was pure; how could the result be other than wonderful?

No face which we can give to a matter will stead us so well at last as the truth. This alone wears well. For the most part, we are not where we are, but in a false position. Through an infirmity of our natures, we suppose a case, and put ourselves into it, and hence are in two cases at the same time, and it is doubly difficult to get out. In sane moments we regard only the facts, the case that is. Say what you have to say, not what you ought. Any truth is better than make-believe. Tom Hyde, the tinker, standing on the gallows, was asked if he had anything to say. " Tell the tailors," said he, " to remember to make a knot in their thread before they take the first stitch." His companion's prayer is forgotten.

However mean your life is, meet it and live it; do not shun it and call it hard names. It is not so bad as you are. It looks poorest when you are richest. The fault-finder will find faults even in paradise. Love your life, poor as it is. You may perhaps have some pleasant, thrilling, glorious hours, even in a poor-house. The setting sun is reflected from the windows of the alms-house as brightly as from the rich man's abode ; the snow melts before its door as early in the spring. I do not see but a quiet mind may live as contentedly there, and have as cheering thoughts, as in a palace. The town's poor seem to me often to live the most independent lives of any. May be they are simply great enough to receive without misgiving. Most think that they are above being supported by the town; but it oftener happens that they are not above supporting themselves by dishonest means, which should be more disreputable. Cultivate poverty like a garden herb, like sage. Do not trouble yourself much to get new things, whether clothes or friends. Turn the old; return to them. Things do not change; we change. Sell your clothes and keep your thoughts. God will see that you do not want society. If I were confined to a corner of a garret all my days, like a spider, the world would be just as large to me while I had my thoughts about me. The philosopher said : " From an army of three divisions one can take away its general, and put it in disorder; from the man the most abject and vulgar one cannot take away his thought." Do not seek so anxiously to be developed, to subject yourself to many influences to be played on ; it is all dissipation. Humility like darkness reveals the heavenly lights. The shadows of poverty and meanness gather around us, " and lo ! creation widens to our view." We are often reminded that if there were bestowed on us the wealth of Crœsus, our aims must still be the same, and our means essentially the same. Moreover, if you are restricted in your range by poverty, if you cannot buy books and newspapers, for instance, you are but confined to the most significant and vital experiences ; you are compelled to deal with the material which yields the most sugar and the most starch. It is life near the bone where it is sweetest. You are defended from being a trifler. No man loses ever on a lower level by magnanimity on a higher. Superfluous wealth can buy superfluities only. Money is not required to buy one necessary of the soul.

I live in the angle of a leaden wall, into whose composition was poured a little alloy of bell metal. Often, in the repose of my mid-day, there reaches my ears a confused *tintinnabulum* from without. It is the noise of my contemporaries. My neighbors tell me of their adventures with famous gentlemen and ladies, what notabilities they met

at the dinner-table ; but I am no more interested in such things than in the contents of
the Daily Times. The interest and the conversation are about costume and manners
chiefly ; but a goose is a goose still, dress it
as you will. They tell me of California and
Texas, of England and the Indies, of the
Hon. Mr. —— of Georgia or of Massachusetts, all transient and fleeting phenomena,
till I am ready to leap from their court-yard
like the Mameluke bey. I delight to come
to my bearings, — not walk in procession
with pomp and parade, in a conspicuous
place, but to walk even with the Builder of
the universe, if I may, — not to live in this
restless, nervous, bustling, trivial Nineteenth
Century, but stand or sit thoughtfully while
it goes by. What are men celebrating?
They are all on a committee of arrangements, and hourly expect a speech from
somebody. God is only the president of the
day, and Webster is his orator. I love to
weigh, to settle, to gravitate toward that
which most strongly and rightfully attracts
me ; — not hang by the beam of the scale
and try to weigh less, — not suppose a case,
but take the case that is ; to travel the only
path I can, and that on which no power can

resist me. It affords me no satisfaction to
commence to spring an arch before I have
got a solid foundation. Let us not play at
kittlybenders. There is a solid bottom
everywhere. We read that the traveller
asked the boy if the swamp before him had
a hard bottom. The boy replied that it had.
But presently the traveller's horse sank in
up to the girths, and he observed to the boy,
" I thought you said that this bog had a hard
bottom." " So it has," answered the latter,
" but you have not got half way to it yet."
So it is with the bogs and quicksands of society ; but he is an old boy that knows it.
Only what is thought, said, or done at a certain rare coincidence is good. I would not
be one of those who will foolishly drive a
nail into mere lath and plastering ; such a
deed would keep me awake nights. Give me
a hammer, and let me feel for the furrowing.
Do not depend on the putty. Drive a nail
home and clinch it so faithfully that you
can wake up in the night and think of your
work with satisfaction, — a work at which
you would not be ashamed to invoke the
Muse. So will help you God, and so only.
Every nail driven should be as another rivet
in the machine of the universe, you carrying
on the work.

Rather than love, than money, than fame, give me truth. I sat at a table where were rich food and wine in abundance, and obsequious attendance, but sincerity and truth were not; and I went away hungry from the inhospitable board. The hospitality was as cold as the ices. I thought that there was no need of ice to freeze them. They talked to me of the age of the wine and the fame of the vintage; but I thought of an older, a newer, and purer wine, of a more glorious vintage, which they had not got, and could not buy. The style, the house and grounds and "entertainment" pass for nothing with me. I called on the king, but he made me wait in his hall, and conducted like a man incapacitated for hospitality. There was a man in my neighborhood who lived in a hollow tree. His manners were truly regal. I should have done better had I called on him.

How long shall we sit in our porticoes practising idle and musty virtues, which any work would make impertinent? As if one were to begin the day with long-suffering, and hire a man to hoe his potatoes, and in the afternoon go forth to practise Christian meekness and charity with goodness aforethought! Consider the China pride and stagnant self-complacency of mankind. This generation inclines a little to congratulate itself on being the last of an illustrious line; and in Boston and London and Paris and Rome, thinking of its long descent, it speaks of its progress in art and science and literature with satisfaction. There are the Records of the Philosophical Societies, and the public Eulogies of *Great Men!* It is the good Adam contemplating his own virtue. "Yes, we have done great deeds, and sung divine songs, which shall never die," — that is, as long as *we* can remember them. The learned societies and great men of Assyria, — where are they? What youthful philosophers and experimentalists we are! There is not one of my readers who has yet lived a whole human life. These may be but the spring months in the life of the race. If we have had the seven-years' itch, we have not seen the seventeen-year locust yet in Concord. We are acquainted with a mere pellicle of the globe on which we live. Most have not delved six feet beneath the surface, nor leaped as many above it. We know not where we are. Beside, we are sound asleep nearly half our time. Yet we esteem ourselves wise, and have an established order on the surface. Truly, we are deep thinkers, we are ambitious spirits! As I stand over the insect crawling amid the pine needles on the forest floor, and endeavoring to conceal itself from my sight, and ask myself why it will cherish those humble thoughts, and hide its head from me who might, perhaps, be its benefactor, and impart to its race some cheering information, I am reminded of the greater Benefactor and Intelligence that stands over me the human insect.

There is an incessant influx of novelty into the world, and yet we tolerate incredible dulness. I need only suggest what kind of sermons are still listened to in the most enlightened countries. There are such words as joy and sorrow, but they are only the burden of a psalm, sung with a nasal twang, while we believe in the ordinary and mean. We think that we can change our clothes only. It is said that the British Empire is very large and respectable, and that the United States are a first-rate power. We do not believe that a tide rises and falls behind every man which can float the British Empire like a chip, if he should ever harbor it in his mind. Who knows what sort of seventeen-year locust will next come out of the ground? The government of the world I live in was not framed, like that of Britain, in after-dinner conversations over the wine.

The life in us is like the water in the river. It may rise this year higher than man has ever known it, and flood the parched uplands; even this may be the eventful year, which will drown out all our muskrats. It was not always dry land where we dwell. I see far inland the banks which the stream anciently washed, before science began to record its freshets. Every one has heard the story which has gone the rounds of New England, of a strong and beautiful bug which came out of the dry leaf of an old table of apple-tree wood, which had stood in a farmer's kitchen for sixty years, first in Connecticut, and afterward in Massachusetts, — from an egg deposited in the living tree many years earlier still, as appeared by counting the annual layers beyond it; which was heard gnawing out for several weeks, hatched perchance by the heat of an urn. Who does not feel his faith in a resurrection and immortality strengthened by hearing of this? Who knows what beautiful and winged life, whose egg has been buried for

ages under many concentric layers of wood-
enness in the dead dry life of society, deposited at first in the alburnum of the green
and living tree, which has been gradually
converted into the semblance of its well-sea-
soned tomb, — heard perchance gnawing out
now for years by the astonished family of
man, as they sat round the festive board, —
may unexpectedly come forth from amidst
society's most trivial and handselled furniture, to enjoy its perfect summer life at last!

I do not say that John or Jonathan will
realize all this; but such is the character of
that morrow which mere lapse of time can
never make to dawn. The light which puts
out our eyes is darkness to us. Only that
day dawns to which we are awake. There
is more day to dawn. The sun is but a
morning-star.

INDEX.

ACTON (Mass.), 192
Æs alienum, another's brass, a very ancient slough, 13
Æsculapius, that old herb-doctor, 217
Age and youth, 16.
Alms House Farm, 397.
America, the only true, 321.
"Amok" against T., society running, 268
Amusements, games and, despair concealed under, 15.
Animal food, objections to, 334
Animal labor, man better without the help of, 91.
Animal life and heat nearly synonymous, 23.
Ants, battle of the, 355-361.
Apples, the world eating green, 123.
Architecture, need of relation between man, truth, and, 75, 76.
Asiatic Russia, Mme. Pfeiffer in, 38.
Atlas, 132.
Atropos, as name for engine, 185.
Auction of a deacon's effects, 107, or increasing, 108.
Average, the law of, in nature and ethics, 448

BAKER FARM, 314-326.
Baker's, barn, 401 ; Farm, 430.
Bands of music in distance, 250.
Bartram, William, quoted, 108.
Baskets, strolling Indian selling, 32.
BEAN-FIELD, THE, 241-259
Bedford (Mass), 192.
Behavior, repentance for good, 19.
Bells of Lincoln, Acton, Bedford, Concord, the, 192.

"Best" room, the pine wood behind house, 221.
Bibles of mankind, 107, 108.
Birds, living with the, 135.
Body a temple, man's, 345.
Bogs with hard bottom, 509.
Books, how to read, 159 ; the inheritance of nations, 162.
Box, living in a, 48.
Brahmins, their forms of conscious penance, 9 ; Walden ice makes T. one with the, 459.
Bread without yeast, 98-101
Breed's hut, 400
Bricks, mortar growing harder on, 373.
Brighton — or Brighttown, 209.
Brister's Hill, 354 ; 397 ; 399 ; 405 ; 412.
Brister's Spring, 406, 408.
BRUTE NEIGHBORS, 347-368.
Bug from an egg in table of apple wood, the, 513.
Building one's own house, significance of, 74.
Business habits indispensable, strict, 33.
Busk, Indian feast of first fruits, 108

Calidas', Sacontala quoted, 491.
Cambridge, college room rent compared with T.'s, 80 , crowded lives of, 212.
Canadian wood - chopper, 224-234.
Canoe, water-logged in Walden Pond, 299.
Cards left by visitors, 203.
Carew, Thomas, quoted, 127.
Caryatides, gossips leaning against barn like, 263.
Cat, the Collins's, 71 ; in the

woods, domestic and " winged,"
361–363.

Cato Major, quoted, 101 ; 132,
133 ; 258 ; 376.

Caves, birds do not sing in, 47.

Celebrating, men, a committee of
arrangements, always, 508.

Celestial Empire, conditions of
successful trade with, 33.

Cellar, a burrow to which house
is but a porch, 72.

Cellini, Benvenuto, quoted, 316.

Chairs for society, three, 218.

Change of air, 493.

Channing, W. E., quoted, 317.

Chapman, George, quoted, 55.

Chastity, the flowering of man,
342.

Chaucer, Geoffrey, quoted, 331.

Chickadees, coming of the, 426.

Chief end of man, 15.

Christianity, adopted as an improved method of *agri*-culture,
61.

Circulating library, 165.

Civilization not all a success, 51.

Classics, a study of the, 158–160 ;
must be read in the original,
163.

Clothing, a necessary of life, 22 ;
not always procured for true
utility, 36 ; new and old, 39.

Cock-crowing, the charms of,
199–201.

Codman place, the, 401.

Cold Friday, dating from, 394.

Collins, James, Irishman whose
shanty T. bought, 69.

Commerce, in praise of, 186–192.

Commonsense, the sense of men
asleep, 501.

Compost, better part of man soon
ploughed into soil for, 11.

CONCLUSION, 493–514.

Concord (Mass.), Walden Pond
in, 7 ; traveled a good deal in,
9 ; the farmers of, 53 , house
surpassing the luxury of, 79 ;
little fresh meal and corn sold
in, 101 , Battle-Ground, 136 ;
effect of a fire bell on people
living near, 147 ; culture, 167 ,
wiser men than produced by
soil of, 169 ; hired man of, 170 ;
liberal education in, 171 ; " its
soothing sound is ——," 180 ;
sign of a trader in, 189 ; bells

of, 192 , two-colored waters of,
275 ; Walden bequeathed to,
303 ; fight of ants, 358 , D Ingraham, Esq., of, 397 , " to the
rescue," 401 ; 408 , 431.

Concord River, 304 , 308, 309.

Confucius, quoted, 20 ; 211.

Cooperation, difficulties of, 114.

Cost, the amount of life exchanged for a thing, 5 ; of
house, items of, 79 ; of food for
eight months, 94 ; total, of living, 96 ; bean-field, 253.

Cowper, William, quoted, 130.

Cummings, slave of Squire, 399.

Damodara, quoted, 138.

Darwin, Charles R , quoted, 22

Davenant, Sir Wm., *Gondibert*
quoted, 402.

Day, deliberately, like nature,
spending one, 153.

Debt, getting in and out of, 13.

Desperation, mass of men lead
lives of quiet, 15.

Dialogue between Hermit and
Poet, 347–350.

Digby, Sir Kenelm, quoted, 253

Discontented, speaking mainly to
the, 28.

Divinity in man ! Look at the
teamster, 14.

Dog in the woods, a village Bose,
361.

Doing-good, a crowded profession, 116.

Drummond of Hawthornden,
William, quoted, 308.

Ducks on Walden Pond, 368.

Dug-out houses of American col-
onists, 63, 64.

Dwelling-house, what not to
make it, 47.

ECONOMY, 7–127.

Education, tuition bills pay for
the least valuable part of, 81.

Egotism in writers, 8.

Eloquence a transient thing, 160.

Elysian life, summer makes possible, 24.

England, last news from, 149.

Epidermis, our outside clothes,
40.

Epitome of the year, the day, 464.

Etesian winds, news simmers
through men like, 262.

Evelyn, John, quoted, 18; 252

Expenses, see Cost, farm, 88, outgo and income, bean-field, 253, 254

Exploration of one's self, 494–497.

Extra Vagance ! depends on how you are yarded, 500.

Face, imaginary formation by thawing of the, 474.

Factory system, not best mode of supplying clothing, 43.

Fair Haven, huckleberries on hill, 269, 271, 290, 308; 317, 385, 421; 430; Ledges, 432; 461, late ice on pond, 468.

Farm, the Hollowell, 131; a model, 308.

Farmer, John, reflections of, 345.

Farmer, visits from a long-headed, 413.

Farmers, interesting in proportion as they are poor, 308.

Fashion, worship of, 42.

Fate, what a man thinks of himself, his, 15.

Father tongue, written language our, 159.

Fenda, wife of "Sippio Brister," 399.

Field, John, an Irishman, story of, 318.

Fine art, no place for a work of, 61, 62.

Fire, purification by, 108; "my housekeeper," 392, man and, 393; an alarm of, 401.

Fishes, schools of, in Walden Pond, 297; of thought, 417.

Fishing, with silent man, 272; at night, 274, alone detains citizens at Walden Pond, 332; impossible to T. without loss of self-respect, 333; in winter, 438.

Fitchburg (Mass.), going to, 85, Railroad, 180.

Flint's Pond, 284; or Sandy, in Lincoln, 304–308; 314, covered with snow, like Baffin's Bay, 418; 461.

Food, a necessary of life, 21; the fuel of man's body, 23; general consideration of, 87–104; objections to animal, 334; desirability of simple, 335–340.

FORMER INHABITANTS AND WINTER VISITORS, 396–418.

Fox, shooting a, 430.

Foxes outside T.'s house, 422.

Freeman, "Sippio Brister," 399.

Frogs, *troonk* of bull-, 197, 198.

Fruits, gathering autumn, 369

Fuel, a necessary of life, 22, of man's body, food, 23.

Furniture, generally considered, 104–110, moved out of doors, 177.

Gazette, news of political parties, not of nature, printed in the, 30

Gilpin, William, quoted, 387; 443.

God, clothes fit to worship, in, 39.

"God's Drop," proposed as name for Walden Pond, 303.

Good Genius, advice of T's, 324.

Gookin, Daniel, quoted, 48.

Goose, stray, cackling like spirit of the fog, 68, honking of, 421, 482.

Goose Pond, 308, musk-rats in, 420.

Gossip, stroll to village to hear, 261.

Ground-nut, the, 370–372

Guns, sound of distant big, 249.

Hare, the, 434.

Harivausa, the, quoted, 135.

Hasty-pudding, friends flee approach of, 380

Hawk, watching a, 487.

Hebe, a worshiper of, 217

Hercules, labors of, trifling compared with those of T.'s neighbors, 10.

Herds, the keepers of men, 90.

Hermit. See Dialogue.

HIGHER LAWS, 327–346.

Hippocrates, on cutting the nails, 18

Hollowell place, the, 129, 131.

Homer, Iliad, 157; never yet printed in English, 163; quoted, 225.

Horses to hang clothes on, wooden, 36.

Hospitalality, not hospitality but, 236.

Hounds hunting woods in winter, 428–433

House, every spot possible site for a, 128, the deal, 377–380.

House-raising at Walden Pond, 73.

HOUSE-WARMING, 369–395

Houses, superfluities in our, 58

Housework, a pleasant pastime, 177.

Huckleberries never reach Boston, 271

Hunters, boys to be made first sportsmen, then, 330.

Hyde, Tom, the tinker, quoted, 505.

Hygeia, no worshiper of, 217.

I, the first person, retained in this book, 8

Ice, looking through the, on Walden Pond, 382; whooping of the, 422, cutting through, to get water, 437, cutting on Walden Pond, 452–460, beauty of Walden, 457; booming of the, 465.

Indian houses in Mass. colony, 49.

Ingraham, Cato, slave of Duncan, 397.

Inherited property a misfortune, 10

Inspector of storms, self appointed, 31.

Iolas, and hydra's head, 10

Irish, physical condition of the poor, 57.

"It is no dream of mine," verse, 303.

Jays, arrival of the, 425.

Jesuits and Indian torture, 119.

Jesus Christ, liberalizing influence of, 170.

Johnson, Edward, quoted, 63.

Khoung-tseu, 150.

Kieou-he-yu, 150.

Kirby, William, and Spence, quoted, 335, 360.

Kittlybenders, let us not play at, 509.

Laborer, choosing occupation of a day, 111; falling in pond with many clothes on, 120

Laboring man has no time to be anything but a machine, the, 12.

Laing, Samuel, quoted, 45

Lake, the earth's eye, a, 291.

Lake Champlain, Long Wharf to, 187

"Leach-hole" in Walden Pond, 450

Leaf, resemblance of sand formation to a, 472.

Lexington (Mass.), 429

Liebig, J. F. von, quoted, 23

Life, cares and labors of, 12; an experiment, 17, students not to play or study life, but to live, 82, purposes of, 143; one has imagined, living the, 498, live your, however mean, 505, in us, like the water in the river, 513.

"Light-winged Smoke, Icarian Bird," verse, 391.

Lilac, growing by deserted houses, 407

Limits of living, 13

Lincoln (Mass.), 136; 192, owls in woods of, 196; 244, Flint's Pond in, 304, chestnut woods of, 370, 397; burying-ground, 399; 419.

Lining of beauty for houses, 65.

Little Reading, 105

Loneliness, desirable, 208, 214.

Loon, hunting and a game with the, 363–368

Luxury, fruit of a life of, 25.

Lyceum, 171 172.

Make-a-Stir, Squire, 14.

Manilla hemp, 187

Maples, autumn colors of, 372

Massasoit, visited by Winslow, 222

Maturing, no need of haste towards, 502.

Mencius, quoted, 342.

Mentors, of little use, 17

Middlesex Cattle Show, 54

Milky Way ' is not our planet in the, 208.

Minding his business, till ineligible as town officer, T, 31.

Minerva, Momus objects to house of, 55.

Mîr Camar Uddîn Mast, quoted, 157.

Mirabeau, on highway robbery, quoted, 497

Model farm, a, 308.

" Modern improvements," an illusion about, 84.

Momus, objection to Minerva's house by, 55.

Monuments, good sense worth more than, 92, 93.

Morning, work, a man's, 59 ; renewal of, 140-142 ; work in the early, 243.

Mortgages, abundance of, in Concord, 53.

Mouse in T.'s house, 351 ; the wild, 433.

Muskrats, colony of, 262 ; in Goose Pond, 420.

Nature, adapted to our weakness as to our strength, 20 ; a liberty in, 202 , no melancholy or solitude in the midst of, 205-207 ; the medicines of, 216 ; known only as a robber by the farmer, 258 ; men who become a part of, 328 , questions and answers of, 436 , our knowledge of the laws of, 448 , helping lay the keel of, 467 , principle of operations of, 475 , man's need of, 489.

Necessaries of life, 21.

Necessity, a seeming fate, commonly called, 11.

Negro slavery, 14

Neighborhood, avoiding a bad, ourselves, 55.

Neva marshes at Walden Pond, no, 35.

New clothes, beware of all enterprises requiring, 39.

New England, *Walden* of and for people of, 9 , hardships endured that men may die in, 25 ; wealth causes respect in, 38 , mean life lived by inhabitants of, 152 , can hire all the wise men of the world to teach her, 173 , natural sports of, 329, Rum, 400 , Night's Entertainment, a, 417

New Hollander, naked when European shivers in clothes, 22.

New Netherland, Secretary of Province, quoted, 63

" News ? What's the," 147 ; futility of the, 148.

Night, walking the woods by, 265-268.

Nilometer. See Realometer

Nine Acre Corner, White Pond in, 280.

" No Admittance," never printed on T.'s gate, 29

Novel reading, 165

Nutting in Lincoln woods, 370

Nutting, Sam, an old hunter, 432.

Olympus, the outside of the earth everywhere, 134.

Opposition to society, 497.

Ornaments, significance of architectural, 77.

Overseer, yourself the worst, 14.

Ovid, quoted, 11, 484 ; 486.

Owl, winged brother of the cat, watching a, 411.

Owls, wailing of, 194-197 , in Walden woods in winter, 420, 421.

Pantaloons not to be mended like legs, 37.

Partridge, the, 352-354 , 426 ; 435.

Pauper, visit from half-witted, 235

Penance, people of Concord doing, 9.

Penobscot Indians, living in cotton tents, 47.

Perfection, artist of Kouroo who strove after, 505.

Pfeiffer, Mme Ida, quoted, 38.

Philanthropy, generally considered, 118-126.

Philosopher, what he is and is not, 20 ; visits from a, 415-418.

Philosophers, ancient, poor in outward, rich in inward riches, 25.

Pickerel, Walden, 439.

Pine-tree, telling, though more its friend than foe, 69.

Plants, the nobler valued for their fruit in air and light, 27.

Plato, 169 ; definition of a man, 232

Pleasant Meadow, adjunct to Baker Farm, 317.

Poet. See Dialogue ; visits from a, 414.

Poets, never yet read by mankind, 164.

PoND IN WINTER, THE, 436-460.

PONDS, THE, 271-313

Poor, houses of the, 56.

Post-office, easily dispensed with, 148.

Present moment, meeting of two eternities, past and future, 29.

Public opinion, compared with private, 14.

Pumpkin, sitting alone on a, 60; none so poor that he need sit on a, 104.

Purslane, dinner of, 98.

Quoil, Hugh, an Irishman, 405.

Rabbit, the, 435.

Railroad, car, growing luxuries in, 60; slowness and heedlessness of, 85, 86; men overridden by, 146; listening with praise to sound of, 180-192; Iron, Trojan Horse running Walden, 301.

Rain, enjoyment of, 208.

Rainbow, standing in light of, 316.

Raleigh, Sir Walter, quoted, 11.

READING, 156-173.

Reality, finding, 154.

Realometer, not Nilometer, but a, 154.

Rent, annual tax that would buy a village of wigwams, 50.

Reporter, with labor for pains, 30.

Resignation, confirmed desperation, 15.

Robin, the evening, 481.

Room for thoughts, 219.

Runaway slave, 257.

Sadi of Shiraz, Sheik, quoted, 125.

Saint Vitus' dance, 147.

Sand formations due to thaw, 469-475.

Sand cherry, tasted out of compliment to Nature, 178.

Sardanapalus, at best houses traveler considered a, 60.

Savage, his advantage over civilized man, 52; life, instinct towards, 326.

Scarecrow taken for man whose clothes it wears, 37.

School, the *uncommon*, 173.

Seeds of virtues, not beans, 255.

Sensuality, in eating and other appetites, 340-346.

Serenade, like the music of the cow, 193.

Sewing, work you may call endless, 38.

Shanty, purchase of Collins's, 69, 70.

Shelter, a necessary of life, 22; how it became a necessary, 45; generally considered, 45-66.

Shingles of thought, whittling, 417.

Shirts, our liber, or true bark, 40.

Simplicity of life, 144.

Skins, sale of, 432.

Sleepers, railroad, 146.

Snake under water in torpid state, 67.

Snow, the Great, 186, 201; dating from the Great, 394, walking in the, 410.

Society, commonly too cheap, 213.

SOUNDS, 174-201.

South, laborers a staple production of the, 58.

Spain, specimen news from, 149.

Sparrow, the first, of spring, 478.

Spectator, the part of man which is, 211.

Spenser, Edmund, quoted, 222.

Sportsmen, making boys, 330.

SPRING, 461-492.

Spring, coming of the, 466, morning, moral effect of a, 484.

Squire Make-a-Stir, 14.

Squirrel, red, watching the, 422-425, in spring, coming of, 478.

Staff, the artist's, which became the fairest creation of Brahma, 503.

Statistics. See Cost.

Stone, nations' pride in hammered, 92.

Stove, disadvantages of cooking-, 394.

Stratten, now the Alms House Farm, 397; family, homestead of, 399.

Students, poor, Walden addressed to, 8.

Sudbury (Mass.), 138; 468.

Sumach growing by T.'s house, 179.

Survey of Walden Pond, 441-452.

Surveyor of forest paths and across lot routes, 31.

Sutton (Mass.), 410.

Tchi·ng-thang, quoted, 140.

Temperature of pond water in spring, 461

Tests, our lives tried by a thousand simple, 18.

Thanksgivings, cattle-shows and so-called, 257.

Thaw, sand formations due to, 469, Thor and, 477.

"They," an authority impersonal as the Fates, 41.

Thieving, practiced only where property is unevenly divided, 270.

Thor and thaw, 477.

Thoreau, Henry David, goes to live by Walden Pond, 7, prefers to talk in the first person singular, 8; beginning in the woods, 66; purchase of Collins's shanty, 69; began to occupy house, 73; planted beans, 87; earnings and spendings, 94-96; making bread, 98, declined offer of a mat, 107; imaginary purchase of Hollowell farm, 131; situation of house, 135, 178; purpose in going to woods, 143; hoed beans, did not read books, 175, listening to various sounds, 180-201; friendship with Canadian wood-chopper, 224-234; devotion to husbandry, 252; earnings and spendings on bean-field, 253, 254, put in jail for not paying taxes, 268, fishing in Walden Pond, 272-275; boiling chowder about 1824, 283, earliest days on Walden Pond, 300, first begins to inhabit house in cold weather, 376; finishes house with plastering, 380, surveys Walden Pond, 441, leaves Walden, Sept. 6, 1847, 492.

Thoughts, sell your clothes and keep your, 506.

Thseng-tseu, quoted, 339.

Tierra del Fuego, inhabitants unable to stand artificial heat, 20.

Time, but a stream to fish in, 155.

Tintinnabulum from without, the noise of contemporaries, 507.

Tools, men the tools of their, 61.

Trees, visits to particular, 315.

Truth, to be preferred to all things, 510.

Turtle-dove, long ago lost hound, bay horse, and, 29.

Varro, Marcus Terentius, quoted, 258.

Vedas, the, quoted, 141; and Zendavestas, 164, quoted, 339.

Vegetable-made bones, oxen with, 17.

VILLAGE, THE, 261-270.

Village, should play part of a nobleman as patron of art, 171-173; a great news-room, 262; running the gauntlet in the, 263.

Vishnu Parana, the, quoted, 418.

VISITORS, 218-240.

Vivid Lake as a name for White Pond, 300.

Wachito River, 148.

Walden, road, townsman on, 209, vale, giving notice, by smoke, to inhabitants of, 391; snow in roads of, 413; vale, making amends for silence, to, 414.

Walden Pond, house on the shore of, 7; purpose in living by, to transact private business, 33, advantages of, as a place of business, 35; March, 1845, went to woods by, 66, of their own natures, fishing in the, 204; no more lonely than, 214, old settler who did, 215; bottomless as, 235; scenery of, 275-304; origin of paving of, 285; temperature of water in, 287, animals in, 288-290, purity of, 302; fishing alone detains citizens at, 332, ducks on, 368; first ice on, 382; dates of first freezing over, 386, 408; bare of snow, 420; fox on thin ice of, 428; 429; pickerel of, 439, surveying and sounding, 441-452; cutting ice on, 452-460; breaking up of ice in, 460-467; dates of complete opening, 467.

Walden Woods, geese alighting in, 385; Cato Ingraham living

in, 398 ; Zilpha living in, 398 ;
Hugh Quoil living in, 405 ; owls
hooting the *lingua vernacula*
of, 420 , 429.
Waldenses, pickerel, 440.
Wasps, visits from, 372.
Water, colors of, 276-278 , transparency of, 278-281.
Wayland (Mass), 244
Weeds, destruction of various,
251.
" Welcome, Englishmen ! " 240
Well-Meadow, 430.
West Indian provinces of the
fancy and imagination, 15.
Weston (Mass.), 431.
" What 's the railroad to me ? "
verse, 192.
WHERE I LIVED, AND WHAT I
LIVED FOR, 128-155.
Whippoorwills, singing of, 194.
White Pond, 280 , 284 , 308-313 ;
plan of, 447.
Wigwam, in Indian gazettes,
symbol of a day's march, 45.

Winslow, Edward, quoted, 222.
WINTER ANIMALS, 419-435.
WINTER VISITORS, FORMER INHABITANTS, AND, 396-418.
Wood, gathering, 386 ; relative
value, in different places, of,
389.
Woodchuck, eating a, 95.
Wood-pile, the, 390.
Woods, turning face to the,
33.
Work, exaggerated importance of
our, 20.
Wyman, the potter, 404.

Yellow-Pine Lake, why suggested
as a name for White Pond,
309.
Young, Arthur, 89.
Youth and age, 16

Zendavestas, Vedas and, 164.
Zilpha, a colored woman, 398.
Zoroaster, let the lured man
commune with, 170.